URBAN LIQUEFACTION

BEFORE YOU START TO READ THIS BOOK, take this moment to think about making a donation to punctum books, an independent non-profit press,

@ https://punctumbooks.com/support/

If you're reading the e-book, you can click on the image below to go directly to our donations site. Any amount, no matter the size, is appreciated and will help us to keep our ship of fools afloat. Contributions from dedicated readers will also help us to keep our commons open and to cultivate new work that can't find a welcoming port elsewhere. Our adventure is not possible without your support.

Vive la Open Access.

Fig. 1. Detail from Hieronymus Bosch, *Ship of Fools* (1490–1500)

First published in 2026 by punctum books, Earth, Milky Way.
https://punctumbooks.com

ISBN-13: 978-1-68571-240-2 (paperbound)
ISBN-13: 978-1-68571-241-9 (PDF)
ISBN-13: 978-1-68571-305-8 (EPUB)

DOI: 10.53288/0532.1.00

LCCN: 2026931294
Library of Congress Cataloging Data is available from the Library of Congress

Editing: Scott Barker and SAJ
Book design: Hatim Eujayl
Cover design: Vincent W.J. van Gerven Oei
Cover image: From the exhibition *Futuro Concreto,* Museum of Contemporary Art of Santiago, Chile (August 2021–March 2022), by Fragüe Colectivo (Gonzalo Barceló, Felipe Cisternas, Pedro Donoso, Juan Gutiérrez, Sebastián Jatz, Felipe Palma and Cristián Simonetti).

p. **punctum**books

spontaneous acts of scholarly combustion

HIC SVNT MONSTRA

Urban Liquefaction

Rethinking the Relationship between Land and Sea

Edited by
Cristián Simonetti,
Michel Lussault, and
Tim Ingold

p.

Contents

Preface

Cristián Simonetti, Michel Lussault, and Tim Ingold

The idea for this volume first arose in the wake of a four-year project (2015–2019), "Solid Fluids in the Anthropocene," funded by the British Academy and led jointly by Cristián Simonetti and Tim Ingold. When, in 2019, the Royal Anthropological Institute announced plans for a major conference designed to explore the interface between the disciplines of anthropology and geography, we thought this would be a great opportunity both to present the findings of our project to a more general audience and to open up a wider inquiry into how tensions between solidity and fluidity have defined the relationship between land and sea, portending alternative futures for the built environment. Having invited Michel Lussault to join us, we submitted a proposal for a panel entitled "Urban Liquefaction: Rethinking the Relationship between Land and Sea." And with the proposal accepted, we set about inviting potential contributors.

The conference, "Anthropology and Geography: Dialogues Past, Present and Future," had been set to take place at the British Museum, London, in June 2020. But like everything else at that time, hit by the COVID-19 pandemic, the conference had to be postponed, and was eventually rolled out in an online format in September of the same year. However, after consulting with our contributors, we decided to withdraw from the conference, preferring to wait for an occasion when we might be able to meet in person, and using the intervening time to work on our papers. But as the pandemic dragged on, and as the prospects for an in-person meeting receded, we eventually concluded that it would be better, after all, to aim for an online workshop. Open only to invited contributors, its purpose would be to lay the foundations for a future edited volume.

We sent out invitations in October 2021, and after some further pandemic-induced delays, finally met online for the two days, June 2 and 3, 2022. These were days of intensive but extremely productive discussion, after which everyone was sent back to the drawing board to get their contributions ready for publication. By October 2022, we had prepared a proposal for submission to our favored open-access publisher, punctum books, and were pleased to have it accepted. Contributors had until February 2023 to send in their final drafts, after which we got on with the job of editing and writing the introductions to each part and to the volume as a whole. Finally, at the end of August 2023, after the usual months of to-ing and fro-ing between authors and editors, we were ready to submit the entire manuscript to punctum.

Ahead of us were still some grueling months of fixing all the final details, including the cover design, but by February 2024 everything was at last in order. There followed a long delay, of about eighteen months, during which the volume languished in a production queue. Punctum had become a victim of its own success, and with so many volumes in the pipeline, we had to wait our turn. But now, finally, it is truly on the way. We would like to thank all our contributors for their patience in staying the distance with what became a very protracted process, and thank also the few who, for one reason or another, have dropped out along the way. Above all, we wish to express our appreciation for Vincent W.J. van Gerven Oei and Eileen A. Fradenburg

Joy, directors of punctum books, for their unwavering support and faith throughout the entire process. In doing so, we call for public and academic institutions to ensure that open-access publishers such as punctum books are funded appropriately as demand for their services grows.

Santiago, Lyon, and Aberdeen
October 20, 2025

1

Introducing
More-Than-Solid Urbanity

Cristián Simonetti, Michel Lussault, and Tim Ingold

From classical times until today, cities have been idealized in the Western imagination as fixed to *terra firma,* dry land, defined in opposition to the fluxes of the sea. Whereas the dry land afforded a durable platform for the establishment of property and citizenship, the fluid sea allowed markets — isolated within the secure boundaries of cities — to be connected across the globe though navigation. Complementary oppositions between solidity and fluidity, permanence and impermanence, substance and change remain at the core of the Western intellectual tradition, often taken to divide what is "social" from what is "natural" in life. In this drama of solidity and fluidity, the principal characters are typically played by the elements of earth and water (Bachelard 1983). Today, however, climate change is forcing us to reassess the relation between solidity and fluidity in the design of the built environment. Eleven of the fifteen largest cities in the world are located in coastal areas, and at least 10 percent of the world's population is likely to be affected directly in coming decades by sea level rise, compromising the infrastructure on which modern life depends. Yet, in reality, urban landscapes have always been in flux, most dramatically revealed to urban dwellers in catastrophic events, such as earthquakes, tsunamis, alluvions, sinkholes, and, above all, soil liquefaction.

This volume opens an inquiry into these more-than-solid cityscapes, in order to speculate on alternative futures for the built environment in the Anthropocene, an epoch defined by humanity's capacity to act as a planetary force, the very same force that is currently driving changes threatening the foundations of modern society. Global warming has been related to numerous changes that risk liquefying solid urbanity, only one of which is sea level rise. Rapid melting of glacial ice and permafrost at high latitudes and altitudes, along with extreme weather events, have been associated with land rebound, earthquakes, volcanic activity, tsunamis, landslides, floods, and increasing soil liquefaction around the world, all of which imperil urban infrastructure. How should urban designers, engineers, architects, builders, and dwellers navigate these turbulent times and the prospect of increasingly unstable grounds? What and how can we learn from peoples more accustomed to living on grounds that, from the viewpoint of their daily practices, never settle permanently into solid or liquid states, such as those given to seasonal melting and flooding, located in river deltas or intertidal zones, or simply suspended in ocean waves? What new practical and intellectual challenges will societies face as they learn to navigate a more-than-solid urbanity?

These are complex questions, and answering them will mean attending to how urban life has come to be so bound to solid land, and to the social, political, and institutional structures predicated upon it. Indeed, the marriage of urbanity and solidity has deep historical roots, to which contemporary urban planning and engineering seem to remain firmly, almost neurotically, attached. Recent scholarship centered around the Anthropocene, however, has done much to destabilize the contrast between solid land and fluid sea. Above all, scholars in the earth sciences and humanities have been forced to rethink the limits of their disciplines, traditionally and paradigmatically founded on an ontological division between the "two worlds" of matter and spirit. Even today, the reputation of the so-called hard sciences, as against the alleged softness of the humanities, owes much to the lingering appeal of this division. Scientific truths are supposed to partake of the hardness of the matter with which they deal, whereas the humanities are fated to float in an ocean of interpretations as ephemeral and evanescent as the spirit of the times, the *Zeitgeist* (Ingold and Simonetti 2022).

It was this confidence in the material foundations of human civilization, progressively revealed by science, that provided a launchpad for the industrial revolution. Yet as it gathered pace, this revolution would go on to unleash the very forces that eventually culminated in the onset of the Anthropocene (Crutzen 2002). Indeed, Karl Marx, writing with his collaborator Friedrich Engels in the mid-nineteenth century, already anticipated the tendency of industrial capitalism to dissolve the foundations upon which its hopes of progress were built, as famously epitomized in their mantra, in *The Communist Manifesto* of 1848, that "all that is solid melts into air" (1978, 476; see also Berman 1982). Marx and Engels were, of course, referring to the way in which capitalism continually eats away at any settled or traditional forms of sociality, inducing a constant state of agitation and disruption in its drive for innovation and profit. In this day and age, however, their dictum deserves to be taken not metaphorically but literally. For what is at stake today, in a time of global warming, is the actual liquefaction of the very ground that Marx (1930, 173) had imagined to be preeminent among the instruments of human labor, insofar as it provides a hard, spatially extensive platform for all productive operations.

The very same forces that Marx identified as having melted traditional social forms, in the early years of the industrial revolution, are still operating in the twenty-first century, but now on a planetary scale, melting the ground itself, and thereby putting at risk the continuity of human existence as we know it. From the viewpoint of the Capitalocene — as some scholars in the humanities have dubbed the new epoch (Moore 2016) — these forces have all along been melting not just the social bonds that hold the lifeworld together but its material bonds as well. Ultimately, anthropogenic processes have merged with the earthly processes that once made space for life on this planet (Clark and Szerszynski 2021) — processes that, arguably, have carried on only because they have been at work in a world that was simultaneously solid and fluid from the start (Simonetti 2022). To imagine alternative futures for humanity, in our times, calls for a kind of planetary thinking, a *Zeitplanet* if you will, that abjures any division between matter and spirit. And it means envisioning urban life in a *solidfluid medium*. The first step toward this involves rethinking the relationship between land and sea.

Land and Sea

Since antiquity, urban life has been predicated on the idea that the land, on which the city is built, confronts the sea. The many city-states of ancient Greece dotted around the islands and peninsulas of the Aegean archipelago, though dependent on the sea for travel and trade, took pains to protect their political order from its transgressive influence (Olwig 2019, 88). The polis had continually to defend itself against attack from the sea and its waterborne forces, never the other way around. In book 4 of the *Laws* (Bury 1926, 257), Plato had the Athenian, a stranger to the isle of Crete, declare that the sea, albeit pleasant enough as a daily companion, can be a "right briny and bitter neighbour," which brings to its shores all manner of raiders, rogues, and tricksters. For safety and security, he insisted, the city should be located well inland. Even Aristotle, in stressing the importance of access to the sea for commerce, acknowledged — in book 7 of the *Politics* (Jowett 1885, 216) — that the influx of strangers caused by the sea's proximity can corrode good government. Every polis, then, figures as an island of order, anchored in the ocean of disorder that threatens to unravel it (Ingold 2022, 172–73). Ever since, land and sea have carried on their uneasy alliance, the former conceived as the fixed enclave of urban life, the latter as a fluid space for the free circulation of goods.

If the polis, with its legal and mercantile institutions, was founded on dry land, so too was the social contract that bound its citizens. Philosopher Michel Serres (1995) has shown that the very idea of "contract," literally a "drawing together," has its source in the stretched cord, tightly tied between those joined by it. From Herodotus, we know that the first cord-stretchers were the *harpedonaptai* of ancient Egypt, royal officials tasked with surveying plots of fertile land after every annual flood of the Nile. The boundaries of each field would be marked out by driving wooden stakes into the earth at the corners and stretching knotted cords between them. The *harpedonaptai,* indeed, were the original earth-measurers, or geometers. Moreover, Serres (1995, 51–52) shows that the birth of geometry, in this act of tying the cord, was also the birth of law, and that both depended upon the possibility of establishing strict lines of demarcation, following the erasures of the flood. These lines would last only so long, however, for with the next flood they would dissolve, returning the land to nature in its primordial sense of a power to give birth to things, to a world.

How different, then, is life at sea! To drive stakes in the earth requires that the soil be solid enough to hold them fast. Likewise, landlubbers, in cementing their social contracts, can normally take for granted that the ground will hold firm beneath their feet. Not so at sea, however, which affords no such support. In an oceanic milieu, existence is possible only thanks to the capacity of one's vessel to stay afloat. The vessel's seaworthiness depends on a pact among the crew that they owe not to the law of contract but to nature itself. Here, as Serres observes, "the collectivity, if sundered, immediately exposes itself to the destruction of its fragile niche, with no possible recourse or retreat" (1995, 40). One cannot simply withdraw to pitch one's tent elsewhere — there is no earth to take the pegs. Not for nothing does the word "ship," used alternately as noun and suffix, connote both the vessel and — as in "fellowship" — a community of sorts (Ingold 2022, 175).

Both Plato's dream of the ideal city, then, and Herodotus's tale of the origins of geometry, presuppose a specifically grounded, land-based sociality, according to which human beings can organize themselves according to laws of their own devising, without having first to surrender to the fellowship of nature. This sense of sociality has been carried over into modern times in the thought of social contract theorists, such as John Locke, Thomas Hobbes, and Jean-Jacques Rousseau, for whom sociality was fundamentally bound to the idea of private property, exclusive to the land. Its continuation well into the twentieth century is exemplified in the writings of the Nazi jurist and political theorist Carl Schmitt, as he witnessed the juridical transformations wrought by the appropriation of the seas and the air. In *The Nomos of the Earth* (2006), written during the early 1940s, Schmitt linked the law to solid land, in explicit contraposition to the fluid sea. The seas, unlike the land, have not been considered state territory in international law, despite their openness to different spheres of human activity, such as fishing, peaceful navigation, and the conduct of war. For Schmitt, this was entirely because of their fluidity. Only on land, he said, can the earthling, "man," make his mark. He can make no mark on the sea, nor engrave any character, since "on the waves there is nothing but waves" (Schmitt 2006, 42–43).

Yet if properly human sociality, for social contract theorists, necessarily rests on a terrestrial foundation — or in Schmitt's (2014) words, "on the firmly-grounded Earth" — the reverse does not hold; terrestrial life does not, in itself, imply that social relations are contractually dependent on the demarcation and appropriation of landed property. This is clearly not the case for the land's nonhuman inhabitants. Nor is it the case for those peoples deemed to be Indigenous, including nominally "nomadic" hunter-gatherers and pastoralists. In the history of colonialism, the supposition that the country was, for native peoples, a *terra nullius* — that they held no more claim to it than the wild animals that freely roamed the same grounds — was repeatedly adduced to justify their eradication or confinement, and the seizure of their lands. But it would also lead to parallels being drawn between the terrains of nomadic life and the sea, which find their echo even in contemporary social theory.

An example lies in the contrast drawn by philosophers Gilles Deleuze and Félix Guattari between "striated" and "smooth" space. Striated space, etched like the farmer's fields with rigs and furrows, belongs to an agrarian regime, rooted in the soil. But in smooth space, lines of movement go every which way, with no consistent direction and responding at every moment to the ever-changing conditions of the sky above and the earth below. Nomads, be they hunter-gatherers or pastoralists, are for Deleuze and Guattari the denizens of smooth space. Yet the sea, they say, "is smooth space par excellence" (Deleuze and Guattari 2004, 529). It is as if hunter-gatherers roamed the terrain, and herdsmen the pastures, as mariners ride the waves. To be nomadic, in this sense, is to be at sea on the land. It is significant, in this regard, that the Vikings, who knew a thing or two about both farming and seafaring, regularly compared their ocean-going longships to horses, but only rarely to ploughs. They could ride the waves, but could not carve their furrows (Jesch 2016, 321; Ingold 2022, 161).

Often enough, of course, the Vikings' maritime expeditions would take them far inland, along broad, navigable rivers, on the banks of which they would go on to found some of Europe's great cities, from Dublin to Novgorod. Yet here, too, the logic of the social contract, with its presupposition of solid ground, dictated that land and water remain strictly separate. Architect Dilip da Cunha (2019) tells of how Alexander the Great, the renowned conqueror of the ancient world and student of Aristotle, initially drew the River Ganges out of pure imagination, for his army never actually reached it. It should look like a ribbon snaking through the land, with a clear boundary on either side. Ever since, cartographers and surveyors have cleaved to what da Cunha calls "river literacy," a geographically disciplined view that pictures the earth's surface as divided between running water and dry land. On the map, these divisions would be indicated by solid lines.

In the case of the Ganges, however, this picture is an abstraction, based on the state of the river in fair weather, ignoring the monsoon season when much of the land is either flooded or saturated. It is an abstraction, according to da Cunha, that aligns with the history of colonialism in India, which, in its drive to appropriate the land, sought to obviate the pervasiveness of phenomena such as the monsoon, the effects of which are to dilute any hard lines on the earth's surface. Da Cunha asks what it would mean to reverse these priorities, to imagine a "wealth of wetness" that is not opposed to dry land but rises and falls with the rains, in an oscillation between water-over-land and land-over-water. Far from being on either side of a hard boundary, both land and water, in a condition of wetness, are everywhere.

Liquefying Knowledge

Just as sociality, in the Western intellectual tradition, has been bound to dry land, so too it has long been assumed that the edifice of knowledge necessarily rises on a solid foundation. As Henri Bergson wrote in his introduction to *Creative Evolution,* we find "that the human intellect feels at home among inanimate objects, more especially among solids, where our action finds its fulcrum and our industry its tools; that our concepts have been formed on the model of solids; that our logic is, pre-eminently, the logic of solids" (Bergson 1922, ix). This logic, philosopher Milič Čapek (1971) has shown, can be traced all the way from Plato to contemporary analytic philosophy. It often takes the form of a search for a stable bedrock, upon which certain knowledge can be built.

For example, René Descartes, reflecting on his method of doubt, declared that his "whole aim was to reach certainty — to cast aside the loose earth and sand so as to come upon rock and clay" (Descartes 1985, 125). In a reanalysis of Descartes's method, the contemporary philosopher Adriaan Peperzak suggests that certitude involves finding solid land in "an ocean of doubt in which we are in danger of drowning" (1995, 137). Similarly, this time in a metaphor strikingly redolent of Plato's scenario of the ideal city, philosopher Edgar Morin (1999), in his celebrated *Seven Complex Lessons in Education for the Future,* famously compared knowing to sailing in and around islands of certitude, in a sea of uncertainties.

Contemporary philosophy, following in Descartes's footsteps, has allowed the assumption of a fixed and stable earth to go largely unchallenged. A relatively recent case in point is Edmund Husserl, founder of phenomenology and an admirer of Descartes, who, in discussing the intellectual claims of modern physics, argued that the Copernican understanding of the Earth, as a body revolving around other planets, depends on a primary phenomenological understanding of the earth as a fixed base. According to Husserl, it is only because the earth presents itself to us as such that we can acquire a sense of both motion and rest. Accordingly, our everyday experience of the earth as static, in relation for instance to other entities, such as the sun, makes up the given background against which is figured physics' comprehension of movement. In Husserl's words, "It is on the Earth, toward the Earth, starting from it, but still on it that motion occurs. The Earth itself, in conformity to the original idea of it, does not move, nor is it at rest; it is in relation to the Earth that motion and rest first have sense" (cited in Derrida 1978, 84n87).

On no account should Husserl's argument be conceived as a return to a pre-Copernican view of the earth as standing at the center of the universe, as Ptolemy and Aristotle had believed. By contrasting the primacy of both understandings of the earth, as a moving body and an immovable base, Husserl seems to challenge the widespread assumption that modern physics managed to establish a planetary view of the Earth by transcending our everyday sensory experience of resting on solid ground. For Husserl, and for most philosophers who have followed in his footsteps, including Martin Heidegger and Hannah Arendt, the opposite would be the case, in that understanding rest and motion in modern physics depends upon the phenomenological encounter with a fixed base.

Although Husserl's argument makes much sense in the light of how modern physics tells the story of its origin, it makes little sense when conceived from the viewpoint of the geological revolution launched two centuries after Copernicus. Whereas the Copernican revolution expanded the limits of space, this new geology, founded by James Hutton with his *Theory of the*

Earth (1795), expanded the limits of time, allowing solid formations of the land, which appear fixed and stable in the shorter
term, to buckle and flow. "What more can we require?" asked
Hutton, to challenge our understanding of earthly formations
in the present. "Nothing but time" (2: 648).

Husserl was not uninterested in the new geology, which was
already well established in his day. Indeed, in his understanding
of time, he was much influenced by it (Simonetti 2018). Yet it
would undermine his most basic premise, namely, that the experience of the earth as a solid substrate beneath our feet is the
sine qua non for all knowledge. Nor was it only on timescales
far exceeding those of human generations that the instability
and even fluidity of the earth's surface would be revealed. It also
came from direct observation of dramatic events, such as earthquakes, tsunamis, mudslides, and the like, vividly described
by such traveling naturalists as Alexander von Humboldt and
Charles Darwin. It is thanks to this revolution in geological
thinking that we are now able to conceive of the interconnect-
edness and ongoing transformation of the planet in deep time.
Today, more than two centuries after Hutton, this has motivated
a *geologic turn* in the humanities, in the face of the current environmental crisis (Ellsworth and Kruse 2012).

The limitations of Husserl's argument from the viewpoint
of geology are nicely illustrated in an anecdote told by the philosopher John Searle. The story is of a visiting philosopher who
attended some seminars in Berkley on the "phenomenological
background" but remained unconvinced by the arguments, until a small earthquake suddenly changed his mind. The visitor
later confessed that "he had not, prior to that moment, had a belief or a conviction or a hypothesis that the earth does not move;
he had simply taken it for granted" (Searle 1992, 185). Once we
shift our perspective from the spatial vastness of early modern
physics to the temporal vastness of modern geology, the earth
can no longer be equated with a stable ground. Given enough
space, all solids seem to remain solid. Yet, given enough time,
all solids melt as they return to the ongoing flows from which
they emerged. It is precisely this fluidity of the earth that the

unprecedented circumstances of the Anthropocene, according to historian Dipesh Chakrabarty (2018), require us to confront.

This call to take our thinking beyond the frameworks of classical science and philosophy is one consequence of the intellectual impetus of the Anthropocene (Demoule and Lussault 2021). Global change, the effects of which we can already verify, confronts us with realities so complex and mixed that the whole decorum of Western thought is disrupted. Chakrabarty has shown that the way we approach time and temporality has been profoundly modified: If the anthropic "forcing" of planetary systems confirms the capacity of human societies to exert geological power, then our very conception of history, along with the concordances of times past, present, and future — whether geological, historical, human, social, or biographical — is completely subverted. It is no coincidence that the current revival of interest in the cosmologies and cosmogonies of Indigenous peoples, on the one hand, and in hypotheses such as Gaia (Latour 2015), on the other, accords real importance to questions of time and temporality. We are in the process of radically altering our regimes of historicity, and this calls for new ways of constructing knowledge (Hartog 2020).

But our thinking about human space is undergoing an equally fundamental upheaval. We are beginning to recognize that the apparent immutability and solidity of the material and geographical foundations of human settlements is a delusion, that these foundations are demonstrably fluid and impermanent. Recent archaeological studies, for example, have revealed the mobility of settlements and dynamism of habitat formation. From geography, through anthropology and philosophy, to architecture and urban planning, paradigms are being proposed that insist on movement, hazard, comings and goings, the temporary nature of things — even things that once seemed the most stable.

This has led, in particular, to an unprecedented and indeed paradigmatic breakdown in the technical and social principles of spatial planning, both urban and nonurban. For these principles are historically founded on the idea of the solidity, immovability, and permanence of a space that can be treated mechanically as a coherent whole, composed of stable and more or less controllable materials. Yet, as the contributions to this volume demonstrate, each in its own way, nothing is without movement and change, in form, status, and appearance. Recognizing this fact, specialists around the world are today attempting to define how protocols of urban planning can adapt to fluidity and liquefaction. These discussions are currently converging on the idea of doing things in ways that assume the temporary nature of occupations and the need to assume their itinerancy, or what some authors call "itinerant" or "transitory" urbanism. For urban planners Patrick Bouchain and Nicola Delon (Delon 2018), this is what makes places "infinite" — their ability to remain perpetually on the move. This is just one illustration of the scale of revisions underway, in a field in which certainty and immutability had once seemed paramount.

Overflowing

It is hard to deny the relevance of cartography to the work of Descartes; it was a field to which he actively contributed. Cartography pins things down. It therefore presumes a solid substrate, which holds everything shown in the map to its proper location. Things that move, that swirl around, creating liquid formations such as waves and vortices, cannot go on the map. We have already seen, in the case of India, how the "river literacy" of surveyors and cartographers facilitated the colonial project of land appropriation, and how this appropriation, in turn, came to lie at the heart of how social contract thinkers understood sociality, and at the same time furnished a justification for the subjugation of Indigenous peoples. But following Descartes, modern philosophy would go on to take a similar approach to mapping the human mind. What can be pinned down by reason goes on the map, represented cartographically as a solid island amidst the unmappable ocean of fluid sensibility. This image empowered authors such as Sigmund Freud to unsettle the foundations of modernity at the turn of the twentieth century. Beneath reason, he thought, upon which modern philosophy builds its intellectual edifice, lies an ocean of unconscious impulses and desires that constantly threaten to overflow. The more humans deny them, the stronger these impulses and desires become.

Inspired by the work of Freud, paleontologist Stephen Jay Gould enumerated a series of dethronements to human exceptionalism brought about by advances in science represented by the figures of Copernicus, Darwin, and Freud, who respectively relegated the Earth to a remote corner of the universe, lowered humans from a God-like figure to a walking ape, and conceived reason as precariously suspended in a turbulent ocean of unconscious drives. Adding to the list, this time from the viewpoint of his own discipline, Gould enumerated a fourth dethronement, from the viewpoint of deep time, which left humans as simply "the last inch in the cosmic mile, or the last second of the geological year" (1989, 44). In the vast ocean of time, to continue with the metaphor, the planet seems indifferent to the supposedly solid islets on which modernity has dreamed of building a comfortable place on earth. And now that the sea is literally and irreversibly overflowing the land, there is no escape for modernity but to face liquefaction.

The reality of global warming requires us to confront difficult decisions that, as recent history demonstrates, are extremely hard to make, especially when it comes to giving up hope for solid land. A recurrent example is New Orleans, a city below sea level that has historically suffered intense flooding, especially during Hurricane Katrina in 2005. Sociologist Andrew Pickering (2008) pointed out in the aftermath of Katrina that no one at the time dared to ask the critical question of whether the moment to give up New Orleans had arrived earlier than expected. All around the world, projects of civil engineering continue largely to protect urban dwellers from inundation, holding onto hopes for solid urbanity that are bound, ultimately, to be dashed. Environmental anthropologist Lukas Ley (2021) — writing of the struggles that people in Semarang, central Java, currently face as a result of flooding — has the impression that urban planners and dwellers simply carry on "building on borrowed time." But if we follow architect Kazi Khaleed Ashraf's analysis of the "wet narratives" currently resurfacing in Dhaka, Bangladesh's capital city, located in the Bengal Delta, then "architecture must recognise that the future is fluid" (2017, 1).

Envisioning a fluid future means challenging a pervasive assumption, in architecture and urban planning, that only the solid lasts. Implicit in this assumption is an understanding of longevity in terms of the preservation of fixed and final forms. But if our concern is with the life history of a thing, with its capacity to keep going or endure, then fluidity is of the essence (Ingold 2013, 104). Things that are locked solid, however much their forms are preserved for posterity, cannot last in this sense. As Serres put it, in a 2009 interview, "It is worth remembering that the soft lasts [dure] longer than the hard [dur]" (cited in Ingold and Simonetti 2022). It is in this sense, too, that we understand the fluid not as the opposite of solid, as nonsolid, but as *more-than-solid*. This is the condition of a world that overflows, whose liquid — primarily watery — element is not channeled between the banks of dry land, confined to pipes, or held at bay by maritime defenses, but omnipresent. In such a world of flux, the solid is but a transient condition. Nothing, indeed, illustrates the illusion of solid urbanity better than concrete, the material most extensively produced and consumed in the history of urban infrastructure. Concrete has long been the material of choice for mammoth infrastructural projects, from dams to seafronts and harbor walls, designed to tame the forces of water. It has been promoted as an icon of modernity by the building industry, which boasts of its exceptional qualities — particularly of endurance and impermeability — under the banner of eternal solidity, while concealing that it is both of maritime origin and ultimately bound to return to the geological cycle from which it originates (Simonetti and Ingold 2018).

As cities move from solid urbanity to embrace what geographer Philip Steinberg (2011, 2113) calls "a post-terrestrial world," perhaps we should start by finally loosening the hold that our assumption of the earth as a solid substrate has on our understandings of citizenship, law, and knowledge. In contemporary cities, concrete has often been used to shore up this assumption in the face of the disruptions brought about by an earth than refuses to conform to it. For in the history of the earth, solid and liquid states have always mingled, and will continue to do so. This should not be confused with an appeal to what sociologist Zygmunt Bauman (2000) has called "liquid modernity." Principally conceived to reflect metaphorically on the increasing mobility and change of relationships, identity, and economics within contemporary society — much as Marx and Engels had done in their mantra that "all that is solid melts into air" — Bauman's liquid modernity leaves somewhat untouched the material foundations of modern life in the Anthropocene. Our contention in this volume, to the contrary, is that the material foundations of urban life — the geological origins of which remain largely invisible within modernity's short-term view of earth history — have been liquefying all along.

In *Down to Earth* (2018), Bruno Latour speculated on the implications of the new climate regime for the possibility of inhabiting common land in the face of imminent ecological disaster. According to Latour, the new climate predicament has begun to quake and stir the ground, unsettling key categories often mobilized to understand contemporary human life, including notions such as "global," "local," "earth," and "place," or even "soil." Among these categories, defined as attractors in geopolitical tension, Latour identifies an emerging term, the "terrestrial," the connotations of which can offer guidance on how to come down to earth in these troubled times. The concept relates to what earth system scientists have described as the *critical zone,* the thin biofilm in which life as we know it has flourished by re-creating the conditions for its own existence over millennia. To conceive the earth as such, as a self-regulating system, is to pull away from any naturalistic view of it, taken from afar, as a planet among other planets, and to embrace it rather as a singularity. In this view, humans never truly own the ground or the soil in which they hope to land, leading arguably to Latour's most important conclusion: "One belongs to it; it belongs to no one" (2018, 92).

There is of course nothing new in this conclusion. Historically, the inversion by which land comes to belong to people rather than people to land is a function of a property regime founded in the social contract whose roots, in Western thought, date back only a few centuries. That the land is the source from which all powers of creation flow, underwriting the kinship of human beings with creatures of every other kind, borne of the same source, is what Indigenous peoples have been telling us all along (Daes 1997, 3). The lesson of this volume, however, is that the terrestrial sphere can overflow with life only because it is not locked solid, because it embraces the liquid expanses of the hydrosphere, including the earth's wetlands, rivers, and seas. Indeed in a living world, states of matter such as solid and liquid can only be abstracted as transient moments of a more fundamental condition of flux. There is no categorical opposition, therefore, between the terrestrial and the riverine or maritime, but rather a continuous process of becoming land, becoming river, and becoming sea. Indeed, it has ever been thus. Yet up to now, urban development has proceeded in a state of denial, as if the land normally presents as a hard surface, and where it does not, draining and paving it to make it so. But these efforts will not withstand the onset of the new climatic regime. Learning to live with it will mean recognizing, after all, that even the cities in which the majority of humans now live rest on a foundation that is as fluid and as open to the elements as the soft earth.

The Book

Divided into four parts, respectively titled "Shifting Grounds," "Life at the Shoreline," "Emerging Lands," and "Rivers and Floods," this volume gathers its contributions from scholars and practitioners in fields interested in urban life in the Anthropocene, from Europe, North America, and South America, working across all continents and from a wide range of disciplines, including anthropology, archaeology, art, architecture, design, human geography, and science studies. Part 1, focusing on the grounds of the city, shows just how much effort and ingenuity has had to be invested in maintaining the illusion, key to the architecture of modernity, that the earth affords a solid and stable platform on which to build. This investment can never rest, but must always continue, for groundwaters are never far beneath the surface, and are liable to rise up if given the chance. The hard surface, whether of asphalt or concrete, by which we are inclined to distinguish the paved ground of the built environment from unpaved countryside, turns out to be but a veneer, temporarily sealing the earth below from the atmosphere above. It is a veneer, moreover, that is liable to sag, should too much of the earth's water content be siphoned off for human use. It turns out, in short, that unbeknownst to the vast majority of their inhabitants, cities are actually floating on water, their buildings, sunk into their foundations, supported by waterlogged earth much as the hulls of ships are supported by the ocean.

In Part 2, we revisit the idea of the shoreline as a well-defined boundary separating land on the one side and sea on the other. Were we to follow this line, it would bend inward at every river mouth, while another line, running roughly parallel, picks up on the other side. Between the two, the river appears to wander through the terrain like a ribbon, bounded by well-defined banks. That, at least, is how it appears on the map. As much engineering effort has been put into maintaining the integrity of these lines, in the form of seawalls and river embankments, as into preserving the solidity of the ground base. Yet like the latter, the effort is doomed to fail, especially as rising sea levels, consequent upon climatic warming, overwhelm sea defenses, and as torrential rains and glacier melt send rivers surging. Urban inhabitants accustomed to life on shorelines or along riverbanks know only too well that shores and banks are not lines of division, between solid earth and liquid water, but zones of intermediacy and overlap, in which earth and water take turns in overreaching one another. It may be better to think of such environments — offering rich possibilities for living organisms to thrive, and for the subsistence of human populations that depend upon them — in terms of gradients rather than absolute lines of demarcation. Such thinking, however, is anathema to nation-states, for which everything depends on the assertion of sovereign control over a well-defined territory.

With Part 3, we enter a world in which the land itself is caught up in processes of material sedimentation and erosion, driven by river flows, ocean currents, and atmospheric cyclones. In these processes, the fate of cities, predominantly built of sedimentary materials, whether silt, clay, or concrete, hangs in the balance. Where land is ever-emergent, and equally prone to disappear beneath the waters, a city's longevity is secured not by its foundation on a fixed base, but by embracing the very opposite — an amphibious and mobile lifestyle that is equally in its element whether on dry land, raised on stilts from an underwater bed, or afloat on boats or rafts. Even as territorially based, political power constantly strives for solidification, it is bound to be overwhelmed in the long run by the movements of materials and people that accompany the formation and dissolution of the land. Fences and walls dividing one state's territory from another — all eventually destined for ruination — are monuments to the futility of attempts to arrest the tide. When the land sinks, centralized power sinks with it, while the future lies with those who can take to the waters or plant their roots in the seabed. What, then, if cities could take leave of the land altogether? Could the ocean become the new frontier, ripe for colonization, offering unparalleled possibilities for both enrichment and leisure for opportunists seeking to avoid the irksome regimes of landlocked polities? Or should we rather look to the past for models of how to inhabit a viscous, elastic world in which land and sea, solidity and liquidity, are no longer opposed?

Finally, in Part 4, the city is restored to the cycles of the geosphere, the hydrosphere, and the atmosphere to which it belongs, and also the archaeosphere, the accumulating pile of rubble that urban life leaves behind it as it grinds on. Inhabitants, far from being insulated from these worldwide currents, find themselves in the thick of it, and, in this era of anthropogenic climate change, more than ever vulnerable to the disruptions visited upon them. Rivers, for example, cutting their way through increasingly built-up areas filled with the rubble of previous occupation, are inclined to flood, wreaking devastation all around. Flooding, as we see in the chapters making up this part, is a consequence of the confinement of river-flow to narrow channels. But these chapters also prove that landscapes never forget. Especially in the wake of European-led colonization, great cities have been designed, with their highways, harbors and airports, on land that formed part of once waterlogged river basins or coastal swamps, ringed with hills and mountains. In the process, hills were violently demolished, while lagoons and swamps were filled with the debris, and rivers embanked, all with the aim of creating a level field on which to build. But periodically, in seasons of heavy rain, the lagoons and rivers remember how they used to lie and flow, leaving citizens knee-deep in mud and sludge, in the ghostly shadow of the hills. Is this an image of the city of tomorrow? Perhaps the lesson of the chapters in Part 4, and indeed of the book as a whole, is that the future of a predominantly urban humanity lies in learning to live with water and its ways, rather than barricading ourselves against it.

References

Ashraf, Kazi Khaleed. 2017. "Wet Narratives: Architecture Must Recognise That the Future Is Fluid." *The Architectural Review,* May 25.

Bachelard, Gaston. 1983. *Water and Dreams: An Essay on the Imagination of Matter.* Translated by Edith R. Farrell. Pegasus Foundation.

Bauman, Zygmunt. 2000. *Liquid Modernity.* Polity.

Bergson, Henri. 1922. *Creative Evolution.* Translated by Arthur Mitchell. Macmillan.

Berman, Marshall. 1982. *All That Is Solid Melts into Air: The Experience of Modernity.* Penguin.

Bury, Robert Gregg. 1926. *Plato: Laws.* Heinemann.

Čapek, Milič. 1971. *Bergson and Modern Physics: A Reinterpretation and Revaluation.* Reidel.

Chakrabarty, Dipesh. 2018. "Anthropocene Time." *History and Theory* 57, no. 1: 5–32. DOI: 10.1111/hith.12044.

Clark, Nigel, and Bronislaw Szerszynski. 2021. *Planetary Social Thought: The Anthropocene Challenge to the Social Sciences.* Polity.

Crutzen, Paul J. 2002. "Geology of Mankind." *Nature* 415, no. 23. DOI: 10.1038/415023a.

da Cunha, Dilip. 2019. *The Invention of Rivers: Alexander's Eye and Ganga's Descent.* University of Pennsylvania Press.

Daes, Erica-Irene. 1997. *Protection of the Heritage of Indigenous People.* United Nations.

Deleuze, Gilles, and Félix Guattari. 2004. *A Thousand Plateaus: Capitalism and Schizophrenia.* Translated by Brian Massumi. Continuum.

Delon, Nicola, ed. 2018. *Lieux infinis: Construire des bâtiments ou des lieux?* B42.

Demoule, Jean-Paul, and Michel Lussault, eds. 2021. *Néolitihique-anthropocène: Dialogue autour des 13000 dernières années.* Editions 205.

Derrida, Jacques. 1978. *Edmund Husserl's Origin of Geometry: An Introduction.* Translated by John P. Leavey. University of Nebraska Press.

Descartes, René. 1985. "Discourse and Essays." In *The Philosophical Writings of Descartes.* Translated by John Cottingham, Robert Stoothoff, and Dugald Murdoch. Cambridge University Press.

Ellsworth, Elizabeth, and Jamie Kruse. 2012. *Making the Geologic Now: Responses to Material Conditions of Contemporary Life.* punctum books. DOI: 10.21983/P3.0014.1.00.

Gould, Stephen Jay. 1989. *Wonderful Life: The Burgess Shale and the Nature of History.* Norton.

Hartog, F. 2020. *Chronos: L'Occident aux prises avec le temps.* Gallimard.

Hutton, James. 1795. *Theory of the Earth with Proofs and Illustrations.* Vols. 1 and 2. William Creech.

Ingold, Tim. 2013. *Making: Anthropology, Archaeology, Art and Architecture.* Routledge.

———. 2022. *Imagining for Real: Essays on Creation, Attention and Correspondence.* Routledge.

Ingold, Tim, and Cristián Simonetti. 2022. "Introducing Solid Fluids." *Theory, Culture & Society* 39, no. 2: 3–29. DOI: 10.1177/02632764211030990.

Jesch, Judith. 2016. "The Threatening Wave: Norse Poetry and the Scottish Isles." In *Maritime Societies of the Viking and Medieval World,* edited by James H. Barrett and Sarah Jane Gibbon. Routledge.

Jowett, Benjamin. 1885. *Politics of Aristotle.* Clarendon.

Latour, Bruno. 2015. *Face à Gaia: Huit conférences sur le nouveau régime climatique.* La Découverte.

———. 2018. *Down to Earth: Politics in the New Climate Regime.* Polity.

Ley, Lucas. 2021. *Building on Borrowed Time: Rising Seas and Failing Infrastructure in Semarang.* University of Minnesota Press.

Marx, Karl. 1930. *Capital.* Vol. 1. Translated by Eden Paul and Cedar Paul. Dent.

Marx, Karl, and Friedrich Engels. 1978. *Manifesto of the Communist Party.* In *The Marx–Engels Reader,* edited by Robert C. Tucker. Norton.

Moore, Jason W. 2016. *Anthropocene or Capitalocene? Nature, History and the Crisis of Capitalism.* PM Press.

Morin, Edgar. 1999. *Seven Complex Lessons in Education for the Future.* UNESCO.

Olwig, Kenneth. 2019. *The Meanings of Landscape: Essays on Place, Space, Environment and Justice.* Routledge.

Peperzak, Adriaan. 1995. "Life, Science and Wisdom according to Descartes." *History of Philosophy Quarterly* 12, no. 2: 133–53. https://www.jstor.org/stable/27744655.

Pickering, Andrew. 2008. "New Ontologies." In *The Mangle in Practice: Science, Society and Becoming,* edited by Andrew Pickering and Keith Guzik. Duke University Press.

Schmitt, Carl. 2006. *The Nomos of the Earth in the International Law of the Jus Publicum Europaeum.* Telos Press.

———. 2014. *Land and Sea.* Counter-Currents.

Searle, John. 1992. *The Rediscovery of the Mind.* MIT Press.

Serres, Michel. 1995. *The Natural Contract.* Translated by Elizabeth MacArthur and William Paulson. University of Michigan Press.

Simonetti, Cristián. 2018. *Sentient Conceptualisations: Feeling for Time in the Sciences of the Past.* Routledge.

———. 2022. "Viscosity in Matter, Life and Sociality: The Case of Glacial Ice." *Theory, Culture and Society* 39, no. 2: 111–30. DOI: 10.1177/02632764211030977.

Simonetti, Cristián, and Tim Ingold. 2018. "Ice and Concrete: Solid Fluids of Environmental Change." *Journal of Contemporary Archaeology* 5, no. 1: 19–31. DOI: 10.1558/jca.33371.

Steinberg, Philip. 2011. "Liquid Urbanity: Re-engineering the City in a Post-Terrestrial World." In *Engineering Earth: The Impact of Megaengineering Projects,* edited by Stanley D. Brunn. Springer Science + Business Media B.V.

PART 1

Introduction to Part 1:
Shifting Grounds

The default assumption of modernist architecture and city planning is that there already exists a flat, solid ground on which to build. But as the chapters making up Part 1 show, the reality could not be more different. The creation and maintenance of this ground call for significant feats of engineering, and their success can by no means be guaranteed, least of all in the long term. Solidity has to be wrested from a medium that is ever susceptible to liquefaction. Liquid water, especially, is never far away, and is prone to reassert its presence, as Paolo Gruppuso discovered in his home city of Latina. About 70 kilometers from Rome, the city was built on land reclaimed in the early 1930s from the Pontine Marshes, under the direction of the fascist regime of Benito Mussolini. The regime decreed that the wetlands should be drained in order to provide a hard surface for building and compact soil for the intensive cultivation of cereal crops. Though water would still have its place in the city, it was ordained to run within the confines of underground pipes or drains, to emerge above ground only as a decorative accompaniment to monumental fountains whose grandiose symbolism would proclaim a message of absolute human control.

Yet Gruppuso shows in Chapter 2 that far from consenting to dance to its master's tune, the water itself has other ideas. It wants to follow its old habits, from its marshy days, sinking and settling into a soft and yielding earth. Gruppuso is surprised to find pools of stagnant water cropping up here and there in the city, around which flourish a wealth of fauna and flora native to the region. Reflected in the still surfaces of the pools he sees the cityscape floating as a mirage, weightless and translucent. Could this floating city, he wonders, be a vision of the future? The fountains of Latina indicate that the modern city is not averse to water so long as it runs or flows along regular channels properly insulated from dry land. What it cannot tolerate is water that not only overspills its proper confines but stays put, refusing to drain away. Going nowhere, stagnant water threatens to dissolve the city's foundations. Here, it is not water's fluidity that comes to the fore but rather its property of what Franz Krause, in Chapter 3, calls *liquescence.*

Krause takes us to Aklavik, a "town" of no more than 600 inhabitants situated in the delta of the Mackenzie River, in the northwest Canadian Arctic. Like other deltas around the world, this is a region in which land and sea blend, continually reshaping the multiple river channels as they do so. The instability of delta regions is such as to overwhelm any human attempts to enforce a rigid division between dry land and running water. Attempts along these lines have generally ended in failure and ruination, making life more difficult, not less, for delta inhabitants. In the Arctic, however, there is an additional factor to contend with, since rising temperatures have caused once permanently frozen ground to thaw. As its ice content melts, the ground — now saturated with liquid water — both softens and swells, leading roads to fracture, bridges to collapse, and buildings to subside, along with dislodging underground water pipes and sewage systems.

Delta inhabitants are accustomed to an unstable ground, where you can never be sure whether it will hold firm beneath your feet. For residents of Aklavik, however, this is compounded by an awareness that the changing climate has not only reduced the overwinter period of solid ice cover but also greatly extended the "in-between" periods during which ice is neither frozen solid nor fully melted. In these periods, things can go one way or the other, depending on increasingly unpredictable weather conditions. The concept of "liquescence," for Krause, captures the affective experience of this uncertainty. It lies in the ever-present potential of grounds to liquefy. A liquescent ground is one whose solidity can never be taken for granted. Many of the world's great cities, originally established in the basins of major rivers that afforded transport and trade, rest on precisely such uncertain foundations.

One such is the city of Paris, and in Chapter 4, Germain Meulemans leads us on an expedition beneath its streets, introducing us to a subterranean world ever on the verge of liquefaction. If Gruppuso sees a vision of a floating city reflected in the stagnant pools of Latina, Meulemans shows us that for Paris the vision is not so far from reality. Unbeknownst to the great majority of its inhabitants, as they go about their business in the city, its buildings and other structures are afloat in a liquescent milieu, subject to unpredictable fluctuations in the underground water table. Life in the city functions according to rules that take for granted the solidity of its foundations, but those who struggle to build and maintain these foundations, Meulemans observes, are obliged to play by different rules.

For more than two centuries, Paris has entrusted the security of its foundations to legions of workmen who originally honed their skills in the labors of mining and well-digging. For them, the city exists as a labyrinth of underground shafts and galleries, propped up with wooden beams, which must be kept in repair lest they collapse, leading — as they say — to the sky to fall in when a sinkhole opens in the ground above. Their work of maintenance literally underpins the city. More recently, however, another approach to shoring up the city's foundations has risen to prominence, drawing on the labors of quarrymen with experience in the construction of earthworks, such as for military fortifications and dam-building. The idea is to drive the water out from under the city by filling the cavities with rubble. What better way could there be to dispose of the immense volume of earth released by the construction of new subway lines?

The approach remains controversial and is countered by supporters of underpinning who argue that filling up existing cavities will not eliminate the underground waters but merely deflect them along different paths. But behind the debate, Meulemans shows, lies a more fundamental contradiction between two ways of understanding the ground of the city. Is it a taken-for-granted background for the life to be carried on at its surface, or something more like a membrane, mediating an ongoing conversation between what is going on above and below, a conversation that we ignore at our peril?

Residents of Colonia z-10, a settlement of around 5,000 souls on the outskirts of Rio de Janeiro and close to the city's international airport, face much the same contradiction. They inhabit an island surrounded by mangrove vegetation, which once supported a thriving fishing economy but is now so fertilized by sewage, coated by plastic bags, polluted by oil spills, and clogged with landfill from urban waste disposal that most former fishermen have had to turn to alternative sources of income. Nevertheless, as Luciana Lang shows in Chapter 5, life in the colony continues to be governed by complex negotiations between the watery environment below, which habitually floods the settlement, and the comings and goings of people and other life-forms above. This requires of residents a certain flexibility, allowing them to adapt to ever-changing conditions.

Urban developers, however, take a different view. In their eyes, architecture should rest on solid foundations. Rather like the reclaimers of the Pontine Marshes, they have no love of marshlands or swamps, regarding them as unhealthy and mosquito-infested, a source of bad air, and good only for landfill. Development means building upward, but this cannot be done on swampy ground until it has first been filled with rubble and then concreted over. This is precisely what has happened in the Colony, with builders putting up two- and three-story houses as investments in real estate. Yet residents worry that the waters sealed below, out of sight and out of mind, will have the last word. One resident told Lang that to mount three floors made from slabs of concrete above a swamp is asking for trouble. Indeed, on the evidence of these chapters, we might wonder whether there is any city, from Paris to Rio, in which liquefaction will not win out in the end.

2

City Wetlands: Unsettling Topography of Urban Liquefaction

Paolo Gruppuso

Architects Anuradha Mathur and Dilip da Cunha have recently challenged the common assumption of a sharp distinction between solid ground and water, letting us imagine an "ocean of wetness"[1] in which water and land intermingle:

> When we experience "water" on the other side of a line that allegedly separates it from "land," we know it to be by design, design that articulates a surface for habitation. This surface has served as a ground for experience, understanding, and knowledge. Today, however, with rising seas, warming temperatures, and the increasing frequency of floods, this surface along with the edifice of civilization and certainty built upon it is threatened, calling into question the act of separation that brought it into being. (Mathur and da Cunha 2017)

---

1   A transdisciplinary design platform initiated by Mathur and da Cunha in 2017: https://www.mathurdacunha.com/ocean-of-wetness.

Following the same line of thinking, Tim Ingold envisions the ground of cities as an ocean and their buildings as ships floating in an unstable medium that challenges the alleged solidity of the city (2022, 166–79). These arguments remind me of what I experienced while exploring abandoned areas in my hometown of Latina, Italy, where spontaneous wetlands emerge whose shallow waters, still and stagnant, mirror the surrounding buildings. The reluctance of these waters to flow triggers imaginaries of marshy, natural, and disorderly environments, commonly perceived as the opposite of the urban built landscape, where water is supposed to run through highly restricted channels, such as fountains, canals, and sewers (Gandy 2014; Gruppuso 2022).

For the people of Latina, a medium-size city on the Italian west coast, 70 kilometers south of Rome, these abandoned areas are vacant sites—gaps in the urban fabric that are unspeakable in the language of urban architecture and unreadable through the lens of economic and ecological rationality. Instead of a solid base, these wet interstices reveal an unstable ground, exposed to the vagaries of the weather and to the anomalies of the climate. In this chapter, I draw on the unsettling images of the built environment mirrored in the shallow waters of urban wetlands, and embrace the provocation of Mathur and da Cunha (2014, 2017) to see water everywhere and to think in terms of wetness, thus revealing a liquid urban topography emerging in the shadow of climate change. My focus will remain on the city of Latina, whose history and relations with water epitomize the predicaments of modernity (Gandy 2014, 4).

Three Fountains: Disciplining Water

Latina was founded in 1932, under the name of Littoria, during the reclamation of the Pontine Marshes, one of the largest forested marshlands in Italy, perceived by the fascist regime as a "watery desert" (Serra 1925, 5). This project of land reclamation, named *Bonifica Integrale* (wholescale reclamation), turned the Marshes into an agrarian space characterized by a sophisticated system of channels, pumps, and dykes, and colonized with settlers brought from northern Italy. Within this engineered landscape, the city was originally envisioned as a center for the new community of settlers, an infrastructure functional to the overall project of Bonifica Integrale, like a channel or a pumping station (Folchi 2015, 70–71). With Latina's foundation, what had once been an anonymous rural village became first a town and, subsequently in 1934, the capital city of the new province of the same name (Cefaly 2021). This development was accompanied by a progressive abstraction of the urban landscape from the waterscape of the region, as can be traced in public architecture. Each of Latina's three main squares is centered on a fountain, which reflects the city's relation with water.

I became aware of these traces thanks to architect and historian Pietro Cefaly, director of the local institute of urban culture,[2] who took me for a walking tour of the city center, showing me its "hydrological paraphernalia" (Gandy 2014, 14). Our walk began in the Piazza del Quadrato, which takes its name from Cancello del Quadrato, one of the key locations in the Marshes before the reclamation (Bianchini and Trabucco 2022, 84). The square is dominated by the headquarters of the Opera Nazionale Combattenti,[3] the organization in charge of the Bonifica Integrale and of the following colonization. At the center of the square lies a fountain with a monument to the Reclaimer, built in the 1920s to celebrate the work of the Opera Nazionale Combattenti, and donated to the city of Latina in the 1950s (fig. 2.1). The monument is dominated by the figure of a sinewy man, the Reclaimer, struggling to hold a sluice gate, and represents reclamation as a material and bodily fight against the stagnant waters of the Marshes. A few hundred meters away is another square, Piazza del Popolo, where the town hall is located. This square pivots around a circular fountain, with a sphere in the center, made of white marble. "Here," my interlocutor Pietro Cefaly explains, "water becomes an abstract element assuming a strong political power in the shadow of the city tower, where Mussolini

2   Casa dell'Architettura di Latina, https://www.casadellarchitettura.eu/.

3   Organization of veterans of World War I.

Fig. 2.1. Fountain with the monument to the Reclaimer. Photograph by the author.

used to give his speeches." The last fountain is in Piazza della Libertà, in front of the prefecture building (Palazzo del Governo), and it depicts a wheat spike, representing the total success of the reclamation that, by taming water, transformed the Marshes into productive fields.

Latina's main squares make up a "hydraulic topography" that represents the progressive control over water established during the reclamation and its abstraction from the city. In the urban context, water runs underground, except in fountains, where its orderly emission attests to the rule of the Bonifica Integrale. This topography describes a foundation myth that pivots on the conversion of the stagnant waters of the marshes into running water. It corresponds to a process of solidification that frames the city within the time and space of modernity, as an artifice "defined against nature [where] the symbolic elements diverged from the increasingly hidden functional realm" (Gandy 2014, 14). Here water runs into an invisible infrastructure, concealed from inhabitants, and removed from their experience.

Viewed thus, the city looks like a platform that stands against the waters thanks to solid foundations firmly anchored to the ground. This image of urban solidity resonates with a hegemonic reading of human history as proceeding from the watery chaos of marshlands to the ordered urban environment (Gruppuso 2022). Yet it also clashes with the image with which I began, of a liquid city reflected in the stagnant waters of emergent and unforeseen wetlands. In the following section, I describe three examples of spontaneous wetland formation that serve as a counterpoint to the monumental fountains built to celebrate the reclamation. In so doing, I trace an alternative topography of urban liquefaction.

Three Wetlands: Revealing Water

Like other cities in the Mediterranean region, Latina has been affected in recent years by an increasing frequency of "flash floods" caused by changes in the regional climate that trigger heavy rainstorms with exceptional precipitations concentrated in a short time (Cioffi et al. 2017). Beyond the unquestionable damage and risk to the city and its inhabitants, these extreme meteorological events have other important effects. First, they reveal the suppressed geology of the city and challenge the rhetoric of the Bonifica Integrale as a technological enterprise that has drained the marshes once and for all. Second, these events make it possible to experience climate change at a human scale (Graef 2017) and in the urban realm. Both these effects materialize in unexpected city wetlands, "where water lies at the intersection of landscape and infrastructure, crossing between visible and invisible urban domains" (Gandy 2014, 1).

I have observed the action of water while walking in my neighborhood after a rainstorm, when I noticed that water in the pavement was not standing still in puddles, but streaming in small rivulets. It took a while for me to realize that it was flowing from an abandoned field higher than the street level, whence it filtered through the ground, ran into the pavement, and flooded the street. This phenomenon challenged the topography of the city by transforming the street into a floodplain for standing water that intercepted streams flowing from a wet field. Intrigued, I followed the water upstream to its origin in the abandoned

Fig. 2.2. Urban pond in an abandoned area. Photograph by the author.

area, where I discovered an interesting environment character-ized by plants and animals, such as reeds (*Phragmites australis*) and cattle egrets (*Bubulcus ibis*), that normally populate the pro-tected coastal wetlands situated a few kilometers away from the city center. I can imagine that these species are attracted by the ecological features of the area, which, though not protected, are typical for a Mediterranean wetland, such as saturated meadow, canebrake, and shallow water.

Beyond the unsettling feeling of sinking into an unstable, wet, and uneven ground, albeit surrounded by concrete, what captured my imagination was the vernal pool I found in the area. This pond, of about 100 square meters, was surrounded by eucalypti. These trees, introduced from Australia in the late nineteenth century when their smell was believed to combat malaria, were extensively planted during the reclamation on ac-count of their hydrophilic properties. The shallow water of the pond mirrored the trees and the buildings behind in a trembling image in which the eucalypti, far from epitomizing the fascist reclamation and its project of solidification, were turned into custodians of a process of liquefaction that was transforming the reclaimed landscape into something reminiscent of the Pon-tine Marshes.

I have encountered a similar phenomenon in other interstitial areas that I have further explored in Latina, where rainstorms bring unexpected ecologies to life by creating wetlands. One example is a small area just behind the most important downtown shopping mall, where a vernal pool lies at the foot of one of the tallest skyscrapers in Italy (fig. 2.2). The pond in this area is probably the result of an uncompleted project that originally involved the construction of a tunnel road underneath a large pedestrian area between the skyscraper and the mall. Neither the tunnel nor the pedestrian zone was ever built, and now the levels are uneven, resulting in a wet area that lies abandoned, at the edge of the street, hidden behind trash cans, a billboard, and a neglected hedgerow. In the middle of the pond are relics of construction materials that emerge during the dry seasons. In winter, instead, water reclaims its space, feeding rush and reeds, as a memento of the natural history of the region. As in the location described previously, here too the pond reflects the surrounding buildings, setting the solidity of construction materials, such as concrete, iron, and glass, in counterpoint to the liquidity of water.

I have found one further instance of the same phenomenon in another abandoned field, usually overgrown with *Arundo donax*, a species of cane that proliferates along drainage channels and in the interstices of the urban environment. Periodically, the city council cuts the cane, revealing an uneven field characterized by small depressions that rainstorms fill with water and a deeper pond colonized by aquatic plants. However, on closer inspection, I discovered that what looked like a pond was instead a section of an old drainage channel that was originally underground. With time, this section of the channel was exposed to the elements, and it is now filled with rainwater, in a palimpsestic process that has allowed the underground infrastructure to emerge in the form of ruins, thus bringing to life new and unexpected environmental relationships. As in the previous locations, the water in this pond also mirrored the surrounding environment, with the tall buildings that characterize the peripheral zone of the city.

The City as Unfolding Wetness

Modernist conceptions of the city envision the urban environment as a well-defined space set apart from a different landscape that is either wild or rural. Proponents of this view argue that in order to protect nature and to face the climate crisis, "the city must retreat into its own territory, develop sharp boundaries, make itself thick and solid like stone" (Magnago Lampugnani 2019).[4] Their mistake is to assume that urban environments can be confined to cities, the combined area of which account for only 3 percent of ice-free land surface (Boeri 2021, 37–38). It results in a picture in which every urban environment resembles an island in an archipelago set amidst a common ocean, in which water is always on "the other side of a line" from land (Mathur and da Cunha 2017). The wetlands I have encountered in Latina unsettle this picture and force us to rethink the relations between land and water. The resulting topography recalls Ingold's (2022, 178) imagining of the city as an "aquapelagic" space, in which water and land intermingle.

This image, moreover, is not far short of being borne out in reality. According to current projections, the expected rise in sea level will put most of the coastal areas in the Mediterranean region at risk of inundation in the next decades (Rizzo et al. 2022; UN Environment Programme 2017; European Environment Agency 2021). However, the present is already challenging for Mediterranean cities, which, like Latina, are experiencing extreme meteorological events with increased frequency. This context of climate uncertainty throws modernist conceptions into doubt, and asks us to rethink urban areas as "a fact in nature" (Mumford 1938, 5). It is interesting that urbanist and cultural historian Lewis Mumford used an aquatic metaphor, likening the city to a "run of mackerel" (5), thus anticipating

---

4   Vittorio Magnago Lampugnani is a well-known architect and emeritus professor at ETH in Zürich. He exemplifies this modernist approach in his recent "The City Is Not the Landscape," published in *L'Architetto*, the journal of the Italian Council of Architects (Magnago Lampugnani 2019). The translation is mine.

contemporary perspectives, such as those of Mathur and da Cunha (2017), who view water and land not as opposing elements but as part of a continuum. Their proposal, from which I began, reimagines the future of cities by questioning the line of separation that divides water from land.

The recurring image I have described, in which the built environment is reflected in the shallow waters of spontaneously formed wetlands, suggests such a reshuffling of the relations between land and water in the urban environment. The example of Latina is important in this regard because, like many cities all over the world, it was constructed by reclaiming a marshland, thus causing a process of solidification of the surrounding landscape that produced soil sealing and compaction. This solidification is nowadays problematic, because it exacerbates the effects of climate change, such as floods and rainstorms. These events unsettle urban topography, revealing the fragility of an old drainage system and the inadequacy of the modernist ideology that underpinned its construction. This is in fact the expression of an unsustainable land-centric perspective, which envisions the water of the marsh as an enemy from which to reclaim land. It is represented in the monumental fountains of Latina, which subjugate water and transform it into a decorative element to celebrate the solidity of the city. When water exceeds human control and "crosses the line," as in the interstitial areas I have described, it is treated as matter out of place, with no other purpose than to flow away as waste. However, water is now claiming back its space, standing in interstitial areas, and refusing to flow. Its reluctance to flow constipates the already slow hydraulic metabolism of the city, and challenges its alleged solidity.

This context of climate uncertainty calls for a new relation between water and cities, as in the urban wetlands I have portrayed, which are symbolically anchored to the past of Latina and thus neglected as vacant spaces or gaps. These areas may remain unnoticed if seen through the technocratic lens of urban planning, because they are not green areas built from a blueprint and may not provide measurable ecosystem services. They grow as convivial experiments in cohabitation among myriad organisms and beings, giving gifts such as climate regulation by moderating the heat island effect, mitigating floods by retaining water, and offering opportunities for multispecies encounters by providing refuge for wildlife. For these reasons, such areas, with their stagnant water, should not only be integrated into the urban fabric; they should also be key to reimagining the sustainable future of the city in the wake of climate change. Such a future is reflected in the image I noticed in the water, in which the city loses its alleged solidity, appearing instead as a zone of intermingling, placed right at the heart of the water cycle and on the intercontinental routes of migratory birds. It is a zone that unfolds through different forms of wetness that coalesce in interstitial ponds, wetlands, and vernal pools, thus exposing the unsustainable solidity of the urban fabric, and anticipating its future liquefaction.

References

Bianchini, Ferruccio, and Marcello Trabucco, eds. 2022. *Latina: Architetture e progetti della città di fondazione, 1927–1944.* Casa dell'Architettura Edizioni.

Cefaly, Pietro. 2021. "Littoria-Latina: Nascita e sviluppo della città." In *Prospettive Pontine: Contributi per una pianificazione del territorio pontino,* edited by Casa dell'Architettura. Casa dell'Architettura.

Cioffi, Francesco, Federico Conticello, and Vincenzo Scotti. 2017. *Analisi degli eventi estremi di tipo idrologico sul territorio di latina, I° Rapporto intermedio della convezione fra il Comune di Latina e il Centro di ricerca e servizi per l'innovazione tecnologica sostenibile del Polo universitario La Sapienza sede di Latina (Ce.R.S.I.Te.S.).* Comune di Latina/ Università La Sapienza.

European Environment Agency. 2021. *Global and European Sea Level Rise.* https://www.eea.europa.eu/ims/global-and-european-sea-level-rise.

Folchi, Annibale. 2015. *Littoria: La pupilla del Duce, 1932–1943.* Arco Edizioni.

Gandy, Matthew. 2014. *The Fabric of Space: Water, Modernity and the Urban Imagination.* MIT Press.

Graef, Dana J. 2017. "Can We 'See' Climate Change?" *Sapiens.* https://www.sapiens.org/column/the-climate-report/climate-change-evidence/.

Gruppuso, Paolo. 2022. "In-between Solidity and Fluidity: The Reclaimed Marshlands of Agro Pontino." *Theory, Culture & Society* 39, no. 2: 53–73. DOI: 10.1177/02632764211038669.

Ingold, Tim. 2022. *Imagining for Real: Essays on Creation, Attention and Correspondence.* Routledge.

Magnago Lampugnani, Vittorio. 2019. "La Città non è il Paesaggio." *L'Architetto* 4 (luglio/agosto): 19–22.

Mathur, Anuradha, and Dilip da Cunha. 2014. *Design in the Terrain of Water.* ORO Editions/Applied Research and Design.

———. 2017. *Ocean of Wetness: A Platform for Design.* https://www.mathurdacunha.com/ocean-of-wetness.

Mumford, Lewis. 1938. *The Culture of Cities.* Harcourt Brace Jovanovich.

Ritchie, Hannah, Veronika Samborska, and Max Roser. 2024. "Urbanization." *OurWorldinData.org.* https://ourworldindata.org/urbanization.

Rizzo, Angela, Vittoria Vandelli, Christopher Gauci, George Buhagiar, Anton S. Micallef, and Mauro Soldati. 2022. "Potential Sea Level Rise Inundation in the Mediterranean: From Susceptibility Assessment to Risk Scenarios for Policy Action." *Water* 14, no. 3: 1–24. DOI: 10.3390/w14030416.

Serra, Pierluigi. 1925. *La bonifica del pantano dei gricilli: Mediante sollevamento meccanico e colmata.* Consorzio della Bonificazione Pontina.

UN Environment Programme, Mediterranean Action Plan Barcelona Convention. 2017. *Climate Change. The Mediterranean Region: A Climate Change Hotspot.* https://www.medqsr.org/climate-change.

3

Building on Shifting Ground: Liquescence in an Arctic River Delta

Franz Krause

Land, Sea, and River Deltas

Aklavik is a hamlet of around 600 inhabitants located in the Mackenzie River Delta at the border of the Inuvialuit and Gwich'in Settlement Regions in the Canadian Arctic. The large majority of its inhabitants belong to the two Indigenous peoples that have long lived in the region and moved into settlements such as Aklavik during the late twentieth century: the Ehdiitat Gwich'in (literally, "those who dwell among the timber stands," i.e., in the Mackenzie Delta), a local band of Dinjii Zhuh, who are also known as Gwich'in people and form part of a wider family of Athabascan-speaking groups spread out across large areas of western North America; and the Inuvialuit (literally, "the real people"), as the Inuit of the western Canadian Arctic call themselves, who refer to the delta population as Uummarmiut (literally, "the people of the evergreen trees") and are related to other Inuit groups across the circumpolar North. Many of its inhabitants refer to Aklavik as "the town" in opposition to "the land," by which they mean the delta, the coast, and the nearby mountains where they maintain camps and hunt, fish, and gather.

Geomorphologically speaking, river deltas can be prime locations from which to rethink the relationship between land and sea — they develop in dynamic processes that are both terrestrial and maritime to the extent that an opposition between the two is all but effaced (Bhattacharya 2006). In deltas, there is no discernible line between land, on the one side, and sea, on the other. Fed by sediments transported over long distances and settling as the current slows down, while simultaneously eroded by tides, currents, and floods, these are transient landscapes both spatially and temporally, where land and sea blend into each other and keep reshaping river channels, wetlands, and sandbanks. Seasonal rhythms, for example of drier and wetter periods, play important parts in these transformations, and in the Arctic, the cycles of freezing and thawing water and ground bring about continual shifts in river deltas (Walker 1998). For parts of the year, bodies of water are mostly covered by ice and precipitation falls as snow, accumulating in the catchment to then melt in spring and flood the river and delta. Ice cover on rivers and along the coast controls erosion in winter, while ice movement during spring can cause extreme flooding and reshape channels.

Also socially speaking, river deltas are often places of mixing and mingling that defy clear-cut boundaries between, for example, land- and sea-based livelihoods or ethnic categories (Krause and Harris 2021). The fertile soils and nutritious waters provide for rich but often fluctuating agricultural, fishery, and other resources that occasional and permanent inhabitants may exploit, often in a seasonal pattern corresponding with water levels, temperatures, or animal migrations. In the Senegalese Sine-Saloum Delta, people say that they have twelve professions in order to get by (Simon 2021), each focusing on a specific affordance with particular spatial and temporal dimensions. The fishing village of Barrinha in the Brazilian Parnaíba Delta grows and shrinks in correspondence with the particular tides that promise rich shrimp catches around the deltaic islands (Horisberger 2021).

Fig. 3.1. Brandon McLeod in front of his Aklavik house, May 2022. The annual spring flood had entered the settlement, but an upstream ice dam kept higher waters away and pushed them into other parts of the delta, so that Aklavik did not have to be evacuated. Photograph by Shandel McLeod.

And in the Ayeyarwady Delta in Myanmar, many dry-season farmers are also rainy-season fishermen, a relationship that a policy of increasing the production of this "rice bowl" has ignored at its own peril and to the detriment of many delta inhabitants (Ivars and Venot 2019). In Aklavik and other Mackenzie Delta settlements, coastal Inuvialuit and inland Dinjii Zhuh live side by side only according to the maps and membership registers that Indigenous organizations adopted as tools to articulate their land entitlement vis-à-vis the Canadian government; in actual life, many Aklavik families have members and ancestors from both of the regional Indigenous peoples and of many other origins (Krause 2022).

Urban infrastructures, including large buildings, paved surfaces, piped water, and sewage services, fit awkwardly into the Mackenzie Delta and other river deltas around the world (fig. 3.1). This is because they are based on the idea — derived from experiences peculiar to temperate climates — that land and sea, solid and fluid, dry and wet are essentially separate realms and, should they be "mixed" in a particular place, can be separated into these two states. Architect Dilip da Cunha (2019) calls this "river literacy," that is, a peculiar way of understanding water in the landscape, confined to a limited segment of the hydrologic cycle, where it flows in a river enclosed by its banks through otherwise dry land on a sunny day. Being schooled in this river literacy means neglecting the largest part of water circulation, when it rains, soaks, floods, lingers, and evaporates. When river-literate planners build cities, they envisage its infrastructures as participating in a world where land and sea can be distinguished, with the former serving as stable substrate for urban life. Architect Lindsay Bremner (2019) has pointed to the various shortcomings of this vision, for example, in relation to floods and sediments.

Da Cunha and Bremner focus on tropical regions in South Asia, where the monsoon plays a pivotal role in upsetting the river literacy of temperate-region planners. Additionally, for the inhabitants of river deltas around the world, recent transformations including climate change, large infrastructures such as dams, and problematic governance present formidable challenges and often cause intense hardships (Nicholls et al. 2020) as they imperil lives and livelihoods modeled on the premises of river literacy. Global awareness of these challenges and hardships is growing, but historians (e.g., Bhattacharyya 2018), geographers (e.g., Lahiri-Dutt and Samanta 2013), and anthropologists (e.g., Dewan 2021) have shown that they tend to have deep colonial roots, often originating in attempts to render productive both people and landscapes by enforcing a material and legal separation of land and water. Ironically, increasingly sophisticated efforts to impose this separation often render people and infrastructures even more vulnerable to a deltaic world that does not conform to the illusion that land and sea are separate realms. As a result, river deltas may appear like dystopias (Cons 2018), in which all that is left to do for people is to cope with continual calamity.

Freeze, Thaw, and Liquescence

In the Mackenzie Delta and other Arctic regions, dwindling ice and permafrost figure centrally in current processes of urban liquefaction. Land and water that tend to be frozen seasonally or even for years on end have long played major roles in the landscape and for its inhabitants. But global heating is contributing to the landscape's liquefaction. This trend is manifest in the Mackenzie Delta, too, where Dinjii Zhuh and Inuvialuit have noted the effects of thawing permafrost (Andrews et al. 2016) and the shortening of the annual period of reliable ice cover on rivers, lakes, and the sea. However, for many people, the result is not simply a more fluid landscape in place of a formerly more solid world, but an extension of the ambivalent intermediary conditions of freeze-up and break-up, when ice and frozen ground form and disintegrate (Krause 2021). Open waters and hard-frozen watercourses pose few problems to Aklavik inhabitants, but the transitions between them can be treacherous and bring many activities to a halt.

Ground that collapses or bulges up with permafrost thaw, and seasonal transitions of states of aggregation, are of course inimical to urban infrastructures that presuppose a solid substrate. This is reflected, for example, in the fact that Aklavik does not distribute its drinking water and collect its sewage through underground pipes, but provides these services with large trucks that pump water from the local treatment plant into, and sewage out from, designated tanks in hamlet buildings. The techniques for constructing these buildings, too, reflect the instability of the ground — the oldest houses still standing hail from the 1960s, according to the estimates of some Aklavik people. These houses were built directly onto the ground. None is inhabited anymore because they have all, to varying degrees, sunk into the softening earth. The next generation of houses are built above the ground, supported by pilings that have been driven many meters deep into the permafrost. However, because the permafrost is thawing, and the pilings themselves conduct summertime warmth into the ground, even these supports have become unreliable, and some of the houses have begun to crack, or their doors and windows no longer open and close properly, because the buildings are shifting. The more recent constructions in Aklavik are supported above ground by so-called pads, which are wooden racks in which most pieces are rectangular, but some wedged, making it possible to adjust their height according to the movements of the liquefying ground. The newest generation of buildings are set on metal frames with variable legs that can likewise be adjusted according to the movements of the ground.

It would be misleading, however, to attribute the shifting substrate only to climate change, although global heating does of course intensify and accelerate these instabilities. But delta ground has always been unstable, erosion and sedimentation happen all the time, and most people, most of the time, are not bothered by them. During an August visit to a camp, I once noticed — just before we were returning to Aklavik — that one of the pans had not yet been cleaned. I hurried to the river to wash it, in a place where the current is slow and tends to add sediment along the shore. Running right into the soft sediments close to the water, I sunk in more than ankle deep, much to the amusement of my companions, and learned my lesson that mud can sometimes, and in some places, be rather treacherous and at times, in other places, fairly firm under one's feet. For delta inhabitants, the issue with solid and fluid mud is not that it can be both at the same time, in the course of a day or across the seasons. Rather, the problem seems to be that it is becoming more fluid, at more times, and in more places than ever before.

The shift from more to less stable surfaces has less to do with a general, objective, and linear process of liquefaction than with what Mark Nuttall (2019) has called "liquescence." Based on his fieldwork in northwest Greenland, Nuttall argues that

> thinking of the experience of climate change as *liquescence* is a way to capture melt and thaw in affective, sensory and embodied ways. People — especially hunters and fishers — move through an environment anticipating encounters with icy, liquescent, and watery spaces often on the same day, what-

> ever the season, and they sense how the weather is, and how,
> through the movement of clouds or a change in wind direc-
> tion, for example, it is likely to alter its mood. (Nuttall 2019,
> 73; emphasis original)

Nuttall emphasizes the affective dimensions of inhabiting liquescence, which is not just about the unidirectional process of
melting or thawing, but mostly about living with the *potentiality*
of things becoming liquid. Understanding a world as liquescent
means acknowledging this potential, and the uncertainty that
goes with it. You never know for sure how the ground will be-
have.

Liquescent Aklavik

Having grown out of an Inuvialuit camp that was joined by a fur
trading post in 1911, Aklavik soon developed into the principal
commercial and administrative hub of the western Canadian
Arctic, with mission churches, hospitals, schools, hotels, and a
police detachment. As a delta settlement, it was well-connected
through shipping channels and surrounded by rich hunting
grounds for fur-bearing animals, but it was also prone to flooding, and its general erosion and muddiness did not chime well
with settler ideas for a twentieth-century town. The Canadian
government resolved in the 1950s that the delta was not a safe
place for Aklavik, and decided to relocate it onto dry, higher
ground on the edge of the delta. This new town, with specially
developed infrastructure to provide water and sewage disposal
despite the Arctic conditions, and other modern, Canadian features, came to be known as Inuvik.

However, not all Aklavik inhabitants were keen on moving to Inuvik, and in recent decades, large floods have become
less frequent, caused by, among other things, a reduction in the
thickness of river ice. Nevertheless, they still happen occasion-
ally. The last major flood occurred in 2006 and meant airlifting a
quarter of Aklavik's population to Inuvik. One of the most striking aspects of this flood was that the water did not actually enter

any houses, since all currently inhabited dwellings are constructed above ground. Also, most families own boats, so getting around would not have been an issue either. What turned the flood into an emergency was that Aklavik, too, had become accustomed to running water, flush toilets, and sewage disposal. With the floods, the trucks supplying fresh water and pumping sewage had trouble reaching some of the houses. Additionally, the road to the place where the sewage truck was supposed to dump its load, affectionately called "Shit Lake" by Aklavik people, was flooded, so that there was no safe place to dispose of the wastewater. In short, it was not the water in itself that made this flood problematic, but the infrastructure that emulated modern, high-ground urbanity, including flush toilets, roads, trucks, and so on.

In the spring of 2020, Aklavik people were again anxious about another possible flood. The ice had been unusually thick in the winter, which made it liable to jam upon breaking up in late May and to cause water levels to rise. The hamlet administration had improved the road to the sewage dumping point and felt fairly confident that they would be able to handle a flood, but it now had something else to worry about. In case they would have to evacuate people to Inuvik, it was not clear at all where they could be lodged, given the ongoing Covid-19 pandemic and its attendant physical distancing rules. In 2006, the evacuated families had stayed with relatives and friends in Inuvik, or were housed in the town's recreational complex for the few days until the waters receded and it was safe to return home. This did not seem a good option in 2020. The flooding issue had thus shifted from sewage infrastructure to epidemiological considerations, but it did not materialize in the end — there was no major ice jam around Aklavik and therefore no flooding or need for evacuations.

However, the hope that physical distancing would prevent a spread of the pandemic to and within Aklavik also inspired the Inuvialuit and Dinjii Zhuh land-claim organizations to distribute grants to families willing to spend extended periods of time at their camps in the delta, the hills, or on the coast. For many Aklavik people, being "on the land" affords a highly desirable opportunity to heal from the ills of settlement life. But they usually have little possibility to leave the settlement, because the economic situation has reversed. Well into the second half of the twentieth century, Dinjii Zhuh and Inuvialuit generated their income on the land — mostly by hunting and trapping, but also in construction and hydrocarbon exploration — and spent it in the settlements at stores and celebrations. More recently, however, income-generating jobs have been concentrated in the settlements, and only those who earn enough can afford the vehicles, buildings, fuel, and other provisions it takes to spend time in camps. For some Aklavik families, Covid-19 grants thus offered a welcome support to allow them to do what they had been wanting to do all along.

These glimpses into Aklavik liquescence suggest that the settlement is located on shifting ground not only in the literal sense of an eroding, flooding, softening, and bulging substrate, which causes problems for urban buildings and infrastructures designed for a solid surface. For in a figurative sense, as well, the economic, social, and political ground on which the settlement rests is shifting. Aklavik itself is a temporal phenomenon that emerged at a particular historical conjuncture, when the fur trade and colonial policies spurred the concentration of mobile populations in fixed centers, but it may also dissolve again as conditions change. The "back to the land" sentiment that flared up during the height of the Covid-19 pandemic, combined with frustrations with unemployment, substance abuse, dependency, and other problems of settlement life, bears witness to this scenario. But rather than describing these dynamics in terms of liquefaction (or something solid becoming liquid), it makes more sense to discuss them in terms of liquescence (or the experience and potentiality of becoming liquid). This shifts the focus from the end point of a unidirectional process to the phase change itself, in which people inhabit an always uncertain, rhythmically hardening and softening landscape, wherein transformations are more significant than imaginary hard or soft ideal types.

References

Andrews, Thomas D., Steven V. Kokelj, Glen MacKay, Julie Buysse, Ingrid Kritsch, Alestine Andre, and Trevor Lantz. 2016. "Permafrost Thaw and Aboriginal Cultural Landscapes in the Gwich'in Region, Canada." *APT Bulletin* 47, no. 1: 15–22. https://www.jstor.org/stable/43799259.

Bhattacharya, Janok P. 2006. "Deltas." In *Facies Models Revisited,* edited by Henry W. Posamentier and Roger G. Walker. SEPM Special Publication 84.

Bhattacharyya, Debjani. 2018. *Empire and Ecology in the Bengal Delta: The Making of Calcutta.* Cambridge University Press.

Bremner, Lindsay, ed. 2019. *Monsoon [+Other] Waters.* University of Westminster.

Cons, Jason. 2018. "Staging Climate Security: Resilience and Heterodystopia in the Bangladesh Borderlands." *Cultural Anthropology* 33, no. 2: 266–94. DOI: 10.14506/ca33.2.08.

da Cunha, Dilip. 2019. *The Invention of Rivers: Alexander's Eye and Ganga's Descent.* University of Pennsylvania Press.

Dewan, Camelia. 2021. *Misreading the Bengal Delta: Climate Change, Development, and Livelihoods in Coastal Bangladesh.* University of Washington Press.

Horisberger, Nora. 2021. "'This Tide Will Be a Good Tide': On Movement, Anticipative Waiting and Tricking on the Islands of the Parnaíba Delta, Brazil." In *Delta Life: Exploring Dynamic Environments Where Rivers Meet the Sea,* edited by Franz Krause and Mark Harris. Berghahn.

Ivars, Benoit, and Jean-Philippe Venot. 2019. "Grounded and Global: Water Infrastructure Development and Policymaking in the Ayeyarwady Delta, Myanmar." *Water Alternatives* 12, no. 3: 1038–63. https://www.water-alternatives.org/index.php/alldoc/articles/vol12/v12issue3/554-a12-3-10/file.

Krause, Franz. 2021. "The Tempo of Solid Fluids: On River Ice, Permafrost, and Other Melting Matter in the Mackenzie Delta." *Theory, Culture & Society* 39, no. 2: 31–52. DOI: 10.1177/02632764211030996.

———. 2022. "Inhabiting a Transforming Delta: Volatility and Improvisation in the Canadian Arctic." *American Ethnologist* 49, no. 1: 7–19. DOI: 10.1111/amet.13051.

Krause, Franz, and Mark Harris, eds. 2021. *Delta Life: Exploring Dynamic Environments Where Rivers Meet the Sea.* Berghahn.

Lahiri-Dutt, Kuntala, and Gopa Samanta. 2013. *Dancing with the River: People and Life on the Chars of South Asia.* Yale University Press.

Nicholls, Robert J., W. Neil Adger, Craig W. Hutton, and Susan E. Hanson, eds. 2020. *Deltas in the Anthropocene.* Palgrave Macmillan.

Nuttall, Mark. 2019. "Icy, Watery, Liquescent: Sensing and Feeling Climate Change on Northwest Greenland's Coast." *Journal of Northern Studies* 13, no. 2: 71–91. DOI: 10.36368/jns.v13i2.950.

Simon, Sandro. 2021. "Gleaning Time: Practice, Pause and Anticipation in the Sine-Saloum Delta, Senegal." In *Delta Life: Exploring Dynamic Environments Where Rivers Meet the Sea,* edited by Franz Krause and Mark Harris. Berghahn.

Walker, H. Jesse. 1998. "Arctic Deltas." *Journal of Coastal Research* 14, no. 3: 719–38. https://www.jstor.org/stable/4298831.

4

Reclamation from Below: Urban Undergrounds as Geosocial Formations

Germain Meulemans

From bidimensional mapping to architectural drawing, modern thinking has tended to approach the ground as a fixed territory to furnish and occupy, as a stable base for buildings or as the surface of a compact and solid mineral world. However, this surface bias has been unsettled by recent calls to revisit urban and landscape studies with greater attention to the "vertical" (Graham 2016) and "volumetric" (McNeill 2020) dimensions of urban life, highlighting the three-dimensional nature of modern territorial governance. These debates also raise questions about anthropology's own lack of conceptualization of the ground, which is still often viewed as mere background for a dynamic social world, a blank canvas upon which human projects, history, and ideas are to be realized.[1]

---

1   I would like to thank the workers and engineers at IGC, CEREMA, Géotec, and the Musée des Arts et Métiers for allowing me to meet them and follow them underground. Many thanks to Yves Wikin and the Musée des Arts et Métiers for hosting the *Paris flotte-t-il ?* residency, and to my accomplice Anaïs Tondeur. Last but not least, thanks to Cristián Simonetti,

In truth, the ground offers a good example of how materials that seem fixed are in fact lively and in motion. Between 2015 and 2019, I conducted ethnographic fieldwork with ground engineers and technicians who attempt — most of the time successfully — to stabilize the ground on, with, and in which Paris is built. I followed them as they went out to monitor construction sites, when they talked about plan modifications with their clients, when they took soil samples in the field, and when they analyzed these samples in the laboratory (Meulemans 2019). In their daily work, these ground specialists constantly encounter ground that is on the verge of flowing, crumbling, fluctuating, collapsing, or settling. They understand the ground not as an independently existing background but as a complex of heterogeneous geo-infrastructural strata, in which mineral particles and water continuously interact with the climate, the surrounding buildings, and the excavation works going on around and about. Always suspended in liquid-solid indeterminacy (Ingold and Simonetti 2022), the urban ground is caught in a field of forces in which flows and resistances are omnipresent and can manifest in a wide variety of ways.

Witnessing maintenance engineers' and workers' daily struggle with the ground and studying the history of their discipline, I realized that the very solidity of the urban ground, instead of being a matter of fact, has always been problematic, and is akin to an ever-renewed performance that relies on perpetual engineering and ground-care practices. The urban ground is something that humans must compose with rather than furnish. In this, my research aligns with Clark and Yusoff's (2017) call to examine "geosocial formations," with the focus on the forces that bring both the social and the geologic into being, and on how specific configurations of contact with the ground and its ecologies afford certain social and political formations.

Tim Ingold, Michel Lussault, the punctum staff, and all the participants in the *Urban Liquefaction* study days that inspired this book, for the stimulating conversations and all the work that went into preparing it.

In this chapter, I follow two threads that allow me to peer through the geosocial history of Paris, a story in which one can always hear the whisper of water as it seeps through the pores and cavities of the ground. The first thread describes how the human procurement of groundwater in Paris led to a dangerous imbalance in the forces that make up the ground. The second follows a team of workers who strive to repair and maintain a network of old underground galleries in danger of collapse because of water infiltration. The two stories conjure up an understanding of ground permanence and stability as achievements rather than ontological properties, the result of constant attention and care that I call "reclamation from below."

The Hydraulic Ruminations of the Underground

Our first thread seeks the whereabouts of underground water tables in the Paris area. Water tables are a key component of the undergrounds. They mark the depth below which the soil is saturated. Any ground cavities such as wells or caves situated below this level will fill with water unless properly waterproofed. The rise and fall of water tables underneath Paris during the past fifty years offers an apt example of how the underground is entwined with aboveground life. Between the early nineteenth century and the 1970s, in the Paris area, ground waters were an essential resource for industry. Water was pumped from underground in large quantities to cool down machines or to wash materials in factories. Because of this intense pumping, water tables dropped by about 15 meters, which made the ground of the city relatively dry down to a certain depth. For more than a century, basements and underground parking lots could be built without much waterproofing. But this made them vulnerable to chronic flooding once pumping was discontinued after the deindustrialization of the 1970s.

In some areas, however, it would not be long before new kinds of pumping were installed, this time in conjunction with the construction of new underground train lines and shopping malls. For example, a powerful pump was installed at the low-

Fig. 4.1. Hommage à David Macaulay, Paris flotte-t-il?, mixed media, 35×50 cm, by Anaïs Tondeur, 2019.

est point of the Conservatoire des Arts et Métiers (3rd arrondissement), when three levels of underground floors were dug to create more class and laboratory space. This pump lifts about 300 cubic meters of water per day, and two floors would be inundated if it failed. The ground on which the Conservatoire sits is an old filled-up branch of the Seine River, and excess water from the nearby river infiltrates faster in the porous alluvium ground than elsewhere — geologists say that the river "remembers." Because of this, four similar pumps were installed within a one-kilometer radius around this one, in order to draw down the table.

Water tables did drop again in many areas, but their fluctuation was intensified, not only as climate change brought about both harder droughts and more severe rain episodes, but also as monoculture based on cereals became widespread in the surrounding countryside, soaking up rainwater before it could penetrate the deeper ground. The resulting fluctuations made it very hard for hydrologists to predict the behavior of underground water. They argue that the effect of human activities on the rhythms of the water cycle has been so disruptive that even advanced models would be of little help to predict future fluctuations.

The chaotic rise and fall of underground water tables soon posed a threat to the stability of buildings. The problem is most dire for old buildings near the Seine, which were built on wooden piles driven into the ground, an ideal foundation in these unstable soggy grounds. Whereas wood can remain in water for long periods without rotting, it will quickly degrade if shifting humidity conditions allow oxygen to penetrate the wood. That is why, between 2001 and 2004, the 3,400 oak trunks that supported the Grand Palais had to be supplanted by 1,800 underground concrete piles, which now firmly anchor the building in the bedrock.

The story of water table fluctuation and of its entwinement with changes in the urban economy, building materials and techniques, and knowledge of the underground shows how a city is never simply laid over the ground. It so thoroughly transforms and is transformed by the currents that underpin it that the surface is only conceivable as a site of exchange and interaction. In a collage series shown as part of a 2019 installation in the Museum of Arts et Métiers, artist Anaïs Tondeur showed what the area would look like if we could see it from below. Concrete casks designed to protect underground parking lots from flooding would look like boat hulls, and one would see many buildings resting on underground stilts, with pumps perpetually bailing out water from basements (fig. 4.1). All of this undermines the idea that a city is simply placed upon a solid base, suggesting rather that it is afloat in a solid fluid ground (Ingold 2022). We could indeed ask, as in the title of Tondeur's installation, "Is Paris floating?"

Stabilizing the Ground in the Aftermath of Extraction

To better understand how the stability of the ground is an achievement rather than an ontological property, let us now pick up another geosocial thread and follow those who work relentlessly to maintain and consolidate the underground. Here, my inspiration comes from maintenance studies (Denis, Mongili, and Pontille 2015), which have shown how artifacts and infrastructures can only hold in time and space thanks to the skillful attention of those who take care of them. Elsewhere (Meulemans 2022), I have argued that in the invisibility of this ground manufacturing and maintenance work lies the great paradox of earthworks and foundations, namely, that once they have been well installed, they allow modern rationality and axioms to unfold in a space that can be ordered and governed, as the modern urban project requires, yet by the same token, they themselves cannot be built by following these axioms. Instead, earth-workers and geotechnicians are forced to acknowledge the ground's dynamism and to strive to compose with it.

In Paris, the water that seeps through the ground often meets ancient cavities that are largely forgotten and sometimes completely unknown. Many of these underground holes are remains of old quarries for gypsum and limestone. Some underground quarries date back to Roman times, but most were excavated in the eighteenth and nineteenth centuries, a time of rapid urban growth and transformation, when a large proportion of the materials used to build the city was extracted, almost equivalent in volume to its aboveground mass. The quarries were outside of the city's limit at the time they were dug, but the city has since expanded and now covers them.

As water slowly creeps into these old tunnels, it dissolves the calcareous stone, which crumbles and eventually collapses entirely, forming a sinkhole that can reach the surface and swallow whatever lies on top. Sinkholes may be triggered by something as mundane as a water leak, and can have dramatic consequences for those who dwell upon the surface. One of the most well-known disasters caused by a sinkhole was the collapse of rue Denfert in 1774, after which a public Directorate for the Inspection of Quarries was established with the task of visiting old quarries, finding out where sinkholes were forming, and undertaking masonry work to stabilize them. This directorate, which still exists today, is now called the IGC (Inspection Générale des Carrières).

The IGC team encompasses several of the specialties related to the underground, and includes geologists, hydrologists, and cartographers. But ever since its inception, it has also included a "well-digger-miner" brigade, a unit of skilled workers tasked with doing the necessary repair jobs in the underground quarries. In the nineteenth century, workers in this team were recruited from among miners and well-diggers with expertise in similar jobs, and the name has persisted. In 2018, I had the chance to shadow a couple of well-digger-miners as they inspected woodwork in the quarry of La Brasserie in the 12th arrondissement of Paris. They showed me how dry rot fungus develops on wooden beams, making them spongy and much more likely to break under the weight of the stone they hold. The props were similar in construction to those used in underground mines, so that excavation and shoring techniques would have circulated as miners were hired by the IGC.

Further along, at a crossroads between two galleries, the two workers show me a pile of rubble on the ground. As we illuminate the ceiling with our headlamps, we see that a sinkhole has begun to form, pushing its way toward the surface. My guides explain that "the sky has fallen down" — "sky" being the word they use for the ceiling of the gallery — "it comes off and falls in patches. It is going to take a bell-shape little by little." The two men look for brown stains formed by humidity around the cracks in the sky. Since they cannot find any stain, they conclude that this sinkhole began to form not long ago. It could soon "come to light," meaning that the rockfall could soon reach the surface, and will need consolidation works. As we can see from this example, hydrologists model the ground and its actual or potential movements at the level of districts, but well-digger-miners are the hands and eyes of the IGC on-site, deploying their expert knowledge of subterranean flows and materials to spot and diagnose disorders in the old galleries. Grasping these processes enshrouded by earth takes not only visual but also tactile and even auditory expertise, and well-digger-miners can sometimes hear the stone "sing," a kind of sucking sound indicating imminent danger of collapse.

Once they spot a new sinkhole, they use a range of techniques to stabilize the moving mass. Woodwork is often used temporarily, until more durable stone vaults, masonry pillars, or dry-stone walls can be built. Dry-stone walls take a bit of expertise, because the lack of cement means that stones have to be placed at the right angles to fit to one another. It is an art to find the right shapes and angles in stones to create a stable assembly, something that can be felt by hand rather than seen by eye. Dry-stone is preferred to cement both because of the risk that cement could react chemically with water that has seeped through the ground and because a wall will not break so easily if it is not too rigid. This approach to stabilization thus rests on a set of careful and exploratory tasks of underpinning that make it possible to negotiate an equilibrium with the forces that shape the ground. Even though the IGC now uses sophisticated lab tests and models, stabilizing the Parisian underground still largely relies on localized ground-stabilization techniques that have not changed much in two centuries.

Subterranean Epistemic Tensions

However, the underpinning approach to reclamation of the IGC has recently come into growing competition with a more radical approach that advocates *filling* the cavities. The underpinning approach is increasingly described as expensive and painstaking, whereas backfilling appears to fix the problem once and for all. Beyond economic considerations, the tension between the two approaches boils down to an epistemic schism. For whereas woodwork and dry-stone masonry belong to the world of miners and well-diggers, backfilling belongs to the world of earthworkers, a field that approaches the ground and underground water problems in a very different way. Even though earthworks have been built since ancient times, modern ground engineering — known as geotechnics — derives from seventeenth-century military engineering, which sought to establish universal principles of ground behavior in order to build fortifications in faraway places. Ground engineering knowledge and techniques were then applied in the field of dam-making in the nineteenth century, and soon became a key discipline in the great urban acceleration of the twentieth century, as new earthworks machinery and techniques allowed cities to grow massively in height and width, into areas where the qualities of the ground would not previously have allowed it (Meulemans 2022).

The clash between underpinning and backfilling approaches is of long standing, but has recently taken on new dimensions. In the Parisian context, the venerable institution of the IGC is still highly regarded and has, for the most part, been able to defend its approach. Their expertise has remained largely uncontested. But it has been increasingly challenged by new actors in the field of urban geology, such as the Société du grand Paris, a public body formed in 2010 to supervise the building of 200 kilometers of new deep-ground subway lines in the Paris area. The Société carried out thousands of core drillings in the subsoil to prepare for digging its subway tunnels, and these extensive boring campaigns have generated much new knowledge about the Paris underground. This made the Société a center of attention, and its specialists are now regarded as the new experts on the Paris subsoil. At the same time, the Société faces an "outlet crisis" for the 40 million tons of excavated rubble that digging these new subway lines will generate. There are simply not enough landfills to accommodate it. This has once again brought the old underground quarries into the spotlight, as places where part of all this waste material could go. Yet, IGC engineers explain that these materials, too, could dissolve or gully, especially in a context of fluctuating water tables. They also insist that compacted earth or solidified cement will not in fact cancel a flow of water, but rather disrupt it, potentially concentrating it elsewhere. "Think of it as a thousand small underground dams," one geologist explained. "The water flow will go around it and concentrate around its edges," accelerating erosion in the surrounding terrain. Well-digger-miners, for their part, point out that once a gallery has been filled, it becomes impossible to go down there to check on the formation of new sinkholes.

These debates about the right way to stabilize the underground once again point to two radically different conceptions of the relationship between human life and the subsurface. In one, the ground is once again relegated to the status of a background, independent of human life on the surface, and to fill it once and for all seems like a good solution that would finally turn it into the solid mass that bureaucratic techniques of spatial discipline require, as a precondition for planning. In the other, human activities (and the construction of the city) can only participate in the ruminations of the subsoil, and to ignore this inevitable relationship could have dangerous consequences.

Conclusion: Reclamation from Below

Modern architecture and urbanism have not only regarded the ground as a stable base for building, but they have also required it to be transformed in order to make it so. Thanks to the development of geotechnics and foundation engineering, this stabilization project has been implemented on a large scale, as is evident from the expansion of cities on previously unstable ground in every part of the world. In recent years, however, critical voices from the worlds of urbanism and the environmental humanities have argued that strict material and conceptual separations between solid and liquid land are futile at a time of rapid rise in sea levels and extreme climatic events (Krause 2017).

In this chapter, I have shown that even in a large European metropolis situated far from the sea and from the effect of tropical hurricanes, a stable urban ground can only hold in time and space thanks to the skills and attention of hundreds of maintenance engineers and workers. Because of Paris's multiple historical layers of extraction, what shifts and crumbles is not a shoreline, but the currents and materials that make up the ground itself. In the face of this volumetric liquefaction, reclamation work is undertaken from below, in a way that belies anthropological distinctions between the detached gaze of the engineer and the improvisatory engagement of the artisan. Indeed, IGC workers rely on both hydrological models and a set of careful and exploratory tasks that make it possible to negotiate an equilibrium with the forces that shape the ground. Today, however, this exploratory approach is increasingly pitched against an approach based on backfilling, which holds out the promise of stabilizing the ground once and for all, while also ridding Paris of the immense quantities of excavated rubble resulting from the construction of new metro lines. This controversy reflects two professional visions, respectively of the miner and the quarryman, but it also speaks to different ways of understanding the ground's materiality and its relationship with the city above — on the one hand, in which the city turns it back on its ground, and on the other, in which the making of the city and the ruminations of the underground can exist only in a common process of geosocial becoming.

References

Clark, Nigel, and Kathryn Yusoff. 2017. "Geosocial Formations and the Anthropocene." *Theory, Culture & Society* 34, no. 2–3: 3–23. DOI: 10.1177/0263276416688946.

Denis, Jérôme, Alessandro Mongili, and David Pontille. 2015. "Maintenance & Repair in Science and Technology Studies." *Tecnoscienza: Italian Journal of Science & Technology Studies* 6, no. 2: 5–15. DOI: 10.6092/issn.2038-3460/17251.

Graham, Stephen. 2016. *Vertical: The City from Satellites to Bunkers.* Verso Books.

Ingold, Tim. 2022. "What If the City Were an Ocean and Its Buildings Ships?" In *Imagining for Real: Essays on Creation, Attention and Correspondence.* Routledge.

Ingold, Tim, and Cristián Simonetti. 2022. "Introducing Solid Fluids." *Theory, Culture & Society* 39, no. 2: 3–29. DOI: 10.1177/02632764211030990.

Krause, Franz. 2017. "Towards an Amphibious Anthropology of Delta Life." *Human Ecology* 45, no. 3: 403–8. DOI: 10.1007/s10745-017-9902-9.

McNeill, Donald. 2020. "The Volumetric City." *Progress in Human Geography* 44, no. 5: 815–31. DOI: 10.1177/0309132519863486.

Meulemans, Germain. 2019. "Fonder les villes: Comment les terrassiers comprennent le sol." *Communications* 105: 149–59. DOI: 10.3917/commu.105.0149.

———. 2022. "Solidifying Grounds: The Intricate Art of Foundation Building." *Theory, Culture & Society* 39, no. 2: 75–94. DOI: 10.1177/02632764211030997.

5

Washed-In and Washed-Out Livelihoods: Shifting Grounds in a Former Fishing Colony

Luciana Lang

Colonia z-10 (the Colony) is a fishing colony with a population of around 5,000 on the urban periphery of Rio de Janeiro, Brazil. Strategically set up just after World War I, the community was the first of 800 cooperative fishing colonies founded along the Brazilian coast between 1919 and 1923 as part of the National Program for Fishing and Sanitation, an initiative to promote literacy and hygiene education to stop the spread of diseases among fishing populations. At a geopolitical level, the initiative was designed to strengthen bonds with the fishermen, who were ideally positioned to contribute to coastal vigilance and national defense.

The Colony is situated on an islet surrounded by mangrove vegetation and by the green grounds where the Brazilian navy radio transmitter is based. Crossing the bridge that leads to the Colony from the bigger island of Ilha do Governador, there is every sign that one has arrived in a fishing community. A fisherman repairs a fishing net, others sell the morning catch surrounded by plastic basins half filled with fish scales, and herons rest on anchored fishing boats ready to grab discarded fish remains. However, the pollution and regular oil spills in the surrounding waters have made fishing very challenging, so much so that first impressions seem more like echoes from a past time. The mangroves that once provided fisherfolk with their livelihoods are now clogged with oil, sewage, plastic, and rubble. A biologist I met at the Colony told me that the proportion of foreign matter in the local mangroves is now so great that they can no longer be regarded as purely botanical phenomena; they have become socio-natural (Farías 2011). In this chapter, I reflect on the impermanent nature of mangroves and on the ways in which the biome has responded to human interference. The mangroves have both informed and defied national developmental agendas for almost two centuries, while their rhizomatic structure has shown phenomenal levels of resilience as they shape-shift to accommodate new contours and incorporate invasive substances.

From Commons to Commodity

As early as 1577, the Portuguese Crown laid out the first regulations concerning mangroves, the wood of which was used for fuel and housing by local populations, and for ship construction. The mangrove's bark also provided coveted tannin, which was extracted to dye fishing nets and cure leather. In 1664, the Crown prohibited the concession of flooded areas, and by the eighteenth century owners of factories producing shoe soles, for whom tannin was essential, denounced the felling of mangrove vegetation by local populations. A warrant from 1760 consequently stipulated that such vegetation could only be used for commercial purposes; anyone caught cutting it for domestic use would be arrested and fined.

As the coastal zones of Rio de Janeiro began to be commodified for their "natural beauty" (Amador 2013), the mangroves on the periphery of the burgeoning city were regarded, by contrast, as mosquito-infested areas. The growing perception that mangroves were "unhealthy" environments paved the way for their destruction. When urban rubbish collection commenced in the second half of the nineteenth century, mangroves were designated as ideal sites for waste disposal. The farm of São Sebastião, located in the swampy areas where the Colony is now based, became a prosperous producer of gravel, shellfish, and lime from shells extracted from the mangroves.

After the farm was sold to the navy in 1871, the Jequiá River, which feeds the mangroves and runs into Guanabara Bay, was widened to allow large boats to enter the Sac of Jequiá to be loaded with lime for industrial use. In 1906, control of the mangrove areas was passed to the federal government, under the administration of the navy, and over the following decades these intertidal ecosystems were landfilled to make room for roads, rubbish dumps, and informal housing (Lang 2020). Arnaldo, an organic environmentalist and the son of a fisherman, summarized the transformation that has taken place since the creation of the Colony: "This here is all an intertidal area. In 1930, the navy took a hill down over there, landfilled this area and created the Colony. Here, there used to be mangroves with some sand, less mud and less mangrove vegetation."

Arnaldo explains that the vast amounts of sewage that flow down the river into the mangroves have caused the quantity of mud and vegetation to increase. Thus, the transformation of the landscape described by the older people to whom I talked included both a decrease of the mangrove area caused by landfilling and an increase of vegetation in the remaining tidal zones caused by the changes in the sediments carried by the Jequiá River, which brought additional nutrients to the plants. Many remarked on the sand that lined the shores of the mangroves when they were children and on how they would collect shrimps with the women as the men went out to sea. "The mangroves were all around us," I was told by older residents. They talked about how the first houses were built on stilts, so that the mangroves were literally below the floorboards of some dwellings, and just outside people's front doors.

In the first half of the twentieth century, natural springs were protected to safeguard the water supply to the city, and legal provisions recognized the value of mangroves for fishing. These provisions, however, although set down on paper, were scarcely enforced in practice. Arnaldo describes how the various industries that established themselves in the area disregarded the value of mangroves: "What started to destroy this area was a factory that produced fat out of coconut; they would throw all the residues in the mangrove. There was a mining company over there. Then Shell arrived, followed by Esso, then Texaco, and lastly Petrobrás."

The 1950s saw the government's investment in the national oil company Petrobrás, which, with its consequent pollution, marked the beginning of the end for local fishermen. The phase of industrialization that followed, intensified under military rule in the 1960s, meant that pollution in Guanabara Bay reached an unprecedented level, accompanied by massive landfilling for further expansion of roads and real estate. Still during the period of military rule, Carlos Lacerda was the director of a "sanitation" project that involved further landfilling of mangroves, lagoons, marshes, and parts of Guanabara Bay, along with the canalizing of rivers. Overall, 95 square kilometers in the area surrounding Guanabara Bay, deemed to be "degraded," were landfilled (Amador 2013, 278). Arnaldo explained the effects of development on the local landscape:

In 1972 there was still sand around, then politicians decided to widen the Jequiá road, so they emptied eight trucks full of clay inside the mangrove. The clay spread and the silting process started, and by 1984 there was already mangrove vegetation, which is now much intensified with the daily pumping of sewage from 95,000 people. Mud occurs naturally in mangroves as a result of natural elements settling to the ground, but here the mud is mostly sewage with a high level of bacteria and algae, stifling growth.

Although mud is an intrinsic part of mangroves, sediments travel down the river and become trapped in the rhizomatic root system of native plants, and sewage causes the waterways to silt up. In this scenario, vegetation thrives, and mud-dwelling crabs find pockets of sludge where they can live, but other forms of fish life are suffocated by cyanobacteria, blue-green algae whose multilayered colonies can create areas of impermeability at the bottom of the mangrove, much as plastic does. A fisherman told me that the seabed is covered in plastic bags that hold the mud in place and prevent fish from breathing under it. "That's what you should be writing about," he told me. Arguably worse than sewage and plastic is the effect of oil spills[1] in the surrounding Guanabara Bay, which, since the first spill in 1975, have allegedly destroyed 35 percent of the original mangrove area. Because the mangroves act as biological filters, they also trap contaminating particles in the sea.

This brief story of local development provides a glimpse into the anthropogenic effects on the mangroves of Jequiá through land drainage (drenagem), landfills, and the recolonization of waterscapes. In the process, both land and labor were converted into marketable commodities. By 2012, when I was doing my fieldwork, former fishermen were competing for jobs offered by the city council to collect rubbish from landfilled sections of the mangroves, to build walls to prevent erosion, and to create makeshift barriers to protect the mangroves from future oil spills (fig. 5.1).

Tide, Time, and Becoming

In Portuguese, the word *tempo* means both "time" and "weather." Local fisherfolk sometimes use *tempo* to refer to tidal fluctuations, which are also affected by lunar cycles. This is a landscape marked by a predictable form of impermanence because the mangroves disappear with the high tide, only to reappear again with a diurnal delay of 45 minutes. This transitional ecosystem

---

1   There have been a number of oil spills since the 1970s. The first one, in 1975, caused a massive fire that locals often talk about in their accounts. The main national oil company, Petrobrás, was held liable for the oil spills of 2000 and 2004, but compensation for the fishermen for loss of productivity has been minimal.

Fig. 5.1. The rhizomatic aerial roots of the mangroves surrounding the colony and the pneumatophores, which enable mangroves to breathe in sewage-waterlogged soil. Photograph by the author.

absorbs both the salt from the sea, and the untreated sewage that flows down the Jequiá River. Life in this ecosystem is characterized by a state of in-betweenness and entails a process wherein its forms have constantly to adapt and shape-shift in response to variable conditions. Immersed in seawater and river water, the mangroves' rhizomes provide a habitat for a range of species that live in low-oxygen soil, in the intertidal zone that is exposed twice a day, and above water during low tide. The acidity, salt, and sediments absorbed by the mangroves' roots, coupled with low concentration of oxygen and high tidal variation, have imposed conditions of adaptation for all life-forms sharing this habitat, both human and nonhuman.

The concept of *tempo*, encompassing weather, time of the day, and the right tide for fishing, was a recurrent point of reference in my conversations with Neco, a fisherman who divided his time between fishing and his duties as a janitor at a local supermarket. I met him a few times before dawn by the bridge, where his little boat was anchored. He would look at the sky and then decide whether we would go fishing; if the tide was low, we would walk through the sewage-filled mud to reach the tiny vessel. The days we could meet followed the tide calendar, which Neco knew by heart, but final decisions about going fishing depended on related factors, such as wind, rain, and currents, all parts of a chain of cause and effect with practical and metaphorical implications. These weather variables were part of local understandings of *tempo,* and kept coming up in people's accounts of everyday life, as Margarida, my hostess in the Colony, remarked while reminiscing about life in the 1960s. "When there was thunder," she said, "the mangrove would become all dark, covered up with crabs."

As this biome changed with different weather conditions, the life-forms living in and by it had to adapt accordingly, as in stories I heard about people getting their best shoes spoiled because of a higher than usual tide. In swampy terrain, both water flow and ground drainage depend on *tempo.* The tide turns with clockwork precision, dictating when to fish, but everyday life in the Colony is marked by impermanence and unpredictability, especially with the challenges associated with the Anthropocene (Tsing 2010; Bear 2012; Lang 2015; McGranahan 2022). Connections were created in the mangrove areas through families, materials, and bridges, but they were also lost as fish life gave way to capitalist ruins. Such gains and losses characterize unfinished processes of becoming in impermanent landscapes such as the socio-natural mangroves of Jequiá.

For urban developers of the nineteenth century who assumed that architecture must be erected on land, and on solid foundations, the only possible use for mangroves was as waste dumps. For them, the constantly shape-shifting mangroves challenged the very logic of planning. Only with the introduction of concrete and rubble, to "contain" the impermanence of the mangroves, did the terrain become more manageable. After separating from his wife, Neco built an additional room at his parent's house by adding a *laje,* the name given to concrete slabs used to create extra floors, characteristic of informal constructions. I will now turn to the fluid and precarious nature of such forms of architecture.

The Urban Fabric: Building on Shifting Grounds

Seas and rivers evoke flux and movement, as opposed to the solidity and stasis associated with the concrete used to build bridges and roads, and to accommodate growing families. However, mangroves complicate this opposition because of their liminal and transient nature that alters with the time of the day. The logic that permeates the organic way of designing housing in the Colony speaks to the "architecture of the commons," a concept that refers to the spatial relations produced by community practices (Stavrides 2016, 16). In the context of the Anthropocene, contemporary designers have increasingly looked for alternative techniques for informal, adaptable, and temporary constructions (Siegal 2008). Designers constructing on water have tried to change the weight distribution of materials to improve flotation and, in the process, provide homes for seaweed and crustaceans (Frearson 2022). Increased nomadism transformed portability into a key component of urban architecture (Shaoqiang 2014). These new trends toward transformable spaces are prompted by dwindling natural resources, climate change, and the ethics of sustainable design. Nevertheless, urban planners do not always appreciate that adaptable design is the default approach of those living in mangrove areas. It is a matter not only of making do with what one has, as is the case with the horizontal and vertical extensions of dwellings in the Colony, but also of learning to construct with, and not against, impermanence.

One example of applying this approach in practice is the traditional house on stilts. During photo-elicitation sessions, older residents would tell of the centrality of tidal mangroves to their everyday life. Born in 1922, Diná had lived in the Colony all her life: "There used to be seawater right here where we are standing. The shack was high up and there were some stairs to get into it. When the tide was high, the water would flow under my house."

Diná remembers when her son was a little boy and would row down the mangroves using an old pan as a boat and a wooden spoon as a paddle. Rita, born in 1936, remembers how her new pair of shoes, which were bought once a year for the St. Peter's procession, were ruined as the high tide invaded the Colony's square. In these accounts, solid surfaces regularly turned to liquid, and back again, with the tides. Developments from the 1970s, including the construction of gates and walls, increasingly separated dwellings from the mangroves. Areas that used to get flooded were safely concreted over. Concrete was also used to restructure housing, reweaving genealogies in more ways than one. Plots of land, originally taken by one family, were subdivided in successive generations as families grew, and to accommodate affines, leading to a layout of houses that reflected the tight network of kinship and affinity. As people say, "Here we are all family":

> My father bought the house at the front here. When I got married, he gave me the back of the house, and when my daughter got married, I gave part of it to her and the upstairs to my son. (Bethania, born in 1947)

> My father had a big plot of land that was given to him by his mother's father; later the land was divided between myself and my brother and sisters. My sister built a house, and then sold it, she now lives out of the Colony. (Carlos, born in 1960)

Thus, material restructuring followed family growth. Margarida was born in 1953 and came to live in the Colony after marrying a fisherman. The outside space, normally used for bingo evenings in Margarida's house, is a long corridor with a dining table. It is clear that the space was once a bigger room, as the main wall has a window that opens into Margarida's sister-in-law's living room. The sewage pipes of these two households are shared with the house of another cousin, since their respective kitchens — now part of three individual dwellings — once belonged to a single household. So, when Margarida's sister-in-law had a problem with the sewage overflowing from her bathroom, bingo had to stop because the floor of Margarida's veranda had to be completely rebuilt.

Sanitation is a common problem with informal housing throughout Brazil, and in the case of the Colony, there are two chronic problems related to sewage. First, the Jequiá River passes through a few communities before arriving at the Colony, and along its course it receives raw sewage from thousands of households. Second, because the Colony is situated in a swamp area that has been landfilled over the years, some houses are below the level of the street, so pipes that transport sewage would have to be raised above ground level for the system to work properly, and the *elevatórias* — the pumping system needed to do this — was never built. Even though the city council made some efforts to solve the problem in the 1990s, residents maintain that the job was carelessly done. The issue is political: The city council places the blame on CEDAE, the State Water and Sewage Company; CEDAE claims that households should cover the costs of restructuring the pipes, while residents refuse to be charged for something they say is not their responsibility. In addition, the large influx of newcomers contributed to "disorderly growth" (*crescimento desordenado*), an expression used by public administrators to describe a favela. As more people moved into the community and space became scarce, houses were entered into the real estate market. Quite a few households were investing in their property by adding self-contained flats for rental. Baixinho, born in 1924 and supposedly the oldest fisherman in the Colony, says that everyone wants to move to the Colony because it is a safe haven in a city otherwise known for its violence. "Some years ago," he commented, "people started selling concrete slabs (*laje*) and everything is becoming a mess."

In 1993, the navy passed the control of the Colony to the city council, and from then on people started to have greater freedom to build upward and to landfill over the mangroves, unleashing a commodification of housing and land. Wilma, born in 1942, came from Maranhão in the north of Brazil and moved to the Colony in 1996. She remembers the changes that took place in the space of two years as part of the development planned for the Colony:

> The construction firm Mendes Junior arrived here in '98; I remember because it was the world cup. I shouted when Brazil scored a goal and ended up falling into one of the construction work holes. Construction had to be quick because jobs done by the government are always rushed. Because these builders liked the place they started to offer people, who are very naïve, to have their house done up in brick [instead of wood] in return for letting them [the builders] put a concrete slab over the top; the builders would then keep the second floor for themselves. So, they got rich, and the people who regretted it later had no comeback, because by the time they realized what they had done, they couldn't get rid of the newcomers.

The dramatic vertical growth since the 1990s supposedly compromises the marshland terrain where the islet is situated, and some residents were scared that the ground would eventually collapse. In Bethania's words: "How can people build three floors on a swamp? This area has been filled with soil; can you see how dangerous it is?"

Jorge, the environmental guard contracted by the city council, was similarly concerned: "In the past, people would go from one place to another in the Colony by canoe; they have now filled the marshes with soil for houses to be built. Those two- and three-story houses put the whole area of the Colony at risk." Bethania and Jorge said that people are building on potentially shifting ground. This form of risk, Arnaldo explained, is directly associated with a transformation of the landscape driven by both industrialization and self-interest. Anxiety over the shifting terrain also exposes tensions that arise from human cravings for things to stay the same (Geismar, Otto, and Warner 2022). The solidity of materials such as concrete, brick, and the plastic of sewage pipes helps to give some permanence to transient tidal mangroves. Yet, the inherent impermanence of waterlogged areas, which are subject to daily tidal changes, seemingly predisposes residents to see fluidity as an inevitable part of life. Flexibility and adaptability have been necessary components of construction toolkits in the Colony ever since the very first houses on stilts were built there, as Diná's account reveals.

Conclusion

In this chapter, I have shown how the mangroves of Jequiá were shaped and sculpted by ever-changing human interests. The drive toward modernity brought unbridled development, cementing over mud and fish life. In the process, the mangroves managed to coexist with stuff rejected by humans, incorporating new substances, such as sewage and oil. Their rhizomes found nourishment in foreign matter and integrated the urban fabric, thus turning the mangroves into a socio-natural biome.

The socioeconomic ripples of development are reflected in the precarious livelihoods of those living in the Colony, who, like the mangroves, are considered peripheral to the city. People have, however, devised homespun strategies for coping with risk and managing infrastructures in this hybrid biome. In 2014, I went back to the field for a visit, and Carlão, one of the few fishermen left in the Colony, told me that fish he had not seen for years had begun to appear again. Locals claim that this is a consequence of a new sewage treatment plant, which is reducing the volume of wastewater flowing into Guanabara Bay. Thus, the mangrove could be seen as work in progress, an open-ended process defined by its dynamic potential and human interventions. As a permeable border, the mangroves around the Colony generate connections and exchange, reconfiguring the tension between permanence and impermanence, and defying the solidity of the urban infrastructure. Their rhizomatic logic invites us to consider the possibilities of socio-natural, co-built environments. The way the mangroves have informed the architecture of the houses prompts us to rethink the relationship between land and sea. Constituted in flux, these socio-natural mangroves with their filtering properties provide stability on shifting grounds and a template for resilience for alternative futures in the Anthropocene.

References

Amador, Elmo da Silva. 2013. *Baía de Guanabara: Ocupação Histórica e Avaliação Ambiental.* Interciencia.

Bear, Laura. 2012. "Sympathy and Its Boundaries: Necropolitics, Labour and Waste on the Hooghly River." In *Economies of Recycling: The Global Transformation of Materials, Values and Social Relations,* edited by Catherine Alexander and Joshua Reno. Zed Books.

Farías, Ignacio. 2011. "The Politics of Urban Assemblages." *City: Analysis of Urban Trends, Culture, Theory, Policy, Action* 15: 365–74. DOI: 10.1080/13604813.2011.595110.

Frearson, Amy. 2022. "Mast Develops Adaptable Flat-Pack System for Building Floating Homes." *Dezeen,* October 14. https://www.dezeen.com/2022/10/14/land-on-water-floating-homes-mast/.

Geismar, Haidy, Ton Otto, and Cameron D. Warner, eds. 2022. *Impermanence: Exploring Continuous Change across Cultures.* UCL Press.

Lang, Luciana. 2015. "Living on the Edge: The Resilience of Marginal Beings in Environmentally Precarious Times." *Etnofoor* 27, no. 1: 53–74. https://www.jstor.org/stable/43410670.

———. 2020. "'That's What Fishers Do Now, We Collect Rubbish': The Making of Environmental Subjects in a Human-Disturbed Environment in Rio de Janeiro." *Ethnos* 85, no. 2: 371–92. DOI: 10.1080/00141844.2019.1604557.

McGranahan, Carole. 2022. "Disinheriting Social Death: Towards an Ethnographic Theory of Impermanence." In *Impermanence: Exploring Continuous Change across Cultures,* edited by Haidy Geismar, Ton Otto, and Cameron D. Warner. UCL Press.

Siegal, Jennifer, ed. 2008. *More Mobile Portable Architecture for Today.* Princeton Architectural Press.

Shaoqiang, Wang. 2014. *New Portable Architecture: Designing Mobile and Temporary Structures.* Promopress.

Stavrides, S. 2016. *Common Space: The City as Commons.* Zed Books.

Tsing, Anna. 2010. *Unruly Edges: Mushrooms as Companion Species.* http://tsingmushrooms.blogspot.co.uk/.

PART 2

Introduction to Part 2:
Life at the Shoreline

Can we draw a line separating land from sea, earth from water? What is it like to live in a zone where land and sea, earth and water meet and mingle? These are the key questions the chapters in Part 2 aim to explore. In Chapter 6, architect Lindsay Bremner opens with a historical account of the ongoing struggle to separate land and sea in Fort St. George, Madras, an English East India Company town on the Coromandel Coast of India, developed since 1630. Bremner shows how cartography and urban planning have shaped imaginaries of coastal zones through a language that promises to delineate clear, unambiguous boundaries between land and sea. This language, dominated by words such as "coast line," "hazard line," "tide line," or "sea level," is temporarily borne out in the hard engineering of linear infrastructure, including, for instance, seawalls. To counteract this language, Bremner recalls the logic of gradients developed by the Arquitect Principe group. This form of architectural imagination, led by Paul Virilio, operates not with lines and levels but with far-from-equilibrium systems, a language more suited to address the current predicament of our planet, dominated by unpredictable climate change, sea level rise, and extreme weather events.

Against Bremner's *cartographic* shoreline, we could set what might be called the *inhabited* shoreline. In traditionally hand-drawn cartography, the former is created as the trace of a human gesture that contravenes the ongoing correspondence between land and sea, a condition only further emphasized by contemporary cartography through its dependence on satellite images taken at fixed points in time. For both traditional and contemporary cartography, the shoreline is atemporal, in contrast to the movement of waves, in a direction orthogonal to this line, the ongoing protraction and retraction of which, rolling up and down with the tides, creates a zone for life to flourish. This advancing and retreating wave front is never fixed but shifts constantly, as successive waves swell and subside. It cannot be determined by averaging the lines formed between high and low tides, because it exists only in the in-between. Never fully formed but constantly in formation, the inhabited shoreline grows and dissolves amidst the imbrication of land and sea, much like in human breathing, which similarly blurs any definitive separation between our inner bodies and the surrounding environment. In this latter case, the boundary, traditionally drawn at the surface of the skin, is equally illusory.

Ultimately, cartographic and inhabited shorelines speak respectively of the prominence of human and nonhuman power, each affording contrasting ways of accommodating to the relationship between land and sea. Whereas human power aims to fix material flows, often for the benefit of a controlling state, nonhuman power turns the continuity of such flows to advantage in opening a living space for organisms of various kinds. Cartography has historically been one of the main tools that nation-states have used to assert sovereignty over the land, its riches, and its people. Accordingly, inhabitants of the shore accustomed to moving between land and sea tend to be regarded as problematic in the eyes of governments. This is what anthropologists Riccardo Ciavolella and geographer Armelle Choplin describe in Chapter 7, in their account of the struggles faced by the Toffinou, an Indigenous community of fishers living in Awansuri-Ladji, a precarious lacustrine village of Cotonou, the economic capital of Benin, located in the West African urban corridor between Abidjan and Lagos. Known as "the people of the water," the Toffinou were regarded by nineteenth-century French colonial authorities as "anarchic water nomads who refused to be taxed." Nowadays, their amphibious ways continue to be threatened by the twin forces of economic development and sea level rise. Forced to solidify their fluid relationships with the city, established through tracing and knotting practices across land and sea, Toffinou people have relied increasingly on concrete as a means to secure official recognition, an effort that is nevertheless materially unsuited to the reality of a changing environment.

The work of Ciavolella and Choplin resonates profoundly with that of anthropologist Lukas Ley, on urban elasticity, set out in Chapter 8. Based on long-term ethnographic research in the Javanese metropolis of Semarang, Ley shows how residents navigate the increasing liquidity of the ground caused by the combined effects of land subsidence and sea level rise. Residents participate in what Ley describes as "vertical reclamation," that is, building practices that work with sand to prolong the duration of the land and people's right to it. These "vertical islands of time," Ley says, reveal a ground that is neither solid nor fluid, but elastic. The lengths to which Semarang residents go to extend the duration of the ground might look futile considering the propensity of sand, thanks to its granular properties, to sink ever farther into the ocean. It is this very granularity of sand, originally extracted from the lacustrine environment people work to reclaim, that prevents residents from securing a permanent foothold on their land. Ley aptly writes that they are "building on borrowed time." In the eyes of residents, however, the point seems to be precisely the opposite, which explains their remarkable resilience. They were conducting vertical reclamation, continuously and without hesitation, long before narratives of sea level rise were established internationally, working *with*, and not *against*, the properties of their fluid environment.

Closing Part 2 is Chapter 9, by anthropologist Cristián Simonetti, who focuses on concrete, a material that, more than any other, has consolidated globally the fracture between land and sea, earth and water, which this volume aims to put into question. It has been the material of choice when it comes to claiming state sovereignty over land or defending coastal infrastructure against rising oceans. In developing countries of the Global South, such as Chile, no building material has contributed more to substantiating modernity's narrative of progress. But although the industry posits concrete as an everlasting substance, on the assumption that the solid alone endures, the reality is that concrete can be only temporarily abstracted from the ongoing flows of the rock cycle from which it originated and to which it will eventually return. Moreover, the maritime and riverine origin of its main ingredients, including cement, sand, gravel, and water, belie any hard opposition between land and sea, earth and water. Indeed, it is this very origin that makes concrete vulnerable and impermanent. A question that lingers from the analysis is whether this so-called synthetic rock has ever allowed urban dwellers to be truly modern and to lay final claim to land against the forces of water. This is a view that flies in the face of the way Roman architects, who first discovered concrete, thought of it. For them it was a concrescence of the elements, including earth, air, fire, and water. Speculating on the possibility of inhabiting a land that is not opposed to the sea, Simonetti describes how the people of the island of Chiloe, off the coast of Chile, have historically "sailed" their buildings over the land, relying on techniques designed for boat construction. These techniques are consistent with the ways the earliest people of the island, at the site of Monte Verde, are thought to have inhabited the landscape. Could they offer a model for the future?

6

Unthinking Coastlines

Lindsay Bremner

Coastal zones have long been reduced by language and cartography to lines and datums. Words such as "coast line," "high or low tide line," "hazard line," "sea level," even "sea level rise" are represented as lines on maps to separate land from sea, reinforced by linear infrastructure, such as groynes and sea walls, to engineer and maintain the separation. In *Soak: Mumbai in an Estuary,* Anuradha Mathur and Dilip da Cunha (2009, 13) argued that these practices were part of a "vocabulary of terrain" that was used by imperial powers to imagine land and sea as divisible and to prepare the ground for colonial extraction. Lines were proxies for power, projecting an image of certainty over uncertainty. Imperial cartographic, engineering, and administrative practices fixed lines between land and sea on paper and in space through forts, ports, and customs regimes, enabling cargo to be inspected and recorded and revenue to be extracted as it crossed the threshold between land and sea (Hofmeyr 2021).

Nowhere was the passage from sea to land more perilous than in Madras, the English East India Company (EEIC) town on the Coromandel Coast of India, which developed around Fort St. George from the 1630s onward (Brouze, McPherson, and Reeves 1987). A shallow sandy continental shelf forced ships to cast anchor beyond the surf, from where goods were transported in "Mussoolas — large, flat-bottom'd sii-shap'd Boats, not nail'd as ours, but sow'd together with Coyr-twine" (Armstrong 1939, 214). Indigenous boats were indispensable to the landing, and boatmen made a living from transporting goods from ships through pounding surf and longshore monsoonal currents, often across shifting sandbars, to the beach. In part to break their monopoly, in part to protect ships and their landings from winds and weather and the shifting sands, a plan to construct a harbor at Madras was approved in 1868 by the colonial British state. The plan included two parallel piers perpendicular to the coast 3,000 feet apart, curving toward each other to make a narrow entrance on the seaward side. Construction started in 1877, but in 1881 a cyclone destroyed the partially built piers and sank two small ships at anchor inside them (Armstrong 1939). The piers were rebuilt in 1895, but they provided inadequate shelter from the restless sea, so the harbor was completely remodeled between 1906 and 1912 (Brouze, McPherson, and Reeves 1987). This story is a reminder of the hubris that propped up colonial ambitions of asserting sovereignty over the conjuncture of land and sea through submarine engineering (Hofmeyr 2021). Stone, cement, and later concrete and steel frequently proved futile against the energy of tectonic plates, expanding clays, alluvial sediments, reversing ocean currents, rising and falling tides, swirling air masses, monsoon rains, and a myriad of life forms, each with their own spatial and temporal scales and cycles.

In the late eighteenth century, after the Seven Years' War (1755–1763), when Britain defeated its colonial rivals on the Coromandel Coast, the directors of the EEIC suggested to the British government that a survey of southern India would be of great value in cementing control over its territories. In 1786, Michael Topping, chief marine surveyor of the EEIC, was appointed to fix the latitudes and longitudes of the principal coastal stations of the Coromandel Coast to supplement company hydrographer Alexander Dalrymple's charts of the Bay of Bengal (Love 1913). From 1788 to 1794, using the private observatory of the governor of Madras as his reference meridian, Topping used a Hadley sextant, a navigational instrument typically employed to fix a ship's position at sea, to triangulate the Coromandel Coast from Madras to Calcutta and then from Madras to Cape Comorin (today's Chennai, Kolkata, and Kanyakumari). In so doing, he produced the first colonial astronomical survey of India and, after it was complete, suggested that his techniques be used to map to the entire Madras Presidency. His proposition was taken up in 1802 by William Lambton, who, abandoning the Hadley sextant for bulky theodolites and a zenith sector, began what became the Great Trigonometrical Survey of India. Lambton defined the coastline of India by combining data on latitude, longitude, and mean sea level. By averaging the mean sea level at nine points on the coast of the subcontinent, he was able to delimit a terrestrial and territorial edge between land and sea in geographic space (Mathur and da Cunha 2009).

I have been able to find only one of Topping's maps in the British Library (fig. 6.1). It was drawn in 1789, at a time before the shift of colonial priorities from the safety of ships at sea to land-based revenue extraction. It is of the Bay of Coringa at the mouth of the Goudavery (now Godavari) River and sketches out the confluence of the river and the sea. The map is dominated by rhumb lines, upon which navigation relied heavily at the time (Arunachalam 1987), radiating from a center aligned with the river mouth. The edges of the sea, represented by a broken line, are crossed by triangulations measured from vertical references — a flagstaff, the East India Company House, a village, pagodas, and so on. The scale of the map's baseline is given in fathoms, traditionally a measurement of depth at sea, whereas bathymetric readings are given in feet from the lowest tide level. The map includes a tide table. The graphic features of the map are accompanied by textual notes on vegetation (covered with woods or lowland covered with jungle), temporal changes (mostly submerged at high water, mostly dry at low tide), and the characteristics of the ground and seabed (hard sandy beach on which the sea breaks heavily, mostly dry at low tides, dry hard ground, mud, soft muddy bottom). The map indicates where country vessels anchor, and warns that no

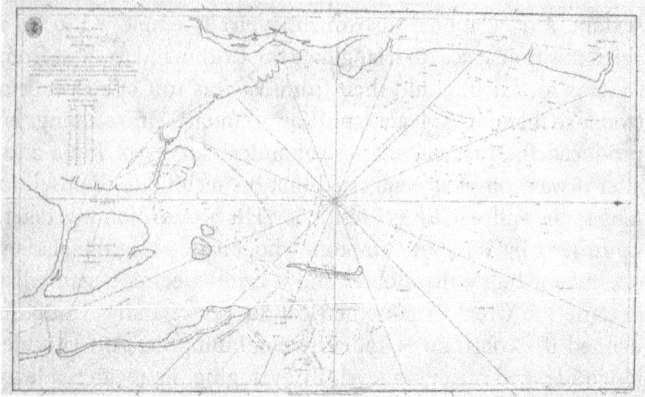

Fig. 6.1. "A Trigonometrical Survey of the Bay of Coringa by Michael Topping" (1789). Source: British Library Shelf Mark: Cartographic Items Maps SEC.12 (828). By permission of the British Library.

part of this tract is navigable with a boat that draws more than two feet of water. Reefs and subsurface shoals are sketched out and the high-tide line has a low-tide shadow. Topping is clearly struggling to ground his line, to get it to hold or to declare with conviction where the sea ends and land begins. By combining land- and sea-based systems of measurement, he hedges his bets on whether what is being measured is part of the land or part of the ocean. The ever-shifting relation between land and sea is emphasized by the notes that make it clear that what is land and what is sea changes all the time.

Gradient

An estuary demands gradients not walls, fluid occupancies not defined land uses, negotiated moments not hard edges. In short, it demands accommodation of the sea, not a war against it which continues to be fought by engineers and administrators as they carry sea walls inland in a bid to both channel monsoon runoff and keep the sea out. (Mathur and da Cunha 2009, 4)

When architects talk about gradients, they refer to the incline of a slope. In the 1960s, the Architecture Principe group (including Paul Virilio, Claude Parent, Morice Lipsi, and Michael Carrade) took up the gradient, or what they called "La Fonction Oblique," as a new technique of the body and principle for architecture (Virilio and Parent 1997). Virilio and his colleagues questioned why the standard measurement of architectural space had always been a static masculine figure (think here of Leonardo da Vinci's Vitruvian man or Le Corbusier's modular), "never a dancer, but always Don Juan's statue of the commander" (Virilio 1997, 8). Instead, starting from *gradior,* the moving body, they proposed that inclined planes would facilitate mobile forms of life, or what they termed "truly habitable circulation, [...] a living ground" (Virilio 1997, 12). The massive ramping concrete megastructures they proposed to achieve this objective might not find favor today, but the proposal of La Fonction Oblique to regard ground as gradient and habitation as mobile retains its sociological and ecological salience. Architecture Principe, responding in the 1960s to Ilya Prigogine's theories of nonlinear thermodynamics, suggests to me a way of conceptualizing the relations between land and sea, and ways of inhabiting them, not through lines and levels, but as far-from-equilibrium systems of sociopolitical, territorial, hydrological, atmospheric, and astronomical fluctuations, pushes and pulls, ebbs and flows.

The Coromandel Coast usefully exemplifies this point. More than many, it defies conceptual and engineering structures of lines and levels. It is a consequence of fluctuating gradients of air pressure, temperature, and humidity, driven by the energy of the sun; where waves crash and tides rise and fall, driven by the pull of the moon and local topography; where riverine sediments are pushed around by rain, currents, gales, and storms; where saline and fresh water mix; where steel corrodes and concrete is worn away; where thresholds between the ocean, sand dunes, tidal flats, wetlands, and creeks move all the time, providing habitats for hundreds of species, including oysters, mussels, barnacles, crabs, shrimps, mangroves, and marsh grasses; and where the humans who live among them exhibit crafty, tenacious ways of living in fluxes and flows. This variable, continuously changing environment, rich in biodiversity and multispecies entanglements, is best thought of as a dissipative system of gradients, thresholds, and phase changes. Karen Barad (2007, 234) would call this zone an "iterative becoming of spacetimemattering" by entangled agencies, mutually constituted in the play of difference.

A dissipative system is a far-from-equilibrium, thermodynamically open system that self-organizes to diffuse intensity differences (Tiezzi et al. 2008). In *Planetary Social Thought: The Anthropocene Challenge to the Social Sciences,* Nigel Clark and Bronislaw Szerszynski argue that the Earth itself is a dissipative system; it is "self-incompatible, always out of step with itself, […] restless, held far from thermal and chemical equilibrium by constant dissipation, as energy from its hot interior and parent star passes through the system, preventing any part of it from settling" (2021, 172). Materially closed but energetically open, the Earth continuously self-organizes by moving energy or matter around to reduce intensity differences (be they of temperature, pressure or density) at all spatial and temporal scales. The resulting material or energy gradients or slopes dissipate difference throughout the system. If gradients have boundaries, these are not sharp lines but indistinct, constantly morphing zones in which differences approach to zero (Lally 2014). Extreme intensity differences that cannot be reduced through gradual dissipation reach critical thresholds or tipping points when phase changes occur, dissipating energy by way of a switch from one state to another, such as when a volcano erupts, a cyclone forms, or ice melts (DeLanda 2005).

This language of dissipative systems (energy, matter, gradients, thresholds, and phase changes) provides a nongeometric vocabulary of space through which to rethink coastal systems and coastal habitats as zones of difference, not as discrete territories demarcated by fixed lines but as material gradients where variable ecological, sociopolitical, aerial, oceanic and terrestrial intensities are generated, meet, mingle, mix, and dissolve. To think in this way acknowledges coastal zones as sites of co-presence and emergence, shaped and saturated by countless inter-related agencies, of which the human is but one.

Among those compelled to think like this were the engineers of the Buckingham Canal, a navigable waterway built in the nineteenth century along the Coromandel Coast. The engineers, whose previous experience was designing canals in temperate climates in which water flowed relatively steadily throughout the year, were confounded by unanticipated problems brought by monsoonal cycles, including torrential rain followed by back-waters that evaporated during hot summer months, shifting sandbars, tidal flows and fluxes, gales, cyclones, storm surges, and much else. Proposals to limit the effects of these phenom-ena by means of flood gates, sluice gates, locks, and embank-ments proved ineffective and had to be revised continuously in the light of how the coastal system responded to previous deci-sions and weather events. Alexander Sherwood Russell, histo-rian of the canal, wrote: "A correct determination of its design demanded…close observation and long practical knowledge of the local and tidal conditions, and of various peculiarities con-nected with rivers, backwaters and sea bars on the Coromandel Coast, and of the natural features of the country generally.… Long experience alone has been the main factor in finally deter-mining the design" (Russell 1898, 4). In other words, fixing and maintaining a line within the ever-changing gradients of the coastal system was an ongoing project that called for constant revision based on experience and embodied knowledge of the fluxes and flows of materials and energy.

Creek

Ennore Creek is a tidal creek and wetland system on the Coro-mandel Coast, extending from the Pulicat Lagoon in the north to the tributaries of the Kosasthalaiyar River in the south. De-scribed by experts as an "interphase between coastal saline re-gions and inland freshwater regions" (Ismail, Narasimhan, and Narasimhan, 2017), it is a system of tidal mudflats, salt marshes, mangroves, and deep and perennial tidal water bodies that meander and shift behind the narrow sand dunes that front the ocean. The creek currently breaches the dunes just south of Kamaraj Port, its opening accreting and eroding with weather events, sediment loads, and reversing littoral current flows. From the north, the Pulicat Lagoon pushes its waters southwards into the creek, where they clash with northward flowing tidal waters. During monsoonal months (October to February, in this part of India), the creek is inundated by depressions and low-pressure systems, by cyclones, gales, and storm surges, and by inland rivers and rivulets carrying torrents of water and sediment toward the sea.

Gradients and thresholds in this complex aerial-terra-aqueous system are constantly shifting, in accordance with intensities of air pressure, temperature, humidity and rainfall, currents, tidal energies, wetness and dryness, freshness and salinity, salt and sediment. Life among the gradients is lived with their ebbs and flows. On the one hand, herbaceous and grass species, dragonflies and butterflies come alive after the monsoon rains each year (Vencatesan 2022). Salt production, on the other hand, can only be undertaken in the dry season when intense heat evaporates water from the salt marshes, leaving a chunky precipitate. During the wet season, paddy cultivation and prawn picking provide alternative sources of livelihood for backwater dwellers. Fishing grounds, too, are tidal and seasonal, with some fish and crustacean species thriving in the fresher-water monsoon months, others in more brackish conditions, some better caught at high tide, others at low. Fishing, in this context, is based on embodied knowledge, observation, and uncertainty. It is a practice that loads everything from breezes, currents, turbidity, temperature, water color, and odor to the texture and shifting depth of sediment with meaning and consequence (Govindan 2021).

In 2008, after a long delay, and framed by the Indian government's push toward liberalizing the country's economy through financial deregulation and industrialization, the Chennai Metropolitan Development Agency rezoned Ennore and its wetlands for heavy industry, in line with the State of Tamil Nadu's developmental priorities (Chennai Metropolitan Development

Agency 2008). Zoning is a modernist planning tool that aligns geographical areas with types of land use and regulates development codes. Based on economic data and abstract city-making principles that pay scant attention to the material reality of the areas it designates, zoning communicates its classifications as bounded, color-coded areas on a map — red for residential, blue for commercial, and so on. In Ennore's 2008 rezoning, the brown (signifying nonurban), white (signifying undefined), and blue (signifying bodies of water) of earlier zoning codes gave way to the unmitigated purple of heavy industry (Bremner 2020).

The color purple had catalytic agency. It either authorized development that had already taken place or instigated further development that had little, if anything, to do with fluctuating meteorological and hydrological gradients and phase changes, or the spacetimematterings of mudflats, wetlands, salt marshes, plants, bodies, and culture, all of which were profoundly altered in consequence. State agencies and private developers acquired land for development by purchase or dispossession. Sand was dredged and pumped to transform wetlands into dry grounds. Mangrove forests, salt pans, and mudflats disappeared, to be replaced by thermal power plants, petrochemical warehouses, fertilizer factories, and steel foundries. A new port was constructed as a coal terminal just north of the southern egress of Ennore Creek, resulting in the rapid buildup of sediment to the south and decreasing tidal flow into the creek. Roads, bridges, pylons, and pipelines, often laid in breach of state regulations, were threaded through and across the creek, blocking tidal and sediment fluxes and flows. Fly ash, a highly abrasive waste product of coal burning, eroded the elevated pipes designed to convey it to ash ponds, causing it to leak into the creek, where it drastically altered hydrological, ecological, and topographical gradients, blanketed fishing grounds, and saturated them with toxic chemicals. The quantity and quality of fish in the creek and their ability to reproduce was compromised, forcing fishers into taking up new occupations, often in the very industries that had callously set in motion the unbounded, toxin-filled process of despoliation in which their lives had become entangled.

These emergent dynamics attest to the unraveling of the lines and flat surfaces of coastal and metropolitan zoning maps and property boundaries, in the face of the far-from-equilibrium material-cultural dynamics of the coastal zone itself. In adjusting to the new lines, levels, leakages, seeps, and mixtures the new economy has brought, former modes of living with the ebbs and flows of the creek have been disrupted and new ones have emerged. Fishers, their livelihoods compromised, have become cartographers and activists; in order to negotiate with the gradients of power in which they are now enmeshed, they have thrown the language of maps, lines, and levels back at the authorities and won a number of court battles to remove fly ash or dredged spoil (e.g., Madras High Court 1996). New multispecies communities have emerged: Crabs have taken up residence among colonies of an invasive species of mussels; mudskippers, not seen for years, have returned; saplings of a tree considered sacred along the Coromandel Coast (*Salvadora persica,* or *ugha* in Tamil), and that had all but disappeared, have been found growing in the fly ash ponds (Vencatesan 2022). In sum, although the lines and levels drawn on maps might describe the way coastal systems are governed, they have nothing to say about the ways they are lived, about navigating loss or negotiating the shifting gradients, thresholds, and phase changes to find opportunities amidst uncertainty and change.

References

Armstrong, G.G. 1939. "Port of Madras for Three Hundred Years." In *The Madras Tercentenary Commemoration Volume,* edited by the Madras Tercentenary Celebration Committee. Oxford University Press.

Arunachalam, B. 1987. "The Haven-Finding Art in Indian Navigational Traditions and Cartography." In *The Indian Ocean: Explorations in History, Commerce and Politics,* edited by Satish Chandra. Sage.

Barad, Karen. 2007. *Meeting the University Halfway: Quantum Physics and the Entanglement of Matter and Meaning.* Duke University Press.

Bremner, Lindsay. 2020. "Planning the 2015 Chennai Floods." *Environment and Planning E: Nature and Space* 3, no. 3: 732–60. DOI: 10.1177/2514848619880130.

Brouze, F.J.A., K.I. McPherson, and P.D. Reeves. 1987. "Engineering and Empire: The Making of Modern Indian Ports." In *The Indian Ocean: Explorations in History, Commerce and Politics,* edited by Satish Chandra. Sage.

Chennai Metropolitan Development Agency. 2008. *Chennai Master Plan 2026.*

Clark, Nigel, and Bonislaw Szerszynski. 2021. *Planetary Social Thought: The Anthropocene Challenge to the Social Sciences.* Polity Press.

DeLanda, Manuel. 2005. *Intensive Science and Virtual Philosophy.* Bloomsbury Academic.

Govindan, Oviya. 2021. "Following Fish-Talk through Industrial Waters." *SSRC Items, Insights from the Social Sciences,* February 16. https://items.ssrc.org/ways-of-water/following-fish-talk-through-industrial-waters/.

Hofmeyr, Isabel. 2021. *Dockside Reading: Hydrocolonialism and the Custom House.* Duke University Press.

Ismail, Sultan Ahmad, D. Narasimhan, and Balaji Narasimhan. 2017. "Environmental Impacts of Coal Ash Pollution on Ennore Creek and Surrounding Areas of North Chennai Thermal Power Station." In Annexure 6 in Joint Expert

Committee, *Report for Assessing the Damages by Fly Ash in the Ennore Backwaters.* Joint Expert Committee, March 2022.

Lally, Sean. 2014. *The Air from Other Planets: A Brief History of Architecture to Come.* Lars Muller.

Love, Henry Davidson. 1913. *Vestiges of Old Madras, 1640–1800.* John Murray.

Madras High Court. 1996. 2 MLJ 175.

Mathur, Anuradha, and Dilip da Cunha. 2009. *Soak: Mumbai in an Estuary.* Rupa + Co.

Russell, Alexander Sherwood. 1898. *History of the Buckingham Canal Project: With a Descriptive Account of the Canal and Its Principal Works and a Guide to Its Future Maintenance.* Govt. Press.

Tiezzi, E.B.P., R.M. Pulselli, N. Marchettini, and E. Tiezzi. 2008. "Dissipative Structures in Nature and Human Systems." *WIT Transactions on Ecology and the Environment* 114: 293–39. DOI: 10.2495/DN080301.

Vencatesan, Jayshree. 2022. "Report on Impact of Fly Ash on Ecology, and Recommendations on Ecological Characterisation and Restoration Strategy for the Ennore Landscape." In *Expert Committee Report for Assessing the Damages by Fly Ash in the Ennore Backwaters.* Joint Expert Committee, March 2022.

Virilio, Paul. 1997. "Disorientation." In *Architecture Principe, 1966 and 1996,* edited by Paul Virilio and Claude Parent, translated by George Collins. Les Editions de l'Imprimeur.

Virilio, Paul, and Claude Parent, eds. 1997. *Architecture Principe, 1966 and 1996.* Translated by George Collins. Les Editions de l'Imprimeur.

7

Between Anchorage and Collapse: Knots, Traces, and Surfaces in a Lacustrian Village in Benin

Riccardo Ciavolella and Armelle Choplin

Along the West African urban corridor between Abidjan and Lagos, people fleeing the internal and the Atlantic slave trades formed communities in the marginal, lacustrine, and lagoon regions on the coast of present-day Benin, where they have lived, dwelt, moved, worshipped, and interacted with their particular social and natural environment for three centuries. Between water and land, liquidity and solidity, they have invented original amphibian ways of inhabiting the world and transforming it in response to social and environmental changes — from slavery through colonization to globalization; from relative village autonomy to their total incorporation into the "modern" urban world; from dependence on natural resources to dependence on the market with the concomitant exposure to social and environmental collapse.

This chapter focuses on one of these communities, the Toffinou, known as *Les hommes de l'eau* ("the people of the water") (Bourgoignie 1972; Coralli and Vido 2017), and on Awansuri-Ladji, a precarious lacustrine neighborhood of Cotonou, Be-

Fig. 7.1. Ladji, a lacustrian precarious neighborhood in Cotonou, Benin, Lozivit, 2018. Photograph by Armelle Choplin.

nin's economic capital. Straddling land and water, this ancient village, now a slum, faces many problems of poverty and lack of infrastructure and basic services (see fig. 7.1). It has long been seen as a hostile and repulsive environment for people from the interior, because of the presence of water and disease. At the beginning of the eighteenth century, it became a place of refuge for people fleeing Dahomean and European slave raids and wars (Manning 1982; Polanyi 1966; Law 1989). These people built a village on stilts in the middle of Lake Nokoué. In the nineteenth century, during the period of colonization, the French considered the villagers to be anarchic water nomads who refused to be taxed, and they went on to destroy the lake piles in 1910 (D'Albeca 1895). By the end of the twentieth century, the village had been completely incorporated into the city, but to this day, administrators continue to consider it off the map, as if it did not exist, which sounds contradictory given that the Toffinou are also supposed to be the "Indigenous" people of Cotonou (Ciavolella and Choplin 2018). Nowadays, the slum suffers from a vicious combination of isolation and incorporation into the city, which perfectly epitomizes the condition of "marginality": poverty, illiteracy, lack of state facilities, almost complete absence of transport or infrastructure, urban pollution, and contamination of the lake, with the consequent depletion of fish stocks.

Drawing on long-term anthropological fieldwork and intense exchanges with this community, carried out between 2016 and 2018, we will unpack the different guises of urban marginality by exploring the links between materiality, culture, and social practice in the historical trajectory of this vulnerable community, affected by demographic growth, frenetic urbanization, globalization, evictions resulting from policies of urban "decongestion and beautification," and coastal erosion and sea level rise caused by climate change.

Inspired by Tim Ingold's work on lines (2007) and surfaces (2017), we will explore the conditions of social and economic vulnerability and precarious dwelling by attending to traces, knots, empty and full or solid volumes (such a plastic containers), and surfaces (such as of concrete or waste), aiming thereby to grasp the material and immaterial aspects of this life on the edge. These are key terms for interpreting the relationship between humans and the environment in a relational way, constituted dynamically by the interweaving of different elements (Ingold 2000). But we also draw inspiration from local conceptions of the *vodun* ("voodoo"), according to which the environment is inhabited by forces that connect, rather than oppose, the social and the natural, the material and the spiritual, the visible and the invisible. Methodologically, the ethnography of traces, nodes, and surfaces is inductive; it is by following the traces, in a literal sense, that one discovers who left them materially. At the same time, on a symbolic level, one understands their meanings and the social relations they represent. It is by grasping the nodes that one can trace the originally disjointed parts they assemble, giving shape to the socio-spatial interweaving of the urban margin. And it is by examining the surface, what is above and below, and what is solid (concrete, waste) or liquid (water), that we can analyze the dialectic of building and dwelling on the margins (Ciavolella 2019).

With this chapter, then, we aim to show how an anthropology of techniques and practices of dwelling enables us to grasp

Fig. 7.2. Child using a plastic container to move around during the floods in Ladji, Cotonou, Benin, 2018. Photograph by Riccardo Cia-volella

the complexity of worlds woven on the urban margins and lake edges, and the tactics inhabitants employ to escape precar-ity. Our analysis calls into question — or rather puts into ten-sion — the capacity of these populations, or what could be called their "elasticity," to renew their culture of adaptation and resil-ience to precarity, while also asserting their capacity to negotiate a "right to the city" at a time when larger logics and interests threaten at once to engulf them and to expel them from the ur-ban world (fig. 7.2).

Traces

The "trace," according to Ingold (2010, 15), is "any permanent mark left in or on a solid surface by a continuous movement." But what happens when we extend the idea of trace beyond solidity? On the liquid surface of Lake Nokoué, linear traces are drawn in a cognitive space that blurs the frontiers between materiality and perception. The lake appears to the eye as a flat, continuous, and uniform surface that conceals its contents, as though a Deleuzean *espace lisse* (smooth space) served as a wrapper for an aquatic dimension. In reality, the lake corresponds more to the notion of the "open" (Ingold 2008), which Ingold perceives as a space of intercourse between the earth and the sky, to which we must therefore add a third component, the aquatic. Human beings live immersed in the material and energetic flows that pass between the constituents of this open space through the mediation of objects, and add their own contribution, through active and practical intervention, to the shaping of the sociobiological and material texture of the environment.

Indeed, on Lake Nokoué and its shores, the history of the relationship between the lake and its inhabitants, in oral tradition, is marked by gestures intended to draw lines joining elements of the lake environment, even if they seem ephemeral, both on the surface and beneath it. The trajectories of canoes, for example, trace lasting lines in the mental geographies of yesterday's fisherman or slave raider, or today's petrol smuggler. According to oral tradition, the instrumental relationship with the lake has its origin in the collective gesture of drawing a line across the entire stretch of water. The first fishing technique, inspired by the hunting systems of lake birds, involved drawing a circle in the water, which was then tightened in order to trap the prey and catch fish by hand. The most recent techniques retain the same principle of drawing lines in the water, but are transformed into fixed fishing parks called *acaja*. Drawing boundaries and demarcating plots in the lake are today at the heart of social conflicts and an index of social inequalities in access to this peculiar type of liquid capital. If we follow other traces in the built environment of the lake dwellings, we see, for example, marks on the houses. There are small signs everywhere, drawn near the entrances, all arranged in a row on an undulating plane, with enigmatic changes of color. In an urban society characterized by social distrust and illiteracy, these signs are a way of keeping track of household debts.

Knots

Fishermen know very well that the knot does not exist in itself, or rather that it is not an object. It is the material consequence of an act on the real, which gives matter a higher value and function. The knot epitomizes the human activity of weaving the world, but also the intervention of objects, natural elements, materials, movements, and, above all, forces. Ingold (2015, 15) writes that "in a world in which things are constantly coming into being through processes of growth and movement — that is, in a world of life — knotting is the fundamental principle of coherence." This statement seems entirely apt for the amphibious context of Ladji, where for decades, if not centuries, inhabitants have been able to make a living from fishing by learning to make nets from woven threads. But even in the urban landscape of Ladji, knots are ubiquitous, albeit hidden. With the exception of more modern concrete structures, the houses on stilts are held together by knots embedded in every corner and joint of their fabric.

Knots also connect the neighborhood to the rest of the city. They can tie connections to urban networks, both infrastructural and social (Green 2014). The inhabitants of Ladji do everything they can to connect with others, to make the *branchement* into what is perceived as a symbol of urban modernity and an indispensable service, namely, the *courant*, as electricity is called locally. Plugging in cables, connecting to the grid — these are actions that give the airspace of the neighborhood the appearance of a *toile d'araignée* (spider's web). Even from the dwellings by the water, which try to avoid the *courant* coming into contact with water by hanging cables and tying them to wooden poles, wires are pulled from the edge of the earth to connect with those who have a new form of infrastructural power, that is, the owners of official meters, who sublet access to electricity and make it possible to light two bulbs at night, recharge an old mobile phone, or turn on the television. But like traces, knots reveal the peculiar relationship of inhabitants not only to the natural or built environment but also to the social inequalities and processes of marginalization of the neighborhood.

Surfaces

In this lacustrine area, the surface is the link between the aquatic, urban, and living worlds. Looking at the "mundane surfaces of everyday life," Ingold (2017, 100) suggests, one can observe many things, empty or full, floating or sinking. The yellow, empty oil-palm jerricans are used as floating canoes or as material for building houses. Vast agglomerations of waste float on the surface until they solidify to form a kind of polder, creating artificial land on which to live. The people of Ladji originally used oysters and shellfish for landfill but are now using the garbage dumped by city dwellers. On the surface, they are pouring concrete and lining up breezeblocks to build houses of concrete rather than bamboo.

For Simonetti and Ingold (2018), concrete is the iconic "solid fluid" of modernity. As such, it is on its way to becoming the dominant material in contemporary urban landscapes, especially in West Africa, where it is an affectively charged material with significant repercussions for political and social relations (Choplin 2023). Concrete is ubiquitous; you can buy bags of cement at any time of the day or night, and also gravel and sand. Concrete is economically important, and the price is displayed every day on shop fronts, like on the stock exchange. Concrete is also socially important, and it has become a symbol of success, wealth, and modernity. In neighborhoods with high levels of economic insecurity, such as Ladji, buying bags of cement and building concrete structures has a special meaning, because during the three months of annual flooding that can sweep everything away, concrete is all that remains. Many urban dwellers see concrete houses as permanent and durable, requiring little maintenance. For George Gnonlonfoun, chief of Ladji neighborhood whom we interviewed in 2018, "building with concrete is the only way to stay out of the rain and the rising waters. And you don't have to rebuild the houses after every rainy season, as you do with mud."

The uncertainties and vulnerabilities associated with mud explain why most households, even poor ones, usually have half a bag of cement stored somewhere. In this case, concrete can be seen as a "spatial fix," to follow David Harvey's (2001) metaphor, with the double meaning of "fix," a way of fixing these precarious lives and of anchoring them in a solid urban world. Buying bags of cement even seems to be a way of fixing or anchoring capital, albeit with a very modest financial outlay. In poor communities such as Ladji, breezeblocks could be seen as "ingots of the poor"; like a bar of gold for the rich, a concrete block is an object that allows poor people to hoard money and commodify this liquid space.

In the face of recurrent evictions, the use of permanent materials and structures — such as concrete — also underpins claims for greater integration into the city and for urban citizenship. In our interview with chief Gnonlonfoun, he continued: "The government can't evict us [*déguerpir,* in French] as if we don't exist. We have invested a lot of money in building concrete houses. If we didn't have the right to stay, if it wasn't our place, we would never have spent so much money." Building in concrete makes it possible to legitimize one's presence, to break away from the precarity of nonpermanent materials, such as wood and earth, and to be no longer at the mercy of eviction policies and floods. Concrete blocks are used to substantiate claims to political legitimacy as citizens. In these drowning areas, they materialize the "right to the city" — to belong to it (Lefebvre 1968).

Maps

This question of eviction is crucial because, since 2016, the Beninese government has decided to carry out a clearance operation from public and state-owned land with the aim of beautifying and reclaiming the city of Cotonou, in line with a broader policy agenda to attract foreign private investment. The urban areas around the lake and the canal are considered priority areas for reclamation, and these precarious waterfront neighborhoods are being transformed from marginal areas of illegal settlement into potential sites for speculative urban megaprojects. Ladji lies on the route of the new road axis planned to decongest the city. The road has already been mapped out on paper in the ministries — it will run along the riverbanks to have its main junction right inside the neighborhood — and the many houses to be demolished to make way for it have been counted. The eviction seemed all the easier because, until 2018, the neighborhood did not even exist on the official map. Working with a local fablab and the local Open Street Map community, we have implemented the Map & Jerry project to create a map with the city residents to bring the slum to the surface (Choplin and Lozivit 2019).[1] After recycling old computers to make new ones, housed in old yellow canisters often found floating in the water, we created the map by collecting points, lines, and areas and giving them toponyms. This bottom-up and participatory map was of huge symbolic significance in connecting the slum to the city. It consolidated local authority, Gnonlonfoun told us: "I am now a real chief because my neighborhood exists on the map." Yet it also showed all the contradictions of this process of material and symbolic integration into the city, as was revealed to us by a government official who remarked, "I don't want your map to give them the impression that they can stay."

Conclusion

Traces, knots, surfaces, materials, and practices that play with emptiness and fullness reveal not only people's resilience in coping with their vulnerability but also their marginalization, which offers no remedy to the threat of collapse. All these practices prevent the margin from succumbing. In a sense, they support it and stop it from physically sinking into the lake or descend-

---

1   See the video of the Map & Jerry project conducted in Ladji: https://youtu.be/8f6sknx7sTQ. For drone images from the Ladji neighborhood, see https://youtu.be/RCuiOwh3dMQ.

ing to lower thresholds of social survival. They leave the people of Ladji clinging to the land of a city — and an economy and a state — which, the more it engulfs their neighborhood, the more they seem to reject it. The world held together by knots, traces, receptacles, and concrete surfaces, however, is not only one of resilient practices of dwelling by shadowy "marginals" but also one of divergent and competing trajectories, of marked underlying inequalities, accumulations and conflicts, and of strong political and economic interests in urban reconfiguration, which give a historical and social face to what may seem at first glance to be a purely physical and natural effusion. This urban connection, this solidification, threatens a new dispossession alongside the dissolution of the amphibian community and the weakening of its resilience. Solidification does not guarantee political inclusion and recognition. Indeed, quite to the contrary, the process of solidification could be seen as a new collapse, a new dissolution or liquefaction that could fragment this precarious community.

If we blur the boundaries between solidity and liquidity and see the relationship between them as an ongoing social-environmental process, then it is clear that solidification and dissolution can occur simultaneously. This is even more apparent with the two most recent and influential processes affecting Lake Nokoué and its precarious dwellings, and reconfiguring social practices of anchoring against collapse. The first is environmental; as a result of climate change, inhabitants are facing rising sea levels and unprecedented flooding. Dissolution looms, and concrete alone will not be enough to keep Ladji and its people out of the water. At the same time, this neighborhood is experiencing a moment of consolidation thanks to the construction of a storm drain founded by a sanitation development project (Projet d'Assainissement Pluvial de Cotonou); a canal is being built to divert water to the lake during heavy rains. But questions are already being raised about its future. Who will maintain the canal? Will it not become a new dumping ground for uncollected waste? This consolidation of infrastructure could presage a new dissolution, in which the neighborhood risks being submerged not only by water but also by waste.

The second element is political, as part of the riverbank is about to be cleared to make way for a bypass. This road infrastructure project will consolidate the neighborhood by connecting it to the rest of the city, but it could also become a symbol of dissolution, since it is not certain that the highway will have a stop in the area. In addition, the construction of the road will entail numerous evictions. Yet although the neighborhood seems to be sinking, and basic services (water, electricity) are still lacking, its leader — whom we met again recently — remains optimistic: "We will soon be connected to fiber optics. Our lives will improve" (interview April 18, 2023). The life of the slum is hanging by a thread.

References

Bourgoignie, Georges. 1972. *Les hommes de l'eau: Ethno-écologie du Dahomey lacustre.* Editions Universitaires.

Choplin, Armelle. 2023. *Concrete City: Material Flows and Urbanization in West Africa.* Wiley.

Choplin, Armelle, and Martin Lozivit. 2019. "Mapping a Slum: Learning from Participatory Mapping and Digital Innovation in Cotonou (Benin)." *Cybergeo.* DOI: 10.4000/cybergeo.32949.

Ciavolella, Riccardo. 2019. "Cosa Trattiene il Margine, Finché non Sprofonda: La Traccia e il Nodo in un Quartiere Precario Lacustre (Cotonou, Benin)." *Tracce Urbane: Rivista Italiana Transdisciplinare di Studi Urbani* 5: 139–75. DOI: 10.13133/2532-6562_3.5.14562.

Ciavolella, Riccardo, and Armelle Choplin. 2018. *Cotonou(s): Histoire d'une Ville sans Histoire.* Cahiers de la Fondation Zinsou, IRD.

Coralli, Monica, and Arthur Vido. 2017. "The Toffinu and the Lebu: Halfway between Indigenous Narrative and Spatial Resistance." In *Correspondences,* edited by Eduarda Neves. CEAA/CESAP.

D'Albeca, Alexandre. 1895. *La France au Dahomey.* Hachette.

Green, Sarah. 2014. "Anthropological Knots: Conditions of Possibilities and Interventions." *HAU: Journal of Ethnographic Theory* 4, no. 3: 1–21. DOI: 10.14318/hau4.3.002.

Harvey, David. 2001. *Spaces of Global Capitalism: A Theory of Uneven Geographical Development.* Verso.

Ingold, Tim. 2000. *The Perception of The Environment: Essays on Livelihood, Dwelling and Skill.* Routledge.

———. 2007. *Lines: A Brief History.* Routledge.

———. 2008. "Bindings against Boundaries: Entanglements of Life in an Open World." *Environment and Planning A: Economy and Space* 40, no. 8: 1796–810. DOI: 10.1068/a40156.

———. 2010. "Transformations of the Line: Traces, Threads and Surfaces." *Textile* 8, no. 1: 10–35. DOI: 10.2752/175183510X 12580391270100.

————. 2015. *The Life of Lines*. Routledge.

————. 2017. "Surface Visions." *Theory, Culture & Society* 34, no. 7–8: 99–108. DOI: 10.1177/0263276417730601.

Law, Robin. 1989. "Between the Sea and the Lagoons: The Interaction of Maritime and Inland Navigation on the Precolonial Slave Coast." *Cahiers d'Etudes Africaines* 29, no. 114: 209–37. https://www.persee.fr/doc/cea_0008-0055_1989_num_29_114_1643.

Lefebvre, Henri. 1968. *Le Droit à la Ville*. Seuil.

Manning, Patrick. 1982. *Slavery, Colonialism and Economic Growth in Dahomey, 1640–1960*. Cambridge University Press.

Polanyi, Karl. 1966. *Dahomey and the Slave Trade: An Analysis of an Archaic Economy*. University of Washington Press.

Simonetti, Cristián, and Tim Ingold. 2018. "Ice and Concrete: Solid Fluids of Environmental Change." *Journal of Contemporary Archaeology* 5, no. 1: 19–31. DOI: 10.1558/jca.33371.

8

Elastic City

Lukas Ley

In a recent piece on sand mining for land reclamation in Singapore, William Jamieson (2021, 276) demonstrates that sediment extracted from rivers or off shore can become alternately fluid or solid.[1] The granularity of sediment allows it to "flow like a liquid or disperse like a gas, jam to a fragile halt or consolidate into solid ground." Focusing on the shifting relations between matter and value, Jamieson underlines sand's fundamental role in Southeast Asian urbanization, where it participates in geomorphological, ecological, and political processes. For example, to facilitate urban extensions, sand is *poured* into bays, transforming a "liquid" milieu into "solid" ground, the condition for economic growth and national stability. Studies of land reclamation, however, demonstrate not only how sand becomes "part of an engineering project" toward territorialization (Arnez 2021, 300) but also how it is used to arrest staggering land subsidence (Siriwardane-de Zoysa et al. 2021) and buttress urban shores. In

---

[1]   In this chapter, I consider three types of sediment, defined as solid material on the move and deposited at a new location: sand, silt, and gravel. These materials are often defined by their grain size, although the criteria for what counts as sand or silt are not globally consistent.

this chapter, I focus on the latter, but instead of looking at large-scale instrumentalizations of sand, I examine coastal adaptation in a minor key, through the lens of smaller, uncoordinated attempts to synchronize with subsidence, such as residential projects that involve techniques of infill, house repair, and street lifting. Together, I argue, these interventions make urban land elastic in a material, symbolic, and temporal sense. By using granular materials such as sand and gravel, residents who live on dissolving shores not only respond to the sheer unboundedness of soils but also shape the outcomes of sea level rise. Based on these observations, I suggest that urban anthropology should pay attention to the fundamental role played by granular material in (un)making urban life. In the face of environmental turmoil, grains of sand and silt afford urban existence itself a certain elasticity — an ability to flexibly bend and twist with precarious grounds and infrastructures that now make up our lifeworlds.

Katherine Dawson (2023, 41–42) suggests that critically "thinking through the city as a sandy landscape," what she calls a "fluid platform, remaking itself over time and space," helps us to account for the material practices and displacements that make it possible for people to live there. In a similar vein, I show how sand and gravel allow residents of coastal Indonesian cities to navigate the liquidity of urban space in the context of retreating urban deltas. Here, the notion of urban liquefaction can be grounded in practices of "vertical reclamation" that produce an urban material form that is neither liquid nor solid, but rather *elastic*. This elasticity is not exactly the same as what the material sciences mean by the term. According to physics, most solid materials exhibit elastic behavior. The limit of elasticity is crossed when solid things remain permanently deformed, rather than returning to their original shape and size. I see elasticity otherwise, as a kind of flexibility afforded to land by the meeting of human action and matter. Together, human responses to flooding and granular stuff make and unmake "urban nature as a dynamic, ever-continuing, social-biophysical process" (Rademacher and Sivaramakrishnan 2021).

Urban Liquefaction

Studies of soil liquefaction — a condition in which the stability of ground soil is suddenly reduced — have shown that the physical properties of rock, the age of mineral deposits, and the depth of groundwater can all contribute to creating favorable circumstances for ground failure (Manoharan and Ganapathy 2023). Earthquakes can liquefy stretches of land and produce sinkholes that swallow houses and vehicles. Ironically, soil can liquefy because of the presence of hard substances, such as silt and sand. "Shake waterlogged sand and liquefaction occurs," warns Michael Welland (2009, 55). Under pressure and in large quantities, sand grains lock together because of their coarse shape; granularity produces friction between grains, strong bonds that cause them to adhere. But this bond is unstable; gravity and other external forces constantly cause grains to separate and settle into new positions and configurations. Sand's participation in soil movement means that the "solidity of the land becomes indistinguishable from the liquidity of water" (Denizen 2019, 100). Similarly, the tensile strength of concrete comes with the risk of liquefaction. The angular-shaped granulates used in concrete produce minute interstices through which corrosive liquids may pass and shatter the structure from within. Thus the materiality of sand and concrete plays an important role in solidifying structures and land, but it can also contribute to their dissolution.

Land subsidence is another example of sediment's role in ground stasis and movement. Subsidence, the gradual sinking of land, involves the disintegration and compression of soil. Coastal flats can sink especially fast because their alluvial soil, expelled from the mouths of sediment-carrying rivers, has had little time to consolidate and solidify. Rapid urbanization of deltas partially explains subsidence, but interdisciplinary research (Siriwardane-de Zoysa et al. 2021) has attributed soil settlement to an interplay of political, historical, and ecological processes.[2] For instance, urban areas that lack access to piped water often sink faster because many residents rely on groundwater, thus depleting urban aquifers and further destabilizing alluvial soils. Studies highlight the many residential responses to sinking land, such as using crab shells as landfill (Keller 2023), forming pumping communities (Kusno 2018; Ley 2022), or relocating to higher ground. However, by far the most common response is to attempt to reverse subsidence by means of granular matter, such as gravel and sand.

In light of Jakarta's problems with sinking land since the 1970s, Batubara, Kooy, and Zwarteveen (2023) argue that subsidence is both a product of, and intrinsic to, urbanization. Adaptation to land subsidence therefore not only reflects uneven urbanization but also produces it. Urban communities living in neighborhoods that *meninggikan* (elevate) streets and houses built on alluvial land do not just carve out a future for themselves. Because "every infill is in reality a reworking" (Ingold 2019, 668), they intervene in the texture of the urban surface and the meanings of land. They translate granular matter into transitory islands of time, a practice I have elsewhere called "building on borrowed time" (Ley 2021). The appropriation of granular matter to raise houses and build impermeable barriers to water makes land elastic, stretching its form and duration. The famous Indonesian concept of *jam karet* (rubber time), which describes an elastic and expansive relation to time, should perhaps be extended to land.

---

2   As a scientific term, the concept of "subsidence" risks displacing Indigenous concepts of ground. After all, the task of "modern geology is to penetrate into the murky world of the ground and synthesize the complexities of topography in order to return with an objective picture that we can all agree upon" (Bobbette and Donovan 2019, 17). Nonetheless, the imagination of sinking land caused by accelerated soil compaction and other forms of ground failure allows us to tune in to the strange movements of the ground and interactions with its more-than-human rhythms. In Indonesia, the concept is doing important political work aimed at preventing the construction of massive seawalls which require evictions and do not provide long-term safety from floods.

Vertical Reclamation

Despite shores that dissolve and retreat, coastal cities in Southeast Asia continue to expand and densify. And instead of withdrawing to higher ground, residents of Jakarta and Manila demonstrate extreme resilience in the face of rising seas and flooding. One reason might be that these cities are used to adjusting to land subsidence and have been engaging in what I call "vertical reclamation" at least since the 1980s, long before sea level rise became an internationally recognized urban hazard. In Semarang, this practice is known as *peninggian* (lifting or elevating). Acts of *peninggian* can extend land downward or upward. Downward reclamation can take the form of solidifying softer ground, such as puddles and fishponds, or preventing upward seepage by covering floors with concrete or tiles. Upward reclamation consists of elevating house foundations, which often creates a need for further adjustments, such as adding stairs to house entrances or elongating walls. These practices not only react to sinking but also intervene in the geologic process of subsidence, for example, by changing the carrying capacity of urban soils or reproducing housing conditions that favor continuous groundwater extraction. Arguably, the ocean-bound sprawl of cities in the Global South required this simultaneous engineering practice that combines "cementitious earthwork" (Elinoff 2019) with vertical reclamation. Practices of vertical reclamation demonstrate how fluid soils force residents to form elastic arrangements with urban infrastructure.

When I arrived in the coastal metropolis of Semarang in 2014 to research the social production of climate vulnerability in flood-prone neighborhoods, I began by investigating government efforts to modernize hydraulic infrastructure in Kemijen, a northeastern subdistrict built on a former wetland. The city was experiencing regular tidal flooding, and because I was interested in local responses, I frequently walked, biked, and drove along the Banger River, a minor drainage canal flowing into the Java Sea, to examine infrastructural interventions in the wake of flooding events. Throughout the day, the Banger River looked like a stagnant body of viscous matter (Ley 2018b). Instead of flowing into the ocean, the dark mass expanded at high tide with an influx of seawater, gradually swallowing footbridges until it overflowed or penetrated its engineered edges, creeping into nearby streets and houses. This cycle of stagnation and excess, far from manifesting a benevolent flux, seemed to represent in microcosm the dissolution caused by climate change around the world.

However, when residents discussed the present and considered their future, they rarely sounded pessimistic. They were "in for it" and "used to it," by which they meant regular flooding. Some even welcomed floods because they attracted the attention of the state and brought infrastructural fixes. I wondered what made this outlook, on life lived on eroding shorelines, possible. My regular walks soon began to take in other riverbank activities. Periodically, trucks arrived to unload mounds of earth and larger rocks. Riverbanks readily served as loading docks for this construction material, but were also used to store bricks, bags of cement, and wood. The constant influx of these materials was in striking contrast to the river's apparent stagnation. Not unlike sediment carried by river water, this matter coursed down the hills of Semarang, where mining companies extracted aggregate and limestone for use in cement, much faster than rivers could erode rock. This engineered flux of granular material into the city was a response to the "sedimentary crisis" caused by dams and canals (Parrinello and Kondolf 2021). Construction materials were used to renovate floors, walls, roofs, and roads in response to recurrent flooding. Garbage was also employed as infill, but hard building materials made up the bulk of what was used for vertical reclamation.

Many of the practices that stretch the spatial and temporal contours of deltaic land cohere around the concept of *gotong-royong,* a foundational principle in Indonesian society centered on reproducing "good" *kampung* life through a system of mutual assistance and shared labor. Jan Newberry has argued that in Java, *gotong-royong* is key to caring for local infrastructure (Newberry 2018). Elsewhere (Ley 2018a), I have suggested that both residential labor and state interventions have facilitated the transformation of downstream edgeland into a "dry" — that is, legitimate — space. Ground lifting and infilling, intended to drain and protect urban land, are forms of collective labor that have literally lifted coastal neighborhoods out of poverty. Filling in and hardening out the marshy contours of the delta through collective work has produced legible and legitimate territory. Vertical reclamation is not just a residential affair. Public funds, humanitarian grants, and corporate money flow into the *kampung* and its ground, and subsidize the elevation of roads and riverbanks. In this way, engaging with sinking land has helped to forge lasting socioeconomic and political relationships.

The Limits of Elastic Land

Residents of coastal plains around the world live on increasingly unstable grounds whose habitability is deeply undermined by erosion, subsidence, and salinization. Following Franz Krause (2022, 39), it is evident that this "is not a problem of losing an alleged permanence in the world, since the cultural, economic, and hydrological relations in the delta have long been unstable and volatile." Rather, it is a problem of upholding and maintaining material presence. In Indonesia, proving legitimate residence is a prerequisite for access to citizenship rights and poverty-relief measures. Vertical reclamation stretches the carrying capacity of land and, by the same token, the expiry date of land-based rights. In so doing, it also stretches the meaning of land, as many urban governments have already begun to designate coastal plains as uninhabitable and to issue master plans that anticipate massive evictions and relocation to higher ground.

Materiality plays an important role in determining the limits of land's elasticity. Layering granular material affords the flexibility to adjust the heights of houses and roads to sea level. But infill and *peninggian* by no means guarantee tenure. Vertical reclamation has allowed residents of Tambak Lorok and Tambak Rejo, frontline coastal neighborhoods of Semarang, to prevent

Fig. 8.1. Drowned two-story house built on reclaimed land in Tambak Rejo that was featured in the site-specific art project "Penta K Labs" organized by the art collective Grobak Hysteria. Photograph by Hysteria Documentation Team. Reproduced with permission.

or at least diminish the effects of flooding, but other infrastructural developments constantly undermine their elastic arrangements with land and water (fig. 8.1). Time and again, residents have noticed sea changes in coastal development that endanger their position at the water's edge. Rerouting the Banger River in the 1990s, the constant expansion of harbor dry docks, and the more recent widening of Semarang's East Flood Canal have all led to a deterioration of the shoreline. Residents claim that dredging in the bay and changing the course of rivers have disadvantaged them by causing more frequent inundations. And fully embanking the flood canal entailed the eviction of hundreds of coastal residents who, against all odds, had managed to eke out a living here. The central government of Indonesia recently started building a toll road connecting the industrial centers of Semarang and Demak, which will require the conversion of 539.7 ha of inhabited coastal land (Batubara et al. 2020, 47). This land is now slated for transport infrastructure and further port expansions. As this example shows, elasticity is as much a function of political and economic as of material conditions.

Coda

Instead of accepting the objective picture of the world beneath our feet, anthropology and critical geography have tried to understand land as a deeply social and cultural achievement, and as a "provisional assemblage of heterogenous elements including material substances, technologies, discourses, and practices" (Li 2014, 589). With its refusal to put human action center stage, this perspective allows us to see land as emerging through shifting relations with materials and their geophysical becoming. In Semarang, Jakarta, and other coastal cities of Southeast Asia, sand and gravel play an important role in making and unmaking land. Raising grounds and houses with granular material, residents preserve an elastic relation to coastal land that is rapidly sinking into the ocean.

Urban liquefaction allows us to consider sand as an active component in reproducing urban life on these shores. In interaction with other substances (such as water or oxygen), with organisms (bacteria or fungi living between sand grains), with aquifers, or with geological disturbances, such as earth tremors, sand informs the material articulations of urban life. These material expressions play a fundamental role in both stabilizing and destabilizing soils. Over the past decade, sand has become the subject of a growing body of literature in geography and development studies (Lamb, Marschke, and Rigg 2019, Jamieson 2021) that center on the epistemic and material practices through which minerals become resources and make their way into global markets and geopolitical schemes (Adriansen 2009). This scholarship has shown how sand comes to matter as a resource in territorial and state-making projects, but it has scarcely explored the role of sand in assembling land and modulating human relations with time and large-scale geologic processes. Granular matter such as sand is especially important for preserving land on urban shores. Sandfill, in particular, constantly produces and reproduces land as "vertical territory" (Bobbette and Donovan 2019, 1). At the same time, the dissipative qualities of sand explain the liquefying contours of land and belonging on urban shores. The urban life that obtains on and between solid and liquid surfaces could itself be qualified as elastic or viscous. Does this prove that organic life is only possible thanks to the "fundamental viscosity of all matter" as Ingold and Simonetti (2022, 21) ask? And where and how does sand allow urban form to preserve some memory of its initial configuration? Where does it also lead to points of no return?

Whenever I return to Kemijen, I still long to see the Banger River. Upon revisiting Semarang in 2018, I noticed that water levels in the canal had dropped drastically. Today, pumps located at the mouth of the Banger River regularly evacuate surplus water into the adjacent East Flood Canal, artificially restoring its flow. The polder (hydraulic system) installed by the municipality simulates gravity, but it is not enough to prevent subsidence — flooding still happens where riverbanks have crumbled as a result of low water pressure and concrete weathering. Another problem caused by the intervention, however, is the water hyacinth, a freshwater plant that flourishes in reservoirs (see Iqbal 2020). Damming the river has prevented brackish water from entering the drainage tract, creating a perfect biological niche for the plant. Only four years after the polder was implemented, a thick layer of branches and leaves already covered the water surface, and the plant's roots increasingly hampered water flow and captured sediment. Paradoxically, attempts to liquefy the river have had the opposite effect; overgrown with biomass and threatening to silt up, the river looked even more stagnant than before the intervention.

References

Adriansen, Hanne Kirstine. 2009. "Land Reclamation in Egypt: A Study of Life in the New Lands." *Geoforum* 40, no. 4: 664–74. DOI: 10.1016/j.geoforum.2009.05.006.

Arnez, Monika. 2021. "The Granularity of Sand: Analogies of Production, Consumption, and Distribution." *Dialogues in Human Geography* 11, no. 2: 298–301. DOI: 10.1177/20438206211004857.

Ashmore, Peter. 2018. "Transforming Toronto's Rivers: A Socio-Geomorphic Perspective." In *The Palgrave Handbook of Critical Physical Geography*, edited by Rebecca Lave, Christine Biermann, and Stuart N. Lane. Springer International.

Batubara, Bosman, Michelle Kooy, and Margreet Zwarteveen. 2023. "Politicising Land Subsidence in Jakarta: How Land Subsidence Is the Outcome of Uneven Sociospatial and Socionatural Processes of Capitalist Urbanization." *Geoforum* 139: 103689. DOI: 10.1016/j.geoforum.2023.103689.

Batubara, Bosman, Henny Warsilah, Ivan Wagner, and Syukron Salam. 2020. *Maleh dadi Segoro: Krisis Sosial-Ekologis Kawasan Pesisir Semarang-Demak*. Lintas Nalar.

Bobbette, Adam, and Amy Donovan. 2019. "Political Geology: An Introduction." In *Political Geology*, edited by Adam Bobbette and Amy Donovan. Springer International.

Dawson, Katherine. 2023. "A Share in the Sands: Trips, Pits and Potholes in Accra, Ghana." *Africa* 93, no. 1: 40–59. DOI: 10.1017/S0001972023000116.

Denizen, Seth. 2019. "Baroque Soil: Mexico City in the Aftermath." In *Political Geology*, edited by Adam Bobbette and Amy Donovan. Springer International.

Elinoff, Eli. 2019. "Cement." Society for Cultural Anthropology, June 27. https://culanth.org/fieldsights/cement.

Ingold, Tim. 2019. "Art and Anthropology for a Sustainable World." *Journal of the Royal Anthropological Institute* 25, no. 4: 659–75. DOI: 10.1111/1467-9655.13125.

Ingold, Tim, and Cristián Simonetti. 2022. "Introducing Solid Fluids." *Theory, Culture and Society* 39, no. 2: 3–29. DOI: 10.1177/02632764211030990.

Iqbal, Iftekhar. 2020. "In the Bengal Delta, the Anthropocene Began with the Arrival of the Railways." In *Feral Atlas: The More-Than-Human Anthropocene,* edited by Anna L. Tsing, Jennifer Deger, Alder Keleman Saxena, and Feifei Zhou. https://feralatlas.supdigital.org/poster/in-the-bengal-delta-the-anthropocene-began-with-the-arrival-of-the-railways.

Jamieson, William. 2021. "For Granular Geography." *Dialogues in Human Geography* 11, no. 2: 275–93. DOI: 10.1177/2043820620950053.

Keller, Kirsten. 2023. "Mussels and Megaprojects: Landscape Structure and Structural Inequality at Jakarta's Coast." *Social Anthropology/Anthropologie Sociale* 31 no. 4: 76–94. DOI: 10.3167/saas.2023.310406.

Krause, Franz. 2022. "The Tempo of Solid Fluids: On River Ice, Permafrost, and Other Melting Matter in the Mackenzie Delta." *Theory, Culture & Society* 39, no. 2: 31–52. DOI: 10.1177/026327642110309.

Kusno, Abidin. 2018. "Where Will the Water Go?" *Indonesia* 105, no. 1: 19–51. https://www.jstor.org/stable/10.5728/indonesia.105.0019.

Lahiri-Dutt, Kuntala, and Gopa Samanta. 2013. *Dancing with the River: People and Life on the Chars of South Asia.* Yale University Press.

Lamb, Vanessa, Melissa Marschke, and Jonathan Rigg. 2019. "Trading Sand, Undermining Lives: Omitted Livelihoods in the Global Trade in Sand." *Annals of the American Association of Geographers* 109, no. 5: 1511–28. DOI: 10.1080/24694452.2018.1541401.

Ley, Lukas. 2018a. "Discipline and Drain: River Normalization and Semarang's Fight against Tidal Flooding." *Indonesia* 105, no. 1: 53–75. https://www.jstor.org/stable/10.5728/indonesia.105.0053.

———. 2018b. "On the Margins of the Hydrosocial: Quasi-Events along a Stagnant River." *Geoforum* 131: 234–42. DOI: 10.1016/j.geoforum.2018.03.010.

———. 2021. *Building on Borrowed Time: Rising Seas and Failing Infrastructure in Semarang.* University of Minnesota Press.

Li, Tania Murray. 2014. "What Is Land? Assembling a Resource for Global Investment." *Transactions of the Institute of British Geographers* 39, no. 4: 589–602. DOI: 10.1111/tran.12065.

Manoharan, Saravana Ganesh, and Ganapathy Pattukandan Ganapathy. 2023. "GIS Based Urban Social Vulnerability Assessment for Liquefaction Susceptible Areas: A Case Study for Greater Chennai, India." *Geoenvironmental Disasters* 10, no. 1: 1–22. DOI: 10.1186/s40677-022-00230-5.

Newberry, Jan. 2018. "A *Kampung* Corner: Infrastructure, Affect, Informality." *Indonesia* 105, no. 1: 191–206. https://www.jstor.org/stable/10.5728/indonesia.105.0191.

Parrinello, Giacomo, and G. Mathias Kondolf. 2021. "The Social Life of Sediment." *Water History* 13, no. 1: 1–12.

Rademacher, Anne, and K. Sivaramakrishnan. 2021. *Death and Life of Nature in Asian Cities.* Hong Kong University Press.

Siriwardane-de Zoysa, Rapti, Tilo Schöne, Johannes Herbeck, Julia Illigner, Mahmud Haghighi, Hendricus Simarmata, Emma Porio, Alessio Rovere, and Anna-Katharina Hornidge. 2021. "The 'Wickedness' of Governing Land Subsidence: Policy Perspectives from Urban Southeast Asia." *PLOS ONE* 16, no. 6: e0250208. DOI: 10.1371/journal.pone.0250208.

Tsing, Anna L., Jennifer Deger, Alder Keleman Saxena, and Feifei Zhou. 2020. *Feral Atlas: The More-Than-Human Anthropocene.* Stanford University Press. https://feralatlas.org.

Welland, Michael. 2009. *Sand: A Journey through Science and the Imagination.* Oxford University Press.

9

Liquefying Concrete: Building, Dwelling, and Thinking at the Shoreline

Cristián Simonetti

Concrete is a material that currently underlines, perhaps like no other, the antithetical relation between land and sea, earth and water, solidity and fluidity, that this volume aims to upset. In its association with steel, it is currently the material of choice for consolidating claims to land and taming the forces of water through hard surfacing, river embankment, and the construction of coastal defenses. In these guises, concrete has been materializing modernity's narrative of progress by providing a durable platform for the enactment of life, over and above the earthly surfaces across which exchanges of nutrients and energy allow life as we know it to flourish. From a geological point of view, concrete is arguably a candidate to mark the origin of the Anthropocene in the stratigraphic record. Enough concrete has been poured since its rediscovery during the industrial revolution to cover the entire surface of the Earth with a layer a few millimeters thick. On a global scale, concrete infrastructure creates what can be described as the largest *geofact* in human history (Simonetti 2023).

In the so-called developing countries of the Global South, such as Chile, concrete has played an important role in consolidating its modern aspirations, a trajectory that started at the turn of the twentieth century, mostly in response to major seismic events. At the time of its introduction, Chilean concrete-manufacturing companies came up with slogans emphasizing the solidity of the material, promoting it as the substance of progress, on the assumption that only the hard will last. In the same vein, the Chilean government decided in 1929 to renovate the country's image by constructing a large concrete building for a prestigious international fair held in Seville, Spain. The building included voluminous walls designed to emulate the white contours of the Andes, suggesting that Chileans were endowed with a tough and industrious character that justified and explained the ascent of the nation (Dümmer 2014), an ideal still often mobilized to advance ideas of progress (Simonetti and Ingold 2018).

Drawing on this national imaginary, one could easily write a history of the country based on its building materials. Stepping beyond the surfaces of the city of Santiago, where nearly half of the country's population lives, quickly brings Chileans in touch with nature. This is what transpires in the work of David Aniñir, a contemporary poet who writes about what it means to be a Mapuche from the city, an experience cast in terms of a tension between concrete and soil (Barros 2007). Compared to the surfaces of the urban landscape, introduced to sanitize the city, the soil that Aniñir's poetry implicitly commemorates and transports the reader to lost forests in the Araucanía region, south of Santiago, to which urban Mapuche no longer seem to belong. This is a truly disturbing image, given the etymology of the term *Mapuche*, referring to people (*che*) of the land (*mapu*), land known to be sentient in the eyes of those who inhabit it (Di Giminiani 2018).[1]

---

1   *Mapu* is an encompassing term that can signify more than just "land," depending on the context. It can refer to the vital space in which humans, other species, and spiritual beings reside, as in the expression *Waj mapu*, which roughly corresponds to ideas of "universe" or "planet" in Western terminology. *Waj* means "to enfold something all around, covering,

Yet, the aura of everlastingness that the building industry has attached to concrete seems suddenly to have been overtaken by the effects of global warming. Not only is the concrete infrastructure in coastal areas — which is key to the connectivity of the globalized world — bound to be submerged by sea level rise, but after nearly a century of concrete building, at a mass scale, concrete structures have also been crumbling, caused in part by the lacustrine origin of the ingredients that make up the material, which has rendered it vulnerable to the characteristic telluric flows of Chile's earthquake-prone geology.

This imminent liquefaction of concrete could be read as the material culmination of what Marx and Engels famously prophesied in their *Communist Manifesto* regarding the dissolution of social structures under capitalism. In their words, "all that is solid melts into air" (1978, 476). It is a prophecy that continues to resonate, for instance, in Zygmunt Bauman's (2000) much discussed notion of *liquid modernity.* Bauman introduced this concept to describe metaphorically how the flow of information, relationships, identities, values, and commodities in contemporary society liquefy established forms of solidarity (from the Latin *solidus,* meaning "solid"), which the founders of modern sociology, such as Émile Durkheim, had placed at the heart of their social theory. Today, however, it is no longer sufficient to treat the ideas of "melting into air" or liquefaction merely as metaphors for social processes conceived to float on a level of their own, independently of the ground that sustains them. From a planetary point of view, they can be applied, quite literally, to the infrastructures in which sociality is grounded, challenging the established idea, in much social thought, that

seeing and relating with what lies inside" (Pichinao Huenchuleo, Mellico Avendaño, and Huenchulaf Cayuqueo 2022, 63; my translation). For the Mapuche, the *waj mapu* has been formed partially through a correspondence between sea and land, as the creation myth of *kay-kay* and *treng-treng* suggests. According to this myth, the landscape formed out of a struggle between two serpents, respectively of the sea and the land, which took place at the beginning of time. I thank Wladimir Martínez for introducing me to the complexity of the term *mapu.*

"solids are cast once and for all" (Bauman 2000, 8). Despite the aura of solidity that the building industry has attached to concrete, its geological origin and destiny suggests that the material transcends any categorial divide between solid and fluid states.

Oceanic Origins

Compared to earth, water has been regarded as the epitome of change and impermanence (Bachelard 1982). This comparison, between the assumed solidity and durability of earth and the liquid changefulness of water, has underpinned the antithetical relation between land and sea since ancient times. Plato, for instance, imagined the ideal city to be built on an island whose rocky foundation held fast against the sea, affording protection for the polis from external influences, including those carried by the forces of water (Steinberg 2011). This opposition between land and sea has once again come to the fore, now that sea level rises and extreme weather phenomena threaten more and more coastal cities, including such iconic examples as New Orleans, Venice, and in the Netherlands, not to mention the islands in the Pacific that are bound to disappear. Concrete has played a crucial part in human efforts to separate earth and water. Yet as the process of its manufacture attests, this separation is illusory.

As soon as we move beyond modernity's shallow understanding of the ground and immerse ourselves in geology's deep time, the solid infrastructure of modern life begins to bend and melt. Indeed, the apparent opposition between solidity and fluidity that concrete establishes, as it arrests exchanges between earth, air, and water, is only transitory. No layer of concrete can permanently seal the earth from the weather or the sea. This is the conclusion that architects Mohsen Mostafavi and David Leatherbarrow (1993) reach as they consider the lives of buildings within a matrix of environmental forces. Moreover, concrete is endowed with a degree of elasticity, with the result that, given enough time and pressure, part of its configuration will resemble waves, much like those of sedimentary formations currently visible in the geological record. Finally, as the earth continues to transform over time, concrete will reenter the on-going rock cycle.

The illusion of eternal solidity offered by concrete infra-structure is belied even further by the lacustrine origins of its principal ingredients. These were mostly deposited in riverine and coastal environments, through the erosion, transport, and compaction of sediments, and subsequently lifted above sea level by the very same telluric forces that now threaten concrete infrastructure in seismic cities, such as Santiago. Cement, for instance, comes from burning limestone, a sedimentary rock composed of the petrified detritus of seashells, the geological origins of which date to the evolutionary appearance of skel-etal material in the oceans nearly 500 million years ago. In the blink of an eye, humans have speeded up earth history, firing limestone, only to subsequently sediment their own "coral reefs" over the land.

Moving down the list of essential ingredients, after cement we find aggregates, particularly sand, originally formed from the slow weathering of rock by rivers as they steadily descend toward the ocean. Lukas Ley points out in Chapter 8 of this volume that the particulate composition of concrete, with its source in lacustrine environments, makes reinforcements vul-nerable to the infiltration of moisture. Last on the list is water, a substance that even more blatantly defies concrete's aura of solidity. Remarkably, the ancient Romans — who are credited with the initial discovery of hydraulic concrete — sourced their water from the sea. Because of its salt content, however, seawa-ter is incompatible with the iron and steel reinforcements used in modern concrete, since salt corrodes metal.

Indeed, from the viewpoint of the Romans — some of whose constructions still stand more or less intact — concrete would never have appeared as the eternal substance, solidified in final forms, on which modernity has pinned its hopes and aspira-tions. Rather, they regarded concrete as the confluence of ma-terials and forces, including those revolving around the element of water. This view is exemplified in Vitruvius's *De Architectura* (1960, 48), written around 25 BCE, which recorded one of the

earliest formulae for the material. According to Vitruvius, cementitious materials, such as lime (*calx*), ash (*pulvis*), and tuff
(*tofus*), extracted from kilns and volcanos, were in urgent need
of moisture when submerged under water, which explained their
tendency to harden into rock. This formation process spoke of a
correspondence between the elements, whereby *earth* burned at
intense temperatures in *fire,* called for *water,* only subsequently
to release latent heat into *air.* This is precisely what occurs with
cementitious or volcanic materials, such as Portland or *pozzola-
na,* which release heat into the atmosphere on contact with water. In fact, concrete never dries out. It rather cures as cement, in
the process of hydration, trapping water molecules in the mix.
That is why the moisture content needs to be kept constant as
the mix hardens, since it would otherwise crack and crumble.
Concrete, as the term suggests, is *concrescence,* a gathering of
forces and materials, of heterogeneous trajectories that extend
deep into the history of planet Earth and of the material flows
that have made this history possible.

This view of concrete, as more-than-solid, has parallels with
the way in which noble building materials, of valued durability,
came subsequently to be understood in medieval times. A remarkable example is marble, a metamorphic material formed of
sedimentary rock, most commonly limestone, again originally
from the sea. According to art historian Barbara Baert (2017),
marble was known among the citizens of Constantinople as
petrified water. This is confirmed by the etymology of the word
"marble," derived from the Sanskrit root *mar,* a term connoting
movement, as of the waves, and commonly used in Romance
languages in reference to the sea. This was the understanding of
marble that, according to Baert, led to its use in Hagia Sophia,
the main cathedral of Constantinople until its fall in 1453. The
nave of the cathedral, resembling the cosmos, included a marble
floor to represent the primordial substance of water. The mar-
bled waves of Hagia Sophia's floor — now known to originate
from the intense pressures at work in the metamorphic formation of the original rock — were, for the descendants of the ancient Romans, a murmur (from the Sanskrit *mar-mar*) of the

sea. To walk and talk on such floors was like sailing with feet and voices on the land, a more-than-solid imagining to which we now turn.

Sailing on Land

Before closing this chapter let me speculate further on what it means to envision a city that is not opposed to the fluid sea, but rather, in the words of geographer Philip Steinberg (2011), "post-terrestrial." My inspiration comes from the inhabitants of the island of Chiloe, situated off the coast of southwest Chile. The life of the Chilotes, as the island's inhabitants are called, literally unfolds in the zone where land and sea meet. The writer Francisco Coloane has told of what it is like to live in such as environment, as he recounts the feeling of growing inside a *palafito,* one of Chiloe's most iconic constructions, raised on stilts in the intertidal zone:

> My house was built half on land and half on the sea. When the tide rose, I felt the sea under my bedroom floor. I can say that I was rocked by the sea since my birth and that its spirit seized me from the first day of my life and in my books with a vital persistence, just like the people, the landscape, and the beasts of the south of Patagonia and the Tierra del Fuego to which I owe so much.

Living their lives between land and sea, these inhabitants of the shoreline have developed construction techniques, inspired by boat building, that some in the island still know well. Traditionally using dowels rather than nails and bolts, these techniques called for an intimate knowledge of the grains and knots of wood. Entire houses constructed in this way could be transported over land to different locations, as part of a ritualistic communal effort known as *mingas.* As they sail their constructions, Chilotes build and dwell on the land much as they do at sea, which presumably they have done since the island's earliest inhabitants arrived from the mainland. The knot depicted in fig-

Fig. 9.1. Clove hitch on tent stick from Monte Verde. Photograph by Tom Dilehay. Reproduced with permission.

ure 9.1, the earliest of its kind to appear in the Chilean archaeo-logical record, comes from one of the buildings of Monte Verde, a site located near Puerto Montt, the main port connecting Chiloe with the mainland. Known as a clove hitch and regarded as one of the most important knots in maritime history, it is usually thought to have originated in the traditions of European seamanship, designed as it is to withstand the ongoing move-ments of a ship in its encounter with oceanic forces without tightening to the point of rigidity.

Contrary to the official narrative, however, this particular knot actually dates from the time of the earliest inhabitants of South America, and was evidently designed to withstand the intense winds that would often have swept up and down over Monte Verde's tents, coming from both the sea and the Andes. Compared with stone artifacts, knots do not figure prominently in our imaginations of prehistory since, because of their organic origin, they tend to be absent from the archaeological record. They are preserved only under exceptional conditions, such as those of the anaerobic bog in which the site of Monte Verde was discovered. Presumably, however, knotting has been present from earliest times, making possible seamanship (arguably crucial to the human peopling of the Americas), tent building (as in Monte Verde), basketry, knitting, and, most certainly, the mounting of arrow heads. Tracing human origins to knotting speaks of a more organic and ductile engagement with nature than that entailed in the production of artifacts of solid stone, a domain traditionally associated in archaeology with the masculine pursuit of hunting (Patou-Mathis 2021).

The inspiration for the knot, moreover, could be traced to the fluid sea, particularly to the seaweed that grows so abundantly in the region's intertidal zone, and that the inhabitants of Monteverde included in their diet (Dilehay et al. 2008). The blades of cochayuyo (*Durvillaea antarctica*), as it is known locally, often tangle into loose knots, as the sea rolls them up and down. These blades are designed to float thanks to a unique honeycomb structure that allows them to withstand the waves. Clove hitches could have been formed in much the same way. The artist Marcos Fisurados — in an exhibition titled *Nodis in Stomachum: Teratomentales,* held in 2023 at the Center for the Promotion of Health and Culture in Quillota, Chile — has explored the relationship between knots in the body and in seamanship through the knotting of cochayuyos found along the Chilean coast.

Admittedly, returning to the Chilotes, the inspiration we can draw from their practices is limited, since in scale and substance their buildings hardly match those of the modern city. For a start, Chilotes build mostly not with concrete but with wood, a material that is substantially more ductile and flexible since it results from a process of organic growth that finds parallels in techniques dependent on the knotting of fibrous materials, such as in knitting or basketry. Yet, as wood is increasingly seen as an alternative material even for tall, multistory urban buildings, perhaps the comparison is not so far-fetched. Unlike concrete, tree growth traps carbon, which remains sequestrated inside buildings (Wiegand and Simonetti 2019). Furthermore, there is perhaps some point in comparing the buildings that make up the urban landscape to ships at sea, immersed in the forces of earth and weather, as Tim Ingold (2022, 166–79) has suggested in a recent speculative exercise. Ultimately, from a geological viewpoint, urban infrastructure is suspended in the flow of soils and tectonic plates that run underneath, as events of liquefaction dramatically illustrate. Though we can acknowledge that foundations are meant to keep buildings in place against these changing flows, perhaps they should be conceived not so much as built *on* the land as temporarily immersed *in* it.

References

Bachelard, Gaston. 1982. *Water and Dreams: An Essay on the Imagination of Matter.* Translated by Edith R. Farrell. Pegasus Foundation.

Baert, Barbara. 2017. "Marble and the Sea or Echo Emerging (A Ricercar)." *Espacio, Tiempo y Forma* 5: 35–54. DOI: 10.5944/etfvii.5.2017.

Barros, M.J. 2007. "'Mapuche de Hormigón,' extranjeros y expatriados urbanos: La poesía de David Aniñir." In *Proyecto patrimonio,* edited by Luis Martínez Solorza. http://www.letras.mysite.com/da1509071.htm.

Bauman, Zygmunt. 2000. *Liquid Modernity.* Polity Press.

Di Giminiani, Piergiorgio. 2018. *Sentient Lands: Indigeneity, Property and Political Imagination in Neoliberal Chile.* University of Arizona Press.

Dilehay, Tom D., C. Ramírez, Mario Pino, M.B. Collins, J. Rossen, and J.D. Pino-Navarro. 2008. "Monte Verde: Seaweed, Food, Medicine, and the Peopling of South America." *Science* 320: 784–86. DOI: 10.1126/science.1156533.

Dümmer, Sylvia. 2014. "Metáforas de un país frío: Chile en la exposición iberoamericana de Sevilla de 1929." In *Una Geografía Imaginada: Diez Ensayos Sobre Arte y Naturaleza,* edited by Amarí Peliowski and Catalina Valdés. Ediciones Universidad Alberto Hurtado.

Ingold, Tim. 2022. *Imagining for Real: Essays on Creation, Attention and Correspondence.* Routledge.

Marx, Karl, and Friedrich Engels. 1978. *Manifesto of the Communist Party (1848).* In *The Marx–Engels Reader,* edited by R.C. Tucker. W.W. Norton.

Mostafavi, Mohsen, and David Leatherbarrow. 1993. *On Weathering: The Life of Buildings in Time.* MIT Press.

Patou-Mathis, Marylene. 2021. *El Hombre Prehistórico es También una Mujer.* Lumen.

Pichinao Huenchuleo, Jimena, Fresia Mellico Avendaño, and Ernesto Huenchulaf Cayuqueo. 2022. *Mapunche gijañmawün gülu ka puwel mapu: La forma Mapunche de pensar y practicar la socialidad religiosa en Gülu y en Puwel Mapu.* Universidad Católica de Temuco.

Simonetti, Cristián. 2023. "Un 'futuro concreto' para la aquitectura en el antropoceno." *Revista 180* 1: 50–61. https://revista180.udp.cl/index.php/revista180/article/view/1293.

Simonetti, Cristián, and Tim Ingold. 2018. "Ice and Concrete: Solid Fluids of Environmental Change." *Journal of Contemporary Archaeology* 5, no. 1: 19–31. DOI: 10.1558/jca.33371.

Steinberg, Philip. 2011. "Liquid Urbanity: Re-engineering the City in a Post-Terrestrial World." In *Engineering Earth: The Impact of Megaengineering Projects,* edited by Stanley D. Brunn. Springer Science + Business Media B.V.

Vitruvius, Marco. 1960. *The Ten Books on Architecture.* Dover.

Wiegand, Eduardo, and Cristián Simonetti. 2019. "Wood Is Coming." *DOMUS* 1040: 1092–98.

PART 3

Introduction to Part 3:
Emerging Lands

Analyzing urbanism, both as a form of thinking and as a set of professional, social, and political practices, is not just a matter of examining how urban forms are concretely planned and built. It is also important to study urbanism as an active geographical and social imagination. Indeed, urban planning practitioners and authorities often idealize what they do, conceiving "perfect" urban forms and related social lives in order to set them down on a geographical surface regarded as a *tabula rasa*. Hence the importance for urban planners of situations where action can be taken from a space not previously built on or that has been cleared by the demolition of what already existed. For some in the profession, this immaculate ground is a kind of holy grail.

Urban planning has only recently begun to present itself as a science of the city, even though the desire to control space is as old as urbanization itself. The role of Ildefons Cerdà i Sunyer in the invention of this new science, with the publication of his *Teoría general del urbanización* in 1867, is now better acknowledged; he can be regarded, at the very least, as an emblematic figure of the period. In 1859, Cerdà, a civil engineer, drew up a plan for the *Ensanche* (extension) of Barcelona, which was partly implemented, and wrote numerous doctrinal texts on the subject. Long unknown, they were rediscovered in archives in 1985, and synthesized in *Teoria general*. The book was intended as a manifesto, laying the foundations for a scientific understanding of the urban phenomenon as a whole and, consequently, for rational intervention aimed at controlling cities, straightening them morphologically and improving them socially. For Cerdà, this control could only be achieved through knowledge of space, from which a conception of geographic organization could be inferred, on the premise that rational thought is to be projected into material form. Cerdà's master plan is an illustration of this morphological work, based on the relationship between the elevation of buildings and the grid of roads. Cerdà was thus implicitly taking up one of the foundations of modern European urban thought, going back to Thomas More's *Utopia* (1516)—the idea that the ideal city, the one that can support the ideal society, should be based on a strictly formal model.

Utopia established the utopian principle at the heart of urban planning. For most agencies involved in the fieldwork of scientific urbanism (urban planners *stricto sensu,* architects, engineers, public authorities, economic stakeholders, and so on), producing and mastering urban organization essentially means projecting a certain way of thinking into morphology and structure. Rational ideation thus becomes the keystone for the construction and arrangement of the material environment, which, once in place, stands as testimony to the essence and substance of the ideas behind it. The causal chain—from sovereign reason to ideal spatial forms to virtuous sociability—seems characteristic of scientific urbanism, which can therefore be considered a utopian practice, serving a positivist conception of progress, often reduced to its technical-functional dimension as an exercise in problem-solving. This scientific urbanism, which has since been exported outside Europe, notably by way of colonization, has been globally prevalent, in one form or another, and has governed the modalities of the most obvious actions of terraforming through urbanization. Urban planning is the latest expression of this trend in the United States, and has been adopted and transposed throughout the world since the 1950s.

This desire to stabilize everything through conceptual thinking is the very antithesis of the principle of urban fluidity that this book is intended to highlight, a principle that nevertheless constantly makes itself felt. Even the slightest observation shows the extent to which cities are social and cultural spaces in which nonpermanence, movement, recursion, uncertainty, informality, incident, the unforeseen, the unfinished, and so on are not just obvious but foundational to urban life. In a way, all manifestations of contingency are continuously working against the will of urban planning to install a world that, if not perfect, is at least stabilized and optimized. The challenge here is to identify the tensions between the desire for a controlled approach inherent in standard, legitimate urban production, particularly on the part of political institutions and the official economy, and the ever-renewing efflorescence of the unexpected, the changing, and the hazardous at the heart of everyday urban life.

The three chapters in Part 3 each examine, in their own way, this utopian dimension and its contradictions. Isabelle Simpson, Martin Hříbek, and Michael Leadbetter analyze very different cases, all of which reveal the more or less pronounced desire (from explicit expression to more discreet trace) to install an optimal urban world. This desire may indeed stem from urban studies themselves, since academic knowledge tends to purify and simplify the realities it observes and reports upon. Against this trend, our three authors set out to decipher the founding social and political imaginaries, and the ways in which urban realities resist the will to capture and control them.

Simpson, in Chapter 10, analyzes a selection of contemporary maritime floating city projects developed around the world, and examines the motivations of their promoters. She links them to the history of scientific urban planning, but also to the history of the fixation of financial capital, and to the political considerations linked to the desire to escape traditional land and territorial controls. She shows us the ambiguity of these dreams of urban islands that are at once fixed and fluid, freely structured but constrained by technical and functional choices, often seemingly libertarian in inspiration but subject to powerful logics of financing and promotion, founded on the affirmation of their hyperlocality and yet highly dependent on globalized circulations, and in which, moreover, concrete urban life often disappears beneath the allegories of an idealized new existence.

Hříbek in Chapter 11, for his part, analyzes spaces whose recent appearance is the result not of any development plan, but of the evolution of the flow of the Bengal River. The very nature of Bengal's hydrographic regime has led to the emergence of new islands, known as *char,* whose status and destination immediately becomes a political and social issue. Hříbek takes a close look at the way in which public and private players seize the opportunity offered by *char* to plan new human settlements, including for Rohingyas fleeing from nearby Myanmar. This is a perfect example of the tensions between permanence and impermanence, between the desire to seize land through political power and development projects, however rudimentary, and the fluidity of changes and practices.

Finally, archaeologist Leadbetter in Chapter 12 draws on examples of cities from outside Europe, in Asia and Central America, to present a picture of urbanism that dissolves the normative, Eurocentric idea of the city as a walled-in space with permanent, immobile buildings and a stationary population. These cities are fluid in two senses. First, their boat-, raft-, or stilt-house-dwelling inhabitants are as much at home on the water as on land, a condition that Leadbetter calls "amphibious urbanism." Second, people continually come and go, sometimes over long distances, alternately aggregating and dispersing, creating far-flung webs of connections. Archaeological studies tell us, moreover, that these "floating cities" were not marginal places of precarity and impoverishment, as for so many on the edge of today's conurbations in the Global South, but major centers of political power and commerce, some of which have endured for thousands of years. As we contemplate a world of rising sea levels, when more and more humans are expected to be on the move, we have much to learn from these examples.

These three chapters have a genealogical dimension, which lies in searching through history for the traces of processes that enable us to better understand the contemporary state of cities. In so doing, the authors aim to provide a critical analysis of contemporary territorial policies and, in particular, of the excessive use of categorizations that fix and freeze urban realities and assign inhabitants to predetermined roles. In contrast to these habits, they underline the liberating potential, for thought and action, of taking into account a fluidity and liquidity so obvious and yet so often obscured by institutional imaginaries.

10

Ocean Urbanization and the Dissolution of the Polis

Isabelle Simpson

The challenges and opportunities brought about by accelerating urban growth and rising sea levels are transforming urban design, architecture, and engineering. This is evidenced by an increased interest in the urban amphibious as an adaptive solution to climate change (Grydehøj and Kelman 2016, 2017), matched by calls to acknowledge that "the future is fluid" and to develop a "wet urbanism" (Ashraf 2017) that can transcend the land–sea, dry–wet dichotomy and achieve what Steinberg (2011) describes as "liquid urbanity." Several proposals to build floating cities have been put forward by entrepreneurs, architects, and state actors who argue that these could provide alternative habitations to coastal populations threated by rising sea levels, bring in much needed income to address the effects of climate change, host climate refugees, and even help regenerate ocean health.

This chapter examines such proposals, which claim to offer solutions to the environmental and political urban challenges accompanying sea level rise. First, I argue that the current push toward ocean urbanization promotes the idea that the consequences of climate change can best be addressed through the acceleration of unregulated capitalist expansion. Floating cities provide a new kind of terraqueous territory that can be used to leverage the characteristics of both land and sea, offering a unique space where capital can accumulate while still preserving its mobility. Second, I argue that the imaginary of the floating city, although couched in the language of innovation and foresight, rejects the interventionist politics of modern cities, and modernism more generally, in favor of a romanticization of "traditional" and classical ways of life. The ocean, conceptualized as a blank slate, is marketed sometimes as a new frontier, reviving the imaginary of the western frontier as a place where individuals, mainly white men, can explore, exploit, and trade as they wish, and sometimes as an opportunity for Indigenous islanders to recover an idealized past, unspoiled by colonization. These two trends are expressed in architectural attempts, in floating cities, to achieve what Ildefons Cerdà i Sunyer conceptualized as "ruralized urbanization" (see Tocquer 2018, 247–50), in which the city is decentralized, a fluid continuum of uninterrupted connections, and exists in harmony with nature, with the important caveat that the universal fraternity, which Cerdà thought ruralized urbanization would both rely on and secure, is replaced by market relations and capitalist expansion.

Capital Flows

Contemporary floating cities are spaces of experimentation for the creation of new sociopolitical networks and finance mechanisms. They can also function as spaces of secession or, conversely, as an urban technology for entrepreneurial states to extend their sovereign territory and attract capital. In both cases, ocean urbanization expands the space in which private trade can be conducted away from the prying eyes of governmental agencies and media, and opens a new frontier for capitalist extraction of resources and labor. This provides common ground for interest groups with diverging and sometimes contradictory objectives, which nevertheless share a vision of climate change as an opportunity for making profit, or what Dawson (2017, 65) describes as "accumulation by adaptation."

Seasteading, a movement to colonize international waters with modular, floating platforms, started as a politically motivated secessionist project and has engaged with issues of climate change only in recent years, an opportunistic shift that "substantially improved" the movement's "branding" (Lutter and Lockhart 2020), but ultimately capitalizes on rising sea levels to advance broader political and economic objectives. Other proposals seek to advance economic or nationalist programs. The Maldives Floating City is a proposed touristic housing development that announces a "new era in which Maldivians return to the water with resilient ecofriendly floating projects" (Maldives Floating City 2021). Saudi Arabia's Oxagon is a planned 7-kilometer-wide port city in the Red Sea described as "a new paradigm where people, industries and technology come together in harmony with nature," offering "unparalleled connectivity to global markets" to include "the largest floating structure in the world," a cruise terminal, blue economy industries, an oceanographic research center, and an offshore community (Oxagon 2023). Advertised as exclusive, live-work-play consumerist communities, these projects are unconcerned with what Henri Lefebvre (1996) famously called "the right to the city," defined by David Harvey as the "collective power over the processes of urbanization" (2008, 23).

Toward a Terraqueous Capitalist Utopia

The Seasteading Institute is a not-for-profit, libertarian-leaning organization co-founded in 2008 by Patri Friedman, a former Google engineer and now an investor, grandson of the neoliberal economist Milton Friedman and son of the anarcho-capitalist theorist David D. Friedman. Seasteaders advocate leveraging the "dynamic geography" (Friedman 2002) of ocean space to "lower barriers to entry" to the "governance industry" by colonizing the high seas with modular, floating platforms (Friedman and Taylor 2011, 2012). Seasteaders would be free to relocate their floating homes to the community that best fits their values, thereby — at least in theory — encouraging competition and driving innovation.

In 2017, the Seasteading Institute announced the signing of a memorandum of understanding with the government of French Polynesia, an overseas collectivity of France, to build the first floating city in the archipelago's territorial waters (see Simpson 2022). The agreement was the result of efforts by Marc Collins Chen, an entrepreneur and former minister of tourism of French Polynesia, who had reached out to the Seasteading Institute in 2016. The Floating Island Project, as it was called, was to function as a prototype for new habitations for Polynesians whose ancestral homes and traditional ways of life are threatened by rising sea levels. It would also, supporters argued, attract capital to the archipelago, help retain talent, and strategically position French Polynesia at the forefront of sustainable development in the Pacific. French Polynesia, it was suggested, could even eventually export floating islands to other small island nation-states threatened by rising sea levels (seasteading 2017). The realization of the project relied on the creation of special economic zones and a new cryptocurrency, Varyon, a name that references "variation in governance," to raise money to finance the construction of the island (Blue Frontiers 2018). Varyon was to be the only currency used on the island, which would create a parallel economy within French Polynesia.

Despite the efforts of foreign and local supporters, including the Édouard Fritch government, the project was received negatively by islanders who feared both losing access to the lagoon where the artificial island would be located and damage to the natural environment. Many felt the creation of an exclusive economic zone in the lagoon would go against Polynesian communal values. The seasteading imaginary relies on the distinction between land as a space controlled by governments and the sea as blank canvas and a space of freedom. This conflicts with the Polynesian understanding of land and sea as a continuum, and with their history of living *with* the sea. Whereas the project boasted of integrating Polynesian culture and ways of life in its design and promised to reserve several units for French Polynesians, islanders argued that the island would be reserved as an exclusive resort for the wealthy. Finally, French Polynesia had been the site of many nuclear tests in the 1960s and 1970s, and many disagreed with the plan to use the archipelago as a laboratory once again.[1]

Seasteaders' ambitions to capitalize on impending climate catastrophe were thwarted when, in 2018, the project became a contentious topic in the French Polynesian territorial election and was put on ice. The signature of an agreement with a government nevertheless marked considerable progress for seasteaders, and it inspired a couple of staunch seasteading supporters and cryptocurrency enthusiasts, Chad Elwartowski and Nadia Supranee Thepdet, to launch their own venture, called Ocean Builders. The company is developing single-family seapods with the objective of creating communities of like-minded individuals. Images of the seapods illustrate the individualistic politics at the core of the concept; each pod is an island of its own, inhabited by individuals, couples, and family units. Both seasteads and seapods offer a calculated, strategic position — not part of the polis, but not so far removed as to impede access to the internet and grocery stores.

In early 2019, Ocean Builders erected a floating structure in the territorial waters of Thailand that stood for approximately three months and functioned as a stage for performative freedom until seized by the Thai military, whereupon Elwartowski and Thepdet, along with a German engineer, fled Thailand on a sailboat (Simpson 2021). The pair have since relocated to Panama where, along with their team, they are working on a planned seapod community, a new urban offshore space that would allow seasteaders to form their own alternative society and benefit Panama by bringing in revenue through commercial activity and tourism. The company faced a considerable setback when, in September 2022, a prototype worth USD $1.5 million

---

1   I was unable to find an official statement from the French government on
     the project.

tipped onto its side after "a ballast tank and pumping system malfunctioned, which caused flooding in the jacuzzi spar" (Romundt 2022).

Even though floating city projects have so far ended in political and technological failure, they remain ideologically compelling and are appealing to powerful nonstate actors, such as UN Habitat. After the defeat of the Floating Island Project, Chen disassociated himself from the seasteading movement and founded another floating city project, OCEANIX, mandating the famed and controversial architecture firm Bjarke Ingels Group to design it. In November 2021, OCEANIX signed a memorandum of understanding with the South Korean city of Busan to build "the world's first Sustainable Floating City" (UN Habitat 2022, 2). At UN Habitat's Second Roundtable on Sustainable Floating Cities, which called for "disruptive innovation on a massive scale" (1), and was attended by such public figures as Maye Musk, OCEANIX was presented as "the definitive blueprint for a sustainable marine metropolis" (2). A roundtable document describes floating cities not only as offering "a clean slate to design climate-neutral cities from the start [and] an innovative way to create new land for coastal cities facing severe housing shortages and looking for sustainable ways to expand onto the ocean," but also as "ideal for disaster relief and other humanitarian emergencies" (2).

The enthusiasm for such ventures from transnational, corporate, state, and nonstate actors is indicative of an inability or a refusal to examine critically the structures that led to the "need" for floating cities in the first place, and reveals the fatalistic approach underlying these endeavors, a collective failure of the imagination to rethink urban spaces and urban life in the Anthropocene. Images of futuristic ecomodernist floating cities, complete with outdoor cafés, green parks, and shopping malls, aim to convince us of their innovative character. Illustrations in vibrant colors are meant to persuade viewers that the future is bright, sustainable, safe, and, reassuringly, not very different from the present. Yet floating cities are not a new idea. They have been proposed as a potential solution to climate change and urban crowding since the 1960s, when the Japanese Me-

tabolists produced multiple mobile, modular, and plug-in floating city designs to address issues of resources and land scarcity,
overcrowding, and mobility (Huebner 2020). Their work continues to inspire today's ecomodernist philosophy, which advocates using technology to decouple human development from
environmental effects and allow continuous industrial growth.
Contemporary floating city proposals, now touted as "part of
the arsenal of climate adaptation strategies available to us" (UN
Habitat 2022), illustrate both the lasting appeal of ecomodern-
ism and the rediscovery of the ocean as a space of industrial
and capitalist expansion, in particular via the development of
the so-called blue economy and the new spatial relationalities it
generates (Choi 2017; Dornan et al. 2018; Steinberg 2001).

Floating cities extend urbanization at sea to achieve total urban liquefaction, "incorporat[ing] nature into the physical and
social structures of society" so as to facilitate the circulation and
accumulation of capital and position their promoters as leaders
in entrepreneurial urbanism and technocentric sustainability
(Steinberg 2011, 2120). The oceanic frontier offers aqua-pioneers
more individual freedom because its fluid nature would boost
"the two fundamental mechanisms of the new global Utopian
system: the right of migration and the abolition of taxes" (Jameson 2007, 219). Developers and inhabitants of floating cities
could take advantage of their liminal territoriality strategically,
to navigate, challenge, or simply avoid those regulations that
complicate or hinder the circulation of capital and capital owners. The choice between permanence and impermanence could
be made in a matter of minutes, giving floating cities owners
even more economic flexibility and resilience. In sum, proposals for floating cities amount to a total surrender to hegemonic
capitalism.

Ocean Urbanization and the Dissolution of the Polis

Framed as entrepreneurial endeavors in sustainable innovation,
floating cities concretize the simultaneous "maritimization of
land" (Adams 2018) — the historical conceptualization of urban

land as a liquid geography undivided by borders but connected by networks — and the urbanization of ocean space for the sake of profit accumulation. This new "liquid urbanity" (Steinberg 2011), rather than providing adaptive solutions to rising sea levels, dissolves the city as a space of democratic engagement and turns it into an amphibious vehicle for the accumulation and circulation of capital.

In 2004, the San Diego company SeaCode, unrelated to the seasteading movement, proposed the idea of housing software engineers on a cruise ship three miles off the California coast, in order to avoid the complexities of the immigration system. SeaCode, according to Steinberg (2011, 2119), depended "on utilizing new technologies to engineer a new integration of the sea into the space of the polis." However, "even as it redefines the polis as a porous entity that incorporates flows, liquid spaces, and border crossings, [SeaCode] does so within the existing structure of the state system." SeaCode, then, was to be "an extension of" rather than "an alternative to" the state system (2120). Ventures such as OCEANIX, the Maldives Floating City, and Oxagon all aim to extend the state system over ocean space. Although projects such as the Seasteading Institute and Ocean Builders present themselves as alternatives to existing state systems, they still rely on the latter for their success and therefore also extend the state system over ocean space in some way. But in doing so, floating cities projects also modify state and ocean politics, and the urban form.

Conclusion

Presented as an innovative solution to urban crowding, forced displacement, and the loss of both land and its history, floating cities materialize broader trends that seek to abolish the political, the "theater of deliberations, powers, actions, and values where common existence is thought, shaped, and governed" (Brown 2019, 56), and to replace the public sphere with privatized politics, institutions, and practices. There is no space for political engagement and for the right to the city in the projects examined here. Proposals to build floating cities instead reflect an accelerating trend toward postdemocratic urbanism, here driven by the belief that capitalist expansion at sea is, paradoxically, the answer to the root causes of inequality, environmental degradation, and rising sea levels. These proposals amount both to a desperate pursuit of a long-promised, technologically advanced, and exciting future, and to a wistful attempt to restore a past imagined as simpler, safer, and greener. Yet, in pretending to address climate change through the construction of liquid urban spaces in harmony with nature, proponents of floating cities in fact advance neoreactionary sociopolitical arrangements that privilege not only the flux of capital and individuals over economic and social stability but also the commitment to ephemeral authoritarian systems over long-term democratic projects. Enthusiasm for floating cities is yet another expression of a broader ambition to "turn freedom into a promise of individual freedom and sever the connection between freedom, participation, and solidarity" (Ludwig 2020, 165). Whether actually built or as sketches in glossy prospectuses, floating city projects bring to the surface the deep ideological currents transforming our cities.

References

Adams, Ross Exo. 2018. "Mare Magnum: Urbanisation of Land and Sea." In *Territory beyond Terra,* edited by Kimberley Peters, Philip E. Steinberg, and Elaine Stratford. Rowman and Littlefield.

Ashraf, Kazi Khaleed. 2017. "Wet Narratives: Architecture Must Recognise That the Future Is Fluid." *The Architectural Review,* May.

Blue Frontiers. 2018. "Varyon — Increasing Variation in Governance." *YouTube,* May 2. https://www.youtube.com/watch?v=LwCu4IuSmvc.

Brown, Wendy. 2019. *In the Ruins of Neoliberalism: The Rise of Antidemocratic Politics in the West.* Columbia University Press.

Choi, Young Raw. 2017. "The Blue Economy as Governmentality and the Making of New Spatial Rationalities." *Dialogues in Human Geography* 7, no. 1: 37–41. DOI: 10.1177/2043820617691649.

Dawson, Ashley. 2017. *Extreme Cities: The Peril and Promise of Urban Life in the Age of Climate Change.* Verso.

Dornan, Matthew, Wesley Morgan, Tess Newton Cain, and Sandra Tarte. 2018. "What's in a Term? 'Green Growth' and the 'Blue-Green Economy' in the Pacific Islands." *Asia and the Pacific Policy Studies* 5, no. 3: 408–25. DOI: 10.1002/app5.258.

Friedman, Patri. 2002. "Dynamic Geography: A Blueprint for Efficient Government." http://patrifriedman.com/old_writing/dynamic_geography.html.

Friedman, Patri, and Brad Taylor. 2011. "Barriers to Entry and Institutional Evolution." Paper presented at the Association of Private Enterprise Education Conference, Nassau, The Bahamas. https://www.academia.edu/27111620/Barriers_to_Entry_and_Institutional_Evolution.

———. 2012. "Seasteading: Competitive Governments on the Oceans." *Kyklos* 65, no. 2: 218–35.

Grydehøj, Adam, and Ilan Kelman. 2016. "Island Smart Eco-Cities: Innovation, Secessionary Enclaves, and the Selling of Sustainability." *Urban Island Studies* 2: 1–24. DOI: 10.20958/uis.2016.1.

———. 2017. "The Eco-Island Trap: Climate Change Mitigation and Conspicuous Sustainability." *Area* 49, no. 1: 106–13. DOI: 10.1111/area.12300.

Harvey, David. 2008. "The Right to the City." *New Left Review* 53: 23–40. https://newleftreview.org/issues/ii53/articles/david-harvey-the-right-to-the-city.

Huebner, Stefan. 2020. "Tackling Climate Change, Air Pollution, and Ecosystem Destruction: How US–Japanese Ocean Industrialization and the Metabolist's Movement Global Legacy Shaped Environmental Thought (circa 1950s–Present)." *Environmental History* 25, no. 1: 35–61. DOI: 10.1093/envhis/emz080.

Jameson, Fredric. 2007. *Archaeologies of the Future: The Desire Called Utopia and Other Science Fictions.* Verso.

Lefebvre, Henri. 1996. "The Right to the City." In *Writing on Cities,* edited by Eleonore Kofman and Elizabeth Lebas. Blackwell.

Ludwig, Gundula. 2020. "The Aporia of Promises of Liberal Democracy and the Rise of Authoritarian Politics." *Distinktion: Journal of Social Theory* 21, no. 2: 162–77. DOI: 10.1080/1600910X.2019.1669688.

Lutter, Mark, and Kurtis Lockhart. 2020. "A Look behind the Charter Cities Movement with Mark Lutter and Kurtis Lockchart." *Charter Cities* podcast, September 21. https://www.chartercitiesinstitute.org/post/episode-13-mark-lutter-kurtis-lockhart.

Maldives Floating City. 2021. https://maldivesfloatingcity.com/.

Oxagon. 2023. NEOM. https://www.neom.com/en-us/regions/oxagon.

Romundt, Grant. 2022. "Ups and Downs along the Road." *Ocean Builders,* September 27. https://oceanbuilders.com/blog/ups-and-downs-along-the-road/.

seasteading. 2017. "Randy Hencken: Who Are We & Why Are We Here?" *YouTube,* June 14. https://www.youtube.com/watch?v=OxoBwXphtMk.

Simpson, Isabelle. 2021. "Performing Freedom: An Examination of Ocean Builders' Successful Failure in Thailand." *Transformations: Journal of Media, Culture, and Technology* 35: 65–87. http://www.transformationsjournal.org/wp-content/uploads/2021/07/Trans35_05_Simpson.pdf.

———. 2022. "'A Brilliant Future of Floating Islands': Sea Level Rise as New Profit Frontier." In *Coastal Urbanities: Mobilities, Meanings, Manoeuvrings,* edited by Rapti Siriwardane-de Zoysa, Kelvin E.Y. Low, Noorman Abdullah, and Anna-Katharina Hornidge. Brill.

Steinberg, Philip E. 2001. *The Social Construction of the Ocean.* Cambridge University Press.

———. 2011. "Liquid Urbanity: Re-engineering the City in a Post-Terrestrial World." In *Engineering Earth: The Impact of Megaengineering Projects,* edited by Stanley D. Brunn. Springer Science + Business Media B.V.

Tocquer, Nicolas. 2018. "La Nature Urbaine Selon Ildefons Cerdá de 'l'idée Urbanisatrice' à 'l'urbanisation Ruralisée.'" PhD diss., Université de Bretagne occidentale.

UN Habitat. 2022. "The Second UN Roundtable on Sustainable Floating Cities: Meeting the Rising Seas with Floating Infrastructure." https://unhabitat.org/sites/default/files/2022/04/1_-_second_un_round_table_floating_cities.pdf.

11

Solidification and Liquefaction: Accounts from the Bengal Delta

Martin Hříbek

Scaling the Delta

The deltaic region of Bengal, the largest river delta in the world, literally sits on moving ground. The habitable area shrinks as seasonal monsoons flood the shores, islands rise and sink, rivers move their course, entire cities are submerged, and new territories are reclaimed. All this happens not on a geological time-scale but on an anthropological one, capable of being witnessed in a single lifetime. Impermanence is a characteristic feature of much of Bengal's landscape, and fluid soil — an in-between of earth and water — is its material basis. At the same time, however, moving substances — the silt, sand, and clay deposited over time — have provided a ready-made source of building materials, evidenced by centuries-old brick-built palaces, terracotta temples, and mosques. Viscous unbaked clay served as the primary material for the built environment in villages, but the fire-processed earth added a porous solidity to cityscapes.

In this chapter, starting from the twin processes of solidification and liquefaction, I will relate the impermanence of the deltaic landscape to that of the social worlds it accommodates. The entire landscape of the Bengal Delta is a hybrid network of plural, natural-cultural agencies. This plurality is far more complex than the readily discernible cultural and religious pluralism of the region. My primary concern will be with the land–water or solid–fluid continuum as it figures in the history of human habitation in the Bengal Delta. Since the effects of global warming loom large over this landscape, the network of agencies contributing to its remodeling, human or otherwise, should be acknowledged, explored, and reconceived (Ghosh 2017). For divinities, earthquakes, migrating rivers, and moving mangrove forests, along with the agency of liquid humanity, have all co-constituted the delta for centuries. This landscape does not, however, lend itself easily to scrutiny. Even to scale the delta requires a transgressive mode of thought, since the objectification of *geos* and parts thereof does not tally with the collectively subjective categories of *demos*. The demographic data are bounded by states, their administrative units and shifting borders, while deltas flow with the rivers.

Bangladesh — a state, and thus a demographic unit, located almost entirely in this flowing delta — is deemed by common consent to be poised on the frontline of global climate change.[1] It is a flat area, smaller in extent than that of England and Wales yet with a population exceeding 170 million, exposed to the seasonal floods of the Ganga-Brahmaputra-Meghna river system,[2] and to cyclones, storm surges, and the continually rising wa-

[1] This claim is made in so many sources that it has almost become a cliché. One example is Michelle Bachelet, the UN high commissioner for Human Rights, who, in a speech to the Bangladesh Institute of International and Strategic Studies in August 17, 2022, identified climate change as a "new frontier of human rights" (UN 2022).

[2] Of the country's total area of 148,460 km², land forms 130,170 km² and water 18,290 km² (CIA Factbook, 2023). During the rainy season, 19 to 66 percent of the total area is flooded, leading to problems of riverbank erosion, the silting of rivers, and the salinization of soil from brackish waters and surges. On the other hand, the dry season brings desertification of up to 25 percent of total area, increased arsenic contamination of ground water and problems with the navigability of waterways.

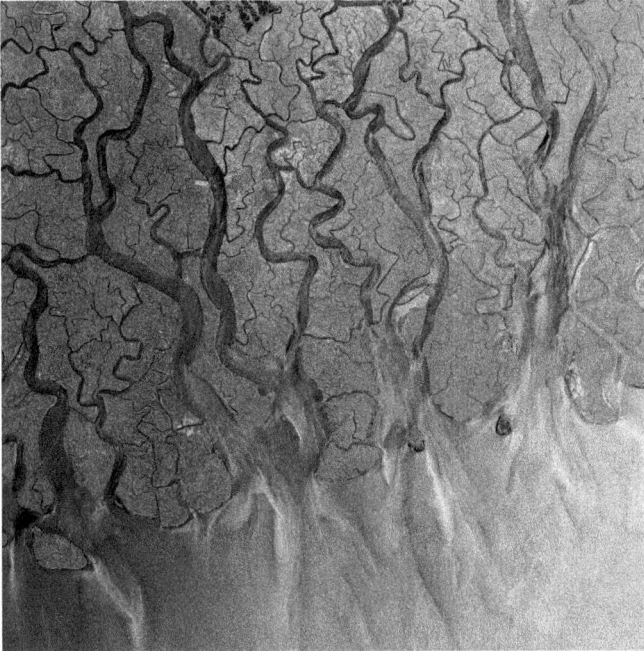

Fig. 11.1. Ganges's dazzling delta, European Space Agency, 2009. Contrary to conventional maps, which give an essentialized representation of land and water, this satellite picture of the Bengal Delta from the European Space Agency captures it rather vividly as a soaking environment. The Envisat Advanced Synthetic Aperture Radar image reflects that dynamism by combining surface backscatter taken in three acquisitions over the first quarter of 2009. The hues represent the variation in the surface across those three instances. Available at: https://www.esa.int/Applications/Observing_the_Earth/Earth_from_ Space_Ganges_dazzling_delta.

ter levels of the Bay of Bengal, the largest bay in the world. The country tops world lists of both population density and environmental pollution (AQLI 2023), it struggles with the spread of Islamic militancy (Riaz 2010; Hossain 2012; Mostofa 2021), generates substantial out-migration (MPI 2023), and, at the same time, copes with almost a million incoming refugees (UNHCR

2023). This concoction of some of the gravest issues facing humanity over the past decades makes it one of the most vulnerable places on Earth.

In the debate on fluid solids in geography, river deltas have already been identified as the "environments in which solid and fluid elements are [most] comprehensively imbricated" (Ingold and Simonetti 2022, 20). The Delta Project (Krause 2018, and Chapter 3 in this volume)[3] has already yielded significant insights, as have the lessons of "oceanic thinking" (Steinberg and Kimberley 2015). The Bengal Delta, however, stands out on several counts. Besides being the largest and the most populated delta in the world, it has always been an area of intense geopolitical contestation.

Historicizing the Flow

During the sixteenth and seventeenth centuries, under Mughal rule, the development of proto-capitalist manufacturing in textiles and shipbuilding, along with extensive networks of international trade, turned Bengal into one of the most economically advanced areas of the world (Ray 2011). The conquest of this rich area in the Battle of Plassey (1757) ultimately made the British the rulers of India, and the wealth of Bengal contributed greatly to Great Britain's industrial revolution.

The fluid landscape was part of this history. Until the sixteenth century, the Ganga River discharged most of its waters through the Bhagirathi–Hugli channel, along which contemporary Calcutta (renamed Kolkata in 2001) is located. Thereafter, its main channel moved eastward, creating the massive body of water Padma after the confluence of Ganga and Brahmaputra. This opened the east of the delta to colonization. Land reclamation in the eastern marshlands was spearheaded by Sufi saints who had been instrumental in the Islamification of Bengal since

---

3   DELTA — *Unstetiges Wasser und das hydrosoziale Anthropozän in großen Flussdeltas* (DELTA — Volatile waters and the hydrosocial Anthropocene in major river deltas); in German at https://delta.phil-fak.uni-koeln.de/.

the early Muslim conquest (Eaton 2011). They motivated colonists to go into dense jungles and turn them into inhabited cultivable land (*ābād*),[4] linked to each other and to trading areas in an extended network of riverways.[5] In fact, environmental changes wrought by moving waterways had been a major factor behind the success and failure of state building in the area, and sometimes caused capital cities to be relocated.

Thus Pandua, capital of the Sultanate of Bengal from 1342, lost its status after the course of the Mahananda River started to shift, and had declined by the end of the fifteenth century. The capital was removed to Gaur-Lakhnauti, the traditional cultural center of Bengal and a former capital city. Gaur, one of the largest urban agglomerations of its time, trading with Europe, the Middle East, Southeast Asia, and China, began to decline soon after, in the first half of the sixteenth century, as the Ganga River, on the eastern bank of which it was located, was silting up and changing course. The initial indications of this decline were invasions and plunder, but both accompanied the process of ecological degradation. When the capital was finally moved to nearby Tanda (literally, "high ground") by the Karrani dynasty in 1565, lack of maintenance of the drainage system soon caused regular flooding in the streets of Gaur, which led to its ultimate abandonment (Ray 2010, 11). The final impetus for abandonment was an epidemic of the plague in 1575 — the pestilential stagnant waters threatened human habitat as much as the fluid earth. Tanda remained the capital for only thirty years; in 1595 the seat of commerce and administration was again moved to

---

4   This Persian word, used as a suffix, remains part of many place names in South and Central Asia, and the verb *ābād karā* in Bengali means "to settle" (literally, to make *ābād*). Other Sufi sheiks helped in the military conquest of East Bengal by Muslim rulers, e.g., Sheik Shah Jalal (d. 1346), who gave the historic name to the town of Sylhet (*Jalalābād*) and to the current name of Dhaka's international airport.

5   Images of the colonization of the Bengal delta's East and of long-distance trade find expression in innumerable examples of medieval Bengali literature.

another nearby city, Rajmahal.[6] These medieval examples show how the solidification of land through its separation from water has always been related to the solidification of political power, and vice versa. Sometimes, however, the flow obliterated this attempted solidity completely, as when Ganga washed away the historical city of Tanda around 1834 (Ray 2010, 11).

At the same time, the flow facilitated trade, which, when unobstructed, made Bengal the richest province of the Mughal Empire. The delta has served as a trading and cultural hub throughout its recorded history, playing a key role, for example, in the spread of Buddhism during the Pala rule (eighth to twelfth century CE) to Southeast Asia and the Tibetan plateau. But it was the advances in seafaring and nautical technologies in Europe that intensified these linkages and made them truly global in scale, and also ultimately brought the delta under colonial control. This control began as the fluid trade brought about a gradual takeover of earthy patches of ground within the riverine network, from a floating ship to a trading outpost, to a solid fortress, and eventually to a claim of sovereignty.

In her groundbreaking historical account of the foundation of Calcutta, the second city of the British Empire, Debjani Bhattacharyya (2018, 5) tells the story of forgetting that "was central to the creation of property for the extraction of value from the marshes. Technologies of fixing (legal and engineering) orchestrated a collective amnesia about the mobility of this landscape." The solidification of what Bhattacharyya (after Mathur and da Cunha 2001) calls "soaking ecologies" turned this originally mobile landscape into pieces of real estate and pockets of wealth and power, leaving the surrounding suburban areas to speculative capital as potential fixed property, which, nevertheless, invited the risk of meltdown. It was in this shady zone that fortunes were made and lost. More distant still were the marshes, removed from the memory of the city. Bhattacharyya's account

---

6   The three cities were located at a short distance from each other near the bank of the Ganga River, approximately 350 kilometers north from the Bay of Bengal.

is original in the way it details the collusion of capitalism, legal procedures, and hydraulic engineering in transforming both the tidal landscape and the way it was understood. The seasonal stagnation of rivers in the original marshland area, for example, came to be regarded as urban waterlogging, while the wealth of wetness was reconceived as a deficiency in solidification that impeded the desired separation of land from water.

Emergent and Collapsing Solidities

Riverbank erosion extending to hundreds of meters, silting, and the shifting courses of rivers still pose an ecological, social, and legal challenge in contemporary Bangladesh and India. Majuli, for example, the largest riverine island in the world — located in the middle of the Brahmaputra in the Indian state of Assam and an important center of neo-Vaishnavite culture dating back to the sixteenth century — is gradually and progressively shrinking. It has been reduced by almost two-thirds over the last eighty years, and what remains, little more than 300 km^2, is set to disappear entirely in the next two decades (Ramachandran 2022).

Perceiving the gradual process of riverbank erosion through the lens of a fixed opposition between agricultural land and wetland also has important social consequences. The two demographically strongest communities of the composite ethnic structure on Majuli are the Assamese and the Mising people, originally a tribal community from the northeastern Indian hill state of Arunachalpradesh. The latter have been integrated into the neo-Vaishnavite milieu of Majuli, but they have still retained habits of meat-eating and rely on fishing, animal farming, and cottage industries such as reed processing, all of which depend on coastal wetlands. The vegetarian Assamese, by contrast, have occupied agricultural land farther from the riverbanks. The Mising community was thus disproportionately affected by riverbank erosion, yet they would have received less recompense from government agencies for the loss of their original habitat because it did not qualify for agricultural land loss compensation. Since their original land was not solid enough — both physically, because it eroded, and legally, as a wetland or marsh notionally opposed to more solid agricultural plots — Mising people often ended up becoming landless agricultural laborers in the Assamese areas of the island (Sahay 2022). This dispossession was triggered by forces of nature, such as the 8.7-magnitude earthquake of 1950. This earthquake set the massive flows on both sides of Majuli on a trajectory of migration, and eroded banks became firsthand victims of this geomorphological process. But ultimately, the dispossession of the Mising people was made possible and brought about by cultural and legal notions, rooted in the idea of solidity, of what possession really is.

But resilience in the face of collapsing solidities may also be effective. During the monsoon, when the island is prone to flooding, its residents in some areas resort to hydroponic farming to compensate for the loss of exploitable land. This practice, only introduced in 2017, is most effective in the areas that remain waterlogged for extended periods (Kumar and Parida 2021). Besides providing subsistence, hydroponic farming also helps to slow the depopulation of Majuli. Floating beds formed of rotting vegetation present yet another queer entity on the land–water continuum in the larger Bengal Delta. However, if we want to find the perfect opposite to a solid piece of real estate, the delta readily provides it: the impermanent, ever-changing alluvial silt islands called *char* that are created, transformed, and destroyed by the twin processes of accretion and erosion. These islands emerge out of the rivers, both inland and in the coastal areas of the delta. Although their lifespan and exploitability for settlement or agriculture are uncertain, some are nevertheless inhabited, while others are used as agricultural outposts.[7] Their emergence represents the plus side of riverbank erosion. In the coastal seas of the delta, however, this process is often related to cyclonic storms and surges.

---

7   Naveeda Khan has recently brought out her years of ethnographic research on the social worlds of *char* islands on the Jamuna River in Bangladesh as a monograph (Khan 2023).

In November 1970, cyclone Bhola struck the Bengal Delta. It was to become the deadliest cyclone in known history, with almost half a million victims. It effectively triggered the Bangladeshi war for independence from Pakistan, which was achieved a year and a month later, at the cost of many more lives than those lost to the cyclone.[8] As a side effect of the storm, a silt island was formed in the Bay of Bengal, directly to the south of the mouth of the Hariabhanga River, which separated India from the recently founded state of Bangladesh. This alluvial accretion went on to become the subject of a territorial dispute, one of many, between the two otherwise friendly nations, with India naming it "New Moore Island" and Bangladesh "South Talpatti." The island itself was uninhabitable, being unsuited for cultivation or any other practical use. Nor did it have any symbolic value. Its importance rather lay in the legal, territorial, and geopolitical potentials tied up in its emergence. These had nothing to do with any claim to ownership of the semisolid land. It was rather all about the flows around it.

With the emergence of the island, the main channel (*thalweg*) of the Hariabhanga, marking the India-Bangladesh border, was diverted to both its eastern and its western flanks. Though the actual course of the main channel was never scientifically determined, both states advanced contradictory claims, pushing the border to one side or the other. Depending on which of the two sides the channel was deemed to run, a straight line drawn from the mouth of the river toward the island, were it extended into the waters of the Bay, would support a much more significant claim under the international law of the seas and, more importantly, would grant a larger exclusive economic zone in the bay. Fishing was a consideration, but the possible existence of reserves of natural gas underneath the ocean bed was a still greater one. Fortunately, the issue was resolved peacefully, as the

---

8   Estimates of the number of victims of the Bangladeshi liberation war differ significantly, from 500,000 to 3 million.

island dissolved into the surrounding waters in 2010, effectively nullifying all claims and counterclaims.[9]

But other *char* islands in the delta have been subject to intensive efforts to solidify the land. For example, Bhasan *char* (literally, "floating island"), which emerged as late as 2006 off the eastern coast of Bangladesh, was still unpopulated and deemed unsuitable for habitation or agriculture a decade later. But in the face of the Rohingya refugee crisis, the government of Bangladesh decided to solidify the *char* with the help of British engineers and a Chinese construction company, so that no less than 100,000 refugees might be relocated there from the squalor of camps around Cox's Bazar in southeast Bangladesh, near the border with Myanmar. Standardized housing, allowing four-by-four meters per family with shared kitchen and sanitary facilities, was built on concrete pillars to protect from the surging sea, complete with schools, health centers, and cyclone shelters — a perfectly dystopian built environment (Islam and Siddika 2022).

After the initial shock and reluctance, when thousands of Rohingyas were physically relocated to the island, the UNHCR agreed to deliver help and monitor their conditions.[10] But the flip side of the resettlement is that the refugees, once settled there, cannot legally leave the island. In a curious twist of irony, the irregular flow of refugees, which effectively forces the liquefaction of state borders, both notionally and practically, has ultimately been contained and encapsuled within an unsolid territory that was unrecognizable on satellite images from not so long ago.

---

9   For a more detailed history of New Moore–South Talpatti, see Tanaka (2011) and Hasan and Jian (2019). Its geopolitical significance aside, the life of this island was not unique in the deltaic sea. In 1996, the populated island of Lohachara, off the coast of West Bengal, India, disappeared, and its inhabitants had to be resettled. The nearby inhabited island of Ghoramara is currently liquefying. Now reduced to less than 10 percent of its original population, it is destined to suffer the same fate as Lohachara.

10 In October 2021, the government of Bangladesh and the UNHCR signed a Memorandum of Understanding to this effect (UN Bangladesh 2021).

A Singleplace of Liquid Humanity

Just as hydraulic engineering works to separate the viscous silt from the flow to produce land from amidst the seas, so does the state management of the erratic flow of humanity strive to solidify national and territorial borders through an infrastructure of separation. The ontological in-betweenness of a temporary silt deposit and of the refugee status fuses here in a singleplace. Bhasan *char* enacts such a singleplace on a dramatic scale. Further up the delta, the Indo-Bangladesh border — with its solid iron fence, particularly on the Indian side to stem the flow of Bangladeshi migrants — has been continually eroded both by the border rivers that shift their course, meandering to leave patches of one state's territory on the other's bank, and by the people who cross these rivers in a liquid way (Lahiri-Dutt and Gopa 2004; Sur 2021). Beyond the Bengal Delta, such singleplaces of in-betweenness are abundant. Installations designed and built to be temporary are primarily intended to insulate the solidity of nation-states from erosive flows of liquid humanity.

Nowadays, the Bengal Delta may not be the economic powerhouse it used to be before the European conquest, nor is it any longer the nexus of capital and power it was under the British Raj. Nevertheless, it is perhaps the world's most contested and most geopolitically significant deltaic region — it connects two large and nuclear-armed Asian neighbors that are increasingly at odds with each other. The densely populated lowland of Bangladesh stands in the middle of their competition. Chinese plans to dam the upper Brahmaputra valley, which would literally impose control through solidification, and any disruption in the riverine system this may cause, would directly affect over a quarter of a billion inhabitants downstream (Donnellon-May 2022). Thus, although relatively unnoticed, the delta remains as much a potential flashpoint in global geopolitical competition as do the reefs solidified as military bases in the South China Sea.

Solidification, at any given point of historical time, is an attempt to achieve temporal fixity and to stabilize a particular projection of power. Every such attempt may display more or less empathy for the wet processes in the ground and, at the same time, may stretch either realistically shorter or imperially longer wings in its bid to take an adventurous flight into eternity. Ultimately, however, the eccentric pull of liquefaction overwhelms the concentric forces of solidification. The push in the latter direction has always been a special instance of an environmental intervention that, from an anthropocentric perspective, manifests as the creation of the built environment. With its largesse, its highly condensed population, and its landscape in motion, the Bengal Delta is not just yet another place on Earth where the effects of climate change can be retrospectively documented and proven. On the contrary, the delta's agential viscosity, capable of establishing a sudden temporal equivalence between geological and anthropological timescales at random intervals, signals to posterity how uncertain is the ground that we, liquid humanity, inhabit.

References

AQLI (Air Quality Life Index). 2023. "Bangladesh." https://aqli. epic.uchicago.edu/country-spotlight/bangladesh/.

Bandyopadhyay, Ritajyoti. 2022. *Streets in Motion: The Making of Infrastructure Property and Political Culture in Twentieth-Century Calcutta.* Cambridge University Press.

Bhattacharyya, Debjani. 2019. *Empire and Ecology in the Bengal Delta: The Making of Calcutta.* Cambridge University Press.

Chatterjee, Ratnabali. 1992. "The Perception of the City in Medieval Bengali Literature." *Proceedings of the Indian History Congress* 53: 187–93. https://www.jstor.org/ stable/44142783.

CIA Factbook. 2023. "Bangladesh." https://www.cia.gov/the-world-factbook/countries/bangladesh/.

Cohen, Jeffrey Jerome, and Lowell Duckert. 2015. *Elemental Ecocriticism: Thinking with Earth, Air, Water, and Fire.* University of Minnesota Press.

Donnellon-May, Genevieve. 2022. "China's Super Hydropower Dam and Fears of Sino-Indian Water Wars." *The Diplomat,* December 9. https://thediplomat.com/2022/12/chinas-super-hydropower-dam-and-fears-of-sino-indian-water-wars/.

Eaton, Richard Maxwell. 2011. *The Rise of Islam and the Bengal Frontier, 1204–1760.* 7th ed. Oxford University Press.

Ghosh, Amitav. 2017. *The Great Derangement: Climate Change and the Unthinkable.* University of Chicago Press.

Hasan, Md. Monjur, and He Jian. 2019. "Protracted Maritime Boundary Dispute Resolutions in the Bay of Bengal: Issues and Impacts." *Thalassas: Revista de ciencias del mar* 35, no. 1: 323–40. DOI: 10.1007/s41208-019-0126-1.

Hossain, Akhand Akhtar. 2012. "Islamic Resurgence in Bangladesh's Culture and Politics." *Journal of Islamic Studies* 23, no. 2: 165–98. DOI: 10.1093/jis/ets042.

Ingold, Tim, and Cristián Simonetti. 2021. "Introducing Solid Fluids." *Theory, Culture & Society* 39, no. 2: 3–29. DOI: 10.1177/02632764211030990.

Islam, Md. Didarul, and Ayesha Siddika. 2022. "Implications of the Rohingya Relocation from Cox's Bazar to Bhasan Char, Bangladesh." *The International Migration Review* 56, no. 4: 1195–205. DOI: 10.1177/01979183211064829.

Khan, Naveeda. 2023. *River Life and the Upspring of Nature.* Duke University Press.

Krause, Franz. 2018. *Delta Methods: Reflections on Researching Hydrosocial Lifeworlds.* Universitäts-und Stadtbibliothek Köln.

Kumar, Sandeep, and Bikash Ranjan Parida. 2021. "Hydroponic Farming Hotspot Analysis Using the Getis–Ord Gi* Statistic and High-resolution Satellite Data of Majuli Island, India." *Remote Sensing Letters* 12, no. 4: 408–18. DOI: 10.1080/2150704X.2021.1895446.

Lahiri-Dutt, Kuntala, and Gopa Samanta. 2004. "Fleeting Land, Fleeting People: Bangladeshi Women in a Charland Environment in Lower Bengal, India." *Asian and Pacific Migration Journal* 13, no. 4: 475–95. DOI: 10.1177/011719680401300404.

Mathur, Anuradha, and Dilip da Cunha. 2001. *Mississippi Floods: Designing a Shifting Landscape.* Yale University Press.

Mostofa, Shafi Md. 2021. *Islamist Militancy in Bangladesh: A Pyramid Root Cause Model.* Palgrave Macmillan.

MPI (Migration Policy Institute). 2023. "Bangladesh." https://www.migrationpolicy.org/country-resource/bangladesh.

Ramachandran, Nira 2022. "Climate Change and Disappearing Habitats: The Case of Majuli Island in Northeast India." In *The Food Security, Biodiversity, and Climate Nexus,* edited by Mohamed Behnassi, Himangana Gupta, Mirza Barjees Baig, and Ijaz Rasool Noorka. Springer.

Ranjan, Amit. 2018. *India-Bangladesh Border Disputes History and Post-LBA Dynamics.* Springer Singapore.

Ray, Aniruddha. 2010. "General President's Address: An Approach to the Study of Morphology of Selected Towns and Cities of Medieval Bengal, c. 1500 to c. 1727." *Proceedings of the Indian History Congress* 71: 1–27. https://www.jstor.org/stable/44147470.

Ray, Indrajit. 2011. *Bengal Industries and the British Industrial Revolution (1757–1857).* Routledge.

Riaz, Ali. 2010. *Islamist Militancy in Bangladesh: A Complex Web.* Routledge.

Sahay, Avijit. 2022. "Riverbank Erosion and Inter-Community Relationships in Majuli: Political Implications of a Changing Landscape in Assam." In *Regional Political Ecologies and Environmental Conflicts in India,* edited by Sarmistha Pattanaik and Amrita Sen. Routledge.

Steinberg, Philip, and Kimberley Peters. 2015. "Wet Ontologies, Fluid Spaces: Giving Depth to Volume through Oceanic Thinking." *Environment and Planning D: Society & Space* 33, no. 2: 247–64. DOI: 10.1068/d14148p.

Sur, Malini. 2021. *Jungle Passports: Fences, Mobility, and Citizenship at the Northeast India-Bangladesh Border.* University of Pennsylvania Press.

Tanaka, Kisei 2011. "The Indo-Bangladesh Maritime Dispute: Conflicts over a Disappeared Island." In *ICE Case Studies,* no. 270, December. http://mandalaprojects.com/ice/ice-cases/talpatti.htm.

UN Bangladesh. 2021. *UN and Government of Bangladesh Sign Memorandum of Understanding for Rohingya Humanitarian Response on Bhasan Char.* October 9. https://bangladesh.un.org/en/150722-un-and-government-bangladesh-sign-memorandum-understanding-rohingya-humanitarian-response.

UNHCR. 2023. "Bangladesh Operational Update December 2022." https://data.unhcr.org/en/documents/details/98261.

UN Office of the High Commissioner for Human Rights. 2022. "New Frontiers of Human Rights." A speech by the UN High Commissioner for Human Rights Michelle Bachelet at the Bangladesh Institute of International and Strategic Studies, August 17. https://www.ohchr.org/en/statements/2022/08/bangladesh-institute-international-and-strategic-studies-climate-change-new.

12

The Shape of Fluid Cities: An Archaeologist's Guide to Amphibious Living

Michael Paul Leadbetter

Introduction

Most humans live in cities. Urbanism is transforming our planet. Understanding urbanism, its processes and long-term effect, is therefore critical to both our present and our future. Archaeology allows us not only to see cities in a landscape, but also to understand how they transform over the vastness of time. Yet despite more than a century of urban research, scholars — especially in archaeology — have still to come up with a coherent definition of what cities are. Archaeologists have often regarded cities as stable and uniform, but they are in fact unstable, fluid, and highly diverse. Not only are modern industrial cities like this, but all urbanism is creative and transformational.[1] Since every city is different, developing through a unique combina-

---

1   Charles Baudelaire (2008) said of nineteenth-century industrial Paris, "Old Paris is no more (the form of a city changes faster, alas! than a mortal heart)." My thanks to Michel Lussault for this reference.

Fig. 12.1. Flying city in the style of 1970s retrofuturism, by Ruby-Anne Birin, using generative machine learning, 2023.

tion of processes, urbanism takes manifold forms. To understand what urbanism really is requires us to be expansive and inclusive, to accommodate and, we hope, to celebrate this diversity, and to ask new questions. Whenever people, materials, and species come together in a landscape, all are irrevocably transformed. For me, urbanism is exactly this, but happening at such a scale, density, and intensity that it can stir up the world in ways that other phenomena cannot. Drawing upon both theory and empirical data, I will explore the fluidity of urbanism through time, with reference to both its local and global contexts. In so doing, I seek to challenge the ways we conceptualize cities in archaeology and more widely across the humanities and social sciences.

Cities of the future are often imagined in fantastical ways — flying across the sky, floating upon the seas, and even soaring through outer space (fig. 12.1). These images stand in stark contrast to the contemporary norm of the "stodgy city," cast in concrete and steel, heavy, inert, and fixed. Yet in truth, cities are already in motion, transforming themselves and the entire planet at an accelerating rate. World archaeology is essential to understanding the diversity of ways in which we live together creatively in large groups, and to showing how, through time, cities connect and transform the world. Fluid cities, and what I call "amphibious urbanism," provide a way to explore urbanism as a generative force of, and with, nature. An archaeology of amphibious urbanism is particularly helpful for understanding its fluidity. At the creative confluence where land and sea merge, such urbanism has been present from earliest times, and continues today in many different forms. Long-term perspectives allow us to see the range of different forms fluid cities can take. In this chapter, I bring together recently published archaeological material, especially from the floating and wetland cities of tropical Southeast Asia and the amphibious Aztec capital in Mexico, in order to better understand what cities are, namely, endlessly fascinating, wonderfully diverse, extraordinarily fluid, and mightily transformational.

When I began my research on urbanism in Southeast Asia, I understood the region's cities as like anywhere else in the world. Archaeologists often visualize cities as compact and dense, with palatial monuments of stone or brick surrounded by houses and temples and ringed by a fortification wall. Some Southeast Asian cities, such as Melaka and Mandalay, were indeed like this, but many were not (Leadbetter 2018). The more archaeological data I gathered and analyzed, the more diversity, fluidity, and mobility I found. My research revealed a colorful mosaic of cities across the region, including sprawling swidden-agricultural cities in Thailand, and cities formed by boats that congregate in vast but temporary aggregations in the wetlands and waterways of the Philippines, Cambodia, Indonesia, and southern China. There is even evidence of public architecture and monumental landscape engineering atop volcanic landscapes (Leadbetter 2021; Leadbetter and Sastrawan 2023; Leadbetter and Phanomvan, forthcoming). This evidence caused me to doubt the conventional category of "cities," and to seek a better understanding of the Southeast Asian experience by way of the concept of *fluidity*.

I have developed the idea of "fluid cities" in two senses. The first specifically relates to amphibious urbanism, and refers to large floating settlements. The second is broader, embracing the ways in which all cities both bring about change and are constituted by it. Fluidity is not of course limited to cities; all life in this world is on the move. But it invites us to understand the dynamism of cities in terms of a philosophy of process (Leadbetter 2021), according to which reality is constituted in movement, becoming, and transformation (Whitehead 1985; Bogaard et al. 2021). The roots of this philosophy lie in mathematics, physics, and the natural sciences, in which it is assumed that things are transforming all the time (Clark et al. 2022). Quarks combine into hadrons, forming the building blocks of atoms. Electrons shift around atoms, in relation with other atoms. Fiery nuclear reactions in the sun, arising from these atomic interactions, light and heat our planet, transforming our Earth. The Earth spins, wobbles, and orbits the aging sun. Water covering much of the surface of our planet flows, moving around the Earth, becoming clouds, driving weather systems. Even the Earth's seemingly solid crust is moving, with violent convections of magma enabling life to emerge in the deepest darkest oceans, and occasional volcanic eruptions transform local landscapes and global weather. Worms turn and transform the soil, creating new opportunities for plants and fungi. You are transforming too — by the time you finish this chapter, your body will have destroyed around a quarter of a million cells and created as many new ones. Within your body a hundred trillion micro-organisms are living, dying, and collaborating, tangling with and sticking to each other.

Cities, likewise, are concrescences, expanding, moving, changing, shifting. Your city or town will be different next week, more so in a decade, and even more so in a century. Treating urbanism as a process, and cities as fluid, offers an alternative understanding of how it is changing our planet and all its inhabitants in the long run. In what follows, I turn to amphibious urbanism, a form of the fluid city that helps us understand the ways people live together with each other and with the water. Southeast Asia is the ideal region in which to study it.

Butuan and Southeast Asia: An Archaeological Guide to
Amphibious Living

The millennium between 600 and 1600 CE was a period of great
variety and experimentation in Southeast Asia. The amphibious
pattern of urban settlement common in the region, typified by
movement and water (Leadbetter 2021), entailed a close creative correspondence between people, wetlands, and organic and
buoyant building materials. Common forms of building include
raft-dwellings, boats, and stilt-houses. These buildings, with
their inhabitants, would congregate, agglomerate, and disaggre-
gate, either permanently or cyclically, whether daily in relation
to tides or seasonally in relation to rains and floods. Amphibious urbanism could be found on its own or in a symbiotic relationship with more exclusively terrestrial urban forms.

At the wetland archaeological site of Butuan, on the northern coast of Mindanao, Philippines, lie the remains of a large
amphibious agglomeration. The site was accidentally discovered
in 1974 and looted by gangs before being excavated archaeologically. Finds from the site include domestic refuse, ceramics, and
iconography showing connections with other parts of Asia,
large quantities of gold, and more than a hundred crucibles for
its production (Burton 1977; Capistrano-Baker, Guy, and Miksic
2011; Estrella 2016). According to historical records, the people
of Butuan traded as far afield as China, while reports of coffee
indicate connections with Africa, Arabia, and across the Indian
Ocean (Capistrano-Baker, Guy, and Miksic 2011, 194). Contra-
dicting our conventional picture of cities, Butuan contained no
walls, irrigation works, temples, palaces, or other monumental architecture. Writing was unknown. However, it did contain watercraft, including boats, which likely served as floating
homes. The many wooden boats discovered so far represent but
a fraction of the watercraft that once plied the local waterways.
Radiocarbon dating places them to between the fourth and thir-
teenth centuries CE, while the recent calibrated dating of smaller
samples places them more precisely to between the eighth and
tenth centuries (Lacsina 2014; Lacsina and Van Duivenvoorde

2014). Ceramics found at the site match chronologically with those from across Asia.

Being an amphibious settlement with boats in a fluid landscape, the rhythm and tempo of movement—including tides, floods, and undertows—were intrinsic to Butuan's operation and existence. Here, each household with its raft or boat would constantly come and go, representing but one moving part of a larger agglomeration. This may account for the presence of materials that can only have been exchanged over long distances. Architecturally, amphibious urbanism is associated with the adaptation and reuse of materials for diverse purposes. The fact that modern communities living amphibiously are often economically and politically marginalized might lead us to regard this reuse or recycling of materials as an index of precarity. Sites such as Butuan, however, show that amphibious urban behaviors have endured with great longevity. Indeed, there are parallels between Butuan and such Southeast Asian cities as Palembang, Indonesia, where amphibious living has persisted for nearly two thousand years. The ability of people and things to flow easily in and out made possible temporary gatherings far in excess of what the surroundings could normally accommodate and supply. Similar temporary gatherings may indeed have formed inland, on the steppes, whose populations would likewise have periodically assembled and dispersed.

With mobility and fluidity at its core, amphibious urbanism has advantages that more permanent settlements lack. In a crisis, watercraft can relocate up and down river, to other islands and deltas and bays, regrouping once the danger has passed, whether it be warfare, floods, or changes in the availability of natural resources. One example comes from a Dutch eyewitness, Olivier van Noort, who in 1600 described an agglomeration in coastal Borneo "made of wood, and built on such light piles that when there is a storm or some other untoward event these houses can be removed from one side of the river to the other" (Nicholl 1975, 96). But, as happened with Palembang, amphibious urbanism can also metamorphose, leaving the water to spread inland.

Indeed, it is always moving and changing, never the same from one moment to the next.

Amphibious agglomerations, large and small, are found around the globe: woven Marsh-Arab settlements; Hong Kong's floating fishing communities; the historic floating and water-village communities of Singapore; water-villages of tens of thousands of people in Brunei Bay; Tenōchtitlan and Mexico City;[2] Jacob's Island in Victorian London; and present-day Makoko in Lagos, Nigeria, with its population of more than 200,000. Venice is the most famous amphibious agglomeration in European history. Amphibious urbanism can also be found far inland: on the edge of Angkor and Tonle Sap Lake south of Siem Reap in Cambodia; in high-altitude Inle Lake, Myanmar; even 3,000 kilometers inland along the Amazon River at Barrio-de-Belén, Peru. North America's first Asian settlement, St. Malo (dating from the mid-eighteenth century) in wetland Louisiana, was an amphibious town built by enslaved Filipino people escaped from Spanish ships (Hearn 1883; Kenny 1994; Salgarolo 2020). During the two centuries from 1765 to 1965, this settlement moved at least four times. Amphibious settlements are found across Europe dating from the Bronze and Iron Ages: Glastonbury Lake-Village; Wasserburg Village; the Zurich lake settlements (Clarke 1973; Heitz et al. 2021). These are all good candidates for helping us break with Eurocentric convention, and to see cities as fluid.

Mexico City: Floating Rainforests and Underwater Basket Weaving

Across the Pacific from Southeast Asia is Mexico City, or what used to be the Aztec capital Tenōchtitlan. Like Butuan, Tenōchtitlan was also colonized by the Spanish. Founded in 1325, it was located across natural and human-made islands in Lake Texcoco, in a valley atop the volcanic Central Mexican Plateau 2,000 meters above sea level. Tenōchtitlan had grand avenues

---

2   In the spelling of "Tenōchtitlan," I follow the language conventions of the Indigenous Nahuatl group.

that crossed the islands and the lake. Its population is debated, but most agree on a figure of around 200,000 (Carrasco and Sessions 1998, 66; Smith 2012, 190), larger than most European cities and among the most extensive cities in the world in the fifteenth century (Smith 2012, 190, 193). Excavations have focused on monumental centers and human sacrifice (Moctezuma 1999; López 2006), but Tenōchtitlan's growth involved an entire ecosystem of corresponding participants.

Tenōchtitlan was a fluid city with stone monuments, indicating the potential size and scale that amphibious urbanism can reach. It had a core of planned monumental ritual buildings, including pyramids, ceremonial precincts, and stone dwellings on a central island (Leadbetter 2021). In 1568, conquistador and eye-witness Bernal Díaz wrote: "When we saw all those cities and villages built in the water...and that straight and level causeway leading to Mexico [Tenōchtitlan] we were astounded. These great towns and cues [pyramids] and buildings rising from the water, all made of stone, seemed like an enchanted vision.... Some of our soldiers asked whether it was not all a dream" (Díaz 1975, 214). Díaz described Aztecs as using floating bridges, causeways, and canoes when resisting conquistador violence. Most of Tenōchtitlan's surface area consisted of floating areas, constructed islands called *chinampas* (Calnek 1972, 108). These appear in Aztec images, were described by conquistadors, and are found in much of Mexico today, especially on the outskirts of modern Mexico City (Calnek 1972). Several archaeological examples have been identified (Berdan 2005, 27; López 2006, 321; Berdan 2014, 80).

Chinampas are based on a traditional agricultural process found across much of Mesoamerica, and offer a microcosm for fluid cities. They were "grown" by humans over time, by weaving together plants, soil, and water (Leadbetter 2021). Each *chinampa* becomes a home, a tiny floating food forest. Creating *chinampas* involves weaving ship-size wooden baskets, 10 to 25 feet wide, 50 to 300 feet long, out of springy willow saplings, which are abundant in wetlands (Carrasco and Sessions 1998, 69). These are filled with about three feet of soil, floated across water, and moored in the lakebed with posts. They are then planted with a complex array of useful plant and tree crops. Over time the soil is replenished, tree roots grow through the bottom of the basket and knit into the lakebed. Meanwhile, floating *chinampas* merge with the lake bed as plants take up the water and their organic matter accumulates.

In ecology, "edge-ecosystems" like this, in which different ecosystems blur, are regarded as particularly productive and biodiverse as they weave together soil-bank and water (Levin et al. 2009, 780). Creating edge-ecosystems means embracing and steering diversity from the small scale up. River deltas are an extreme example, but the *chinampas* process relies on humans and plants working together to create new, delta-like environments. This process constituted most of Tenōchtitlan. Like cities, *chinampas* are never finished, never completed; they are always in a state of transformation and becoming.

Tenōchtitlan's urban fabric was organically woven, grown, planted, harvested, pruned, consumed. This involved relations between humans, plants, animals (including insects), fungi, and microbes, all in perpetual movement. No two *chinampas* are identical; each has different plants, setting up relations that unfold in diverse ways. *Chinampas,* and the city that emerges from their large-scale use, are themselves diverse microcosms, floating and fluid rainforests. But they also construct a way of being involving the creative transformation of land, water, people, and plants. As the fabric of Tenōchtitlan, they offered a creative form of multispecies collaboration. In short, the Aztec capital was not simply built; Tenōchtitlan was *grown.* The nature–culture divide makes little sense in places like this, where urbanism is a force of, and with, nature.

Chinampas have now been pushed to Mexico City's geographic and social margins, yet they still flourish there. Colonizers tried to drain Lake Texcoco, filling the canals with stone from smashed Aztec monuments, so as to make Tenōchtitlan more static and stable. Mexico City suffers from numerous problems as a result: during the dry months from water shortages; during the wet months, from the attempts of Lake Texcoco to return, which often lead to catastrophic floods. Because Mexico City was built on a lake bed, this heavy megacity of 22 million inhabitants is sinking rapidly into the soft soil (Chaussard et al. 2021), in some areas at a rate of 30 centimeters per year, or 3 meters per decade. The lake bed beneath the city is so waterlogged that during earthquakes solid soil liquefies (Samui, Dixon, and Tien Bui 2020, 153–63). This caused thousands of deaths during the 1985 Mexico City earthquake. Tragically, as a result of colonial and modern attempts to impose permanence, Mexico City is on the move.

Conclusion: Moving, Brimming, and Bubbling with Creativity

Cities transform the world. For example, buildings now outweigh plants (Elhacham et al. 2020), and enough concrete has been cast since World War II to cover the whole surface of the Earth (Farrier 2021). These transformations require huge amounts of energy. For instance, 96 percent of Earth's total mammal biomass now constitutes food for humans, mostly feeding urban areas (Bar-On, Phillips, and Milo 2018). The stakes have never been higher for cities, which are growing to unprecedented sizes, while also facing and creating unparalleled threats to both themselves and life on earth (Clark et al. 2022).

Urbanism must be understood over the long term, and archaeology is uniquely equipped to provide insights into transformations of material culture in deep time. However, though archaeology has an established record of describing linear change, approaches to the exploration of process, fluidity, and transformation are still in their infancy (Flad 2018; Bogaard et al. 2021; Leadbetter 2021; Kim and McAnany 2023). These approaches matter, because archaeology does more than merely provide the contextual backdrop for creative processes; it can help us think through how humans, along with beings and things of other kinds, participate, connect, and negotiate with one another in creative assemblages (Masterson 2022; Chen 2023; Pearson 2023). Fluid cities are ecologically embedded, rather than environmentally determined. They are large-scale processes, connecting and reshaping the world as they grow and as their relationships diversify and complexify. They generate things at a scale that other kinds of human settlement do not (Leadbetter 2021). As they draw in more of the world's inhabitants, they also increase in size, animating relationships of collaboration, creation, destruction, and transformation. This fluidity is nowhere more noticeable than in cases of amphibious urbanism.

Cities are composed of a great many small and diverse things in generative assemblages, coming together in new ways, moving toward a point of greater complexity and elaboration. They operate as assemblages of existing technologies (Arthur 2009). They encompass houses, people, animals, plants, infrastructure, and materials. Archaeologically, we see these joining up and transforming landscapes through time. Many other things are also generative, of course; what is special about cities is the scale of transformations and the changes generated. As transformational hubs, cities connect everything up. They become machines full of small assemblages; they grow by incorporating, connecting, and collaborating with more assemblages, including people, material, species, and landscapes, becoming hungrier for connections with yet more assemblages (Deleuze and Guattari 2018, 24). At a certain scale, transformations begin to generate new phenomena of their own, resulting in a cascade of transformative creativity, an "autocatalytic loop" (De Landa 1997, 62, 94). Transformations bring new problems, in turn requiring more technologies and generative assemblages to solve. These transformations are nondeterministic; they do not follow a set ladder of urban progress. Cities are as diverse as their own varied assemblages. Nevertheless, agglomerations are subject to constraints, which limit and shape their forms. Constraints emerge from generative processes themselves, such that assemblages become self-shaping (Fletcher et al. 2008; Gosden and Malafouris 2015). This helps us understand the fluid and transformational power and scale of urbanism.

Fig. 12.2. NASA's Mobile City of the Future "The Stanford Torus," Rick Guidice, NASA 1975 ID Number AC75-1086-1.

The cities of the future are often imagined as mobile, in fabulous and fantastical ways. NASA artist Robert McCall created inspiring visualizations of our techno-scientific future: idealized images of flying cities, water cities, orbital cities, cities in which to cross the stars. These would explore, rearrange, and transform the universe, moving, brimming, and bubbling with creativity. Such cities represent an explicit and deliberate break with the present and the past. However, when we turn to the archaeological evidence, we find that mobile, fluid, creative, transformational cities, futuristically imagined by NASA's techno-scientists (fig. 12.2), have actually flourished throughout human history. Fluidity and mobility are not exotic and extraterrestrial; they are here on earth, both archaeologically and anthropologically, as we have seen in the examples described here.

This surprising parallel between NASA futurism and the archaeological record tells us something very important about the relationship between archaeologists and future-makers, whether they be techno-scientific-urbanists, policymakers, or social scientists. In order to communicate with these stakeholders, archaeologists have often tried to narrow human behavior to averages, serving as a baseline of "normality." There comes a point, however, when this baseline ceases to be an artifact of statistical analysis, and becomes instead a projection of what most societies are thought to be like. The trouble with such normative projection, however, is that it tends to be Eurocentric, with the result that the progression from the prehistoric past to a Western present appears natural and preordained. Beyond telling us that all of human history inevitably leads to the problems of today, this kind of narrative is not very instructive when it comes to future strategies for living. It leads future-makers either to appropriate archaeology in order provide a context for our contemporary predicament, or simply to treat it as an irrelevance, as did NASA's futurists. Blinded by their own preconceptions, they fail to appreciate the many alternative ways, such as amphibious urbanism, in which people live and have lived.

Focusing on fluidity and transformation offers a radically different approach (Ingold and Simonetti 2022). By embracing a richer empiricism that acknowledges and embraces the diversity of human activities, we can view the archaeological record as open-ended, creative, and generative. This is about thinking and researching *with* the world (Ingold 2021, 198). We can step outside of the closed, the straight, the teleological, and even the authoritarian (Gruppuso 2021) to embrace worlds that seem to unsettle the narrow conceptions of ways of being that have resulted in global problems like climate change. An important role for archaeology is to focus at high resolution on the creativity of people who lived in the past. Instead of imagining impossible and unprecedented future worlds, we can then see that strategies and solutions for amphibious living are not merely possible, but have thrived for thousands of years (Leadbetter 2021; Hammer 2022; Zhuang, Zhang, and Xu 2023).

Futurists often imagine mobile cities to be isolated and cut off from the rest of the world, but archaeology tells us that amphibious urbanism connects the world in inventive, creative, and surprising ways. When we ask, "How can archaeology help us imagine what a good life on this planet means for all its inhabitants?" these ways must be part of the answer. The philosopher Baruch Spinoza (1632–1677) (2002, 280) once said that we do not yet know all the things that humans can do. Long-term averages of human behavior do of course have something important to tell us, but so too do the extraordinarily creative ways that people through the ages have devised to live well with each other and other creatures on the planet. As a discipline that draws its inspiration from the lived experiences of humanity, archaeology has much to teach us about how the boundaries of land and sea can be blurred, and about how to live with literal and metaphysical fluidity. The lesson we should learn from it is that to resolve the major issues of our time, we must become amphibians ourselves.

References

Arthur, W. Brian. 2009. *The Nature of Technology: What It Is and How It Evolves.* Allen Lane.

Bar-On, Yinon M., Rob Phillips, and Ron Milo. 2018. "The Biomass Distribution on Earth." *PNAS (Proceedings of the National Academy of Sciences of the United States of America)* 115, no. 25: 6506–11. DOI: 10.1073/pnas.1711842115.

Baudelaire, Charles. 2008. *The Flowers of Evil* (1857). Translated by James McGowan and Jonathan D. Culler. Oxford University Press.

Berdan, Frances F. 2005. *The Aztecs of Central Mexico: An Imperial Society.* Thomson Wadsworth.

———. 2014. *Aztec Archaeology and Ethnohistory.* Cambridge University Press.

Bogaard, Amy, Robin Allaby, Benjamin S. Arbuckle, Robin Bendrey, Sarah Crowley, Thomas Cucchi, Tim Denham, Laurent Frantz, Dorian Fuller, Tom Gilbert, Elinor Karlsson, Aurélie Manin, Fiona Marshall, Natalie Mueller, Joris Peters, Charles Stépanoff, Alexander Weide, and Greger Larson. 2021. "Reconsidering Domestication from a Process Archaeology Perspective." *World Archaeology* 53, no. 1: 56–77. DOI: 10.1080/00438243.2021.1954990.

Burton, Linda M. 1977. "Settlement and Burial Sites in Butuan City: A Preliminary Report." *Philippine Studies* 25, no. 1: 95–112. https://www.jstor.org/stable/42632370.

Calnek, E.E. 1972. "Settlement Pattern and Chinampa Agriculture at Tenochtitlan." *American Antiquity* 37, no. 1: 104. DOI: 10.2307/278892.

Capistrano-Baker, Florina H., John Guy, and John N. Miksic. 2011. *Philippine Ancestral Gold.* Ayala Foundation; NUS Press.

Carrasco, David, and Scott Sessions. 1998. *Daily Life of the Aztecs: People of the Sun and Earth.* Greenwood Publishing.

Chaussard, E., E. Havazli, H. Fattahi, E. Cabral-Cano, and D. Solano-Rojas. 2021. "Over a Century of Sinking in Mexico City: No Hope for Significant Elevation and Storage

Capacity Recovery." *Journal of Geophysical Research: Solid Earth* 126, no. 4: 1. DOI: 10.1029/2020JB020648.

Chen, Guo Peng. 2023. "Boundary-Crossing as Resilience: The Colonisation of the Maya at Lamanai, Belize in the 16th Century." *Journal of Social Archaeology* 24, no. 2. DOI: 10.1177/14696053231196887.

Clark, Nigel, Sasha Engelmann, Paolo Gruppuso, Tim Ingold, Franz Krause, Gavin Lucas, Germain Meulemans, Cristián Simonetti, Bronislaw Szerszynski, and Laura Watts. 2022. "A Solid Fluids Lexicon." *Theory, Culture & Society* 39, no. 2: 197–210. DOI: 10.1177/02632764211030976.

Clarke, David. 1973. "Archaeology: The Loss of Innocence." *Antiquity* 47, no. 185: 6–18. DOI: 10.1017/S0003598X0003461X.

De Landa, Manuel. 1997. *A Thousand Years of Nonlinear History.* Zone Books.

Deleuze, Gilles, and Félix Guattari. 2018. *A Thousand Plateaus: Capitalism and Schizophrenia.* Translated by Brian Massumi. Bloomsbury.

Díaz, B. 1975. *The Conquest of New Spain.* Penguin Classics.

Elhacham, Emily, Liad Ben-Uri, Jonathan Grozovski, Yimon M. Bar-On, and Ron Milo. 2020. "Global Human-Made Mass Exceeds All Living Biomass." *Nature* 588, no. 7838: 442–44. DOI: 10.1038/s41586-020-3010-5.

Estrella, V. 2016. "The Gold-Working Sub-Assemblage from Butuan, Northeast Mindanao, Philippines." *Proceedings of the Society of Philippine Archaeologists* 8: 17–34.

Farrier, David. 2021. "How Cities Will Fossilise." *BBC,* May 6. https://www.bbc.com/future/article/20210505-how-cities-will-fossilise.

Flad, Rowan. 2018. "Urbanism as Technology in Ancient China." *Archaeological Research in Asia* 14: 121–34.

Fletcher, Roland, Dan Penny, Damian Evans, Christophe Pottier, Mike Barbetti, Matti Kummu, and Terry Lustig. 2008. "The Water Management Network of Angkor, Cambodia." *Antiquity* 82, no. 317: 658–70. DOI: 10.1017/S0003598X00097295.

Gosden, Chris, and Lambros Malafouris. 2015. "Process Archaeology (P-Arch)." *World Archaeology* 47, no. 5: 701–17. https://www.jstor.org/stable/26160322.

Gruppuso, Paolo. 2021. "In- Between Solidity and Fluidity: The Reclaimed Marshlands of Agro Pontino." *Theory, Culture & Society* 39, no. 2: 53–73. DOI: 10.1177/02632764211038669.

Hammer, Emily. 2022. "Multi-Centric, Marsh-Based Urbanism at the early Mesopotamian City of Lagash (Tell al-Hiba, Iraq)." *Journal of Anthropological Archaeology* 68: 101458. DOI: 10.1016/j.jaa.2022.101458.

Hearn, Lafcadio. 1883. "Saint Malo: A Lacustrine Village in Louisiana." *Harper's Weekly: A Journal of Civilization,* March 31, 196–69.

Heitz, Caroline, Martin Hinz, Julian Laabs, and Albert Hafner. 2021. "Mobility as Resilience Capacity in Northern Alpine Neolithic Settlement Communities." *Archaeological Review from Cambridge* 36, no. 1: 75–105. DOI: 10.17863/CAM.79042.

Ingold, Tim. 2021. *Correspondences.* Polity Press.

Ingold, Tim, and Cristián Simonetti. 2022. "Introducing Solid Fluids." *Theory, Culture & Society* 39, no. 2: 3–29. DOI: 10.1177/02632764211030990.

Kenny, Jim. 1994. "Dancing the Shrimp." *Philippine Studies: Historical and Ethnographic Viewpoints* 42, no. 3: 385–90. DOI: 10.13185/2244-1638.4805.

Kim, Nam C., and Patricia A. McAnany. 2023. "Experimenting with Large-Group Aggregation." *Journal of Urban Archaeology* 7: 17–30. DOI: 10.1484/J.JUA.5.133448.

Lacsina, Ligaya. 2014. "Boats of the Precolonial Philippines: Butuan Boats." In *Encyclopaedia of the History of Science, Technology, and Medicine in Non-Western Cultures,* edited by Helaine Selin. Springer Science+Business Media. DOI: 10.1007/978-94-007-3934-5_10279-1.

Lacsina, Ligaya, and Wendy Van Duivenvoorde. 2014. *Report in C-14 AMS Analysis of Butuan Boats.* National Museum of the Philippines.

Leadbetter, Michael Paul. 2018. "A Critical Glocal Archaeology of Southeast Asian Settlements." *Archaeological Review from Cambridge* 33, no. 1: 82–105.

———. 2021. "The Fluid City, Urbanism as Process." *World Archaeology* 53, no. 1: 137–57. DOI: 10.1080/00438243.2021.2001367.

Leadbetter, Michael Paul, and Phacharaphorn Phanomvan. Forthcoming. "The Archaeology of Zomia in Southeast Asia." In *Medieval Zomias: Alternative Global Histories,* edited by Minoru Ozawa, Amanda Power, and Ian Forrest. punctum books.

Leadbetter, Michael Paul, and Wayan Jarrah Sastrawan. 2023. "Do Mountains Kill States? Exploring the Diversity of Southeast Asian Highland Communities." *Journal of Global History,* December 1, 1–26. DOI: 10.1017/S1740022823000268.

Levin, Simon A., Stephen R. Carpenter, H. Charles, J. Gofray, Ann P. Kinsig, Michel Loreau, Jonathan B. Losos, Brian Walker, and David S. Wilcove. 2009. *The Princeton Guide to Ecology.* Princeton University Press.

López, L. 2006. *La Casa de las Aguilas.* 2 vols. Fondo de Cultura Económica.

Masterson, Molly. 2022. "Tree Aesthetics at Holme I, Norfolk." *Archaeological Review from Cambridge* 37, no. 2: 158–75.

Moctezuma, Eduardo Matos. 1999. *Excavaciones en la Catedral y el Sagrario Metropolitanos.* Instituto Nacional de Antropología e Historia.

Nicholl, Robert, ed. 1975. *European Sources for the History of the Sultanate of Brunei in the Sixteenth Century.* Muzium Brunei.

Pearson, Natali. 2023. "The Multispecies Shipwreck." *International Journal of Heritage Studies* 30, no. 6: 673–86. DOI: 10.1080/13527258.2023.2284719.

Salgarolo, Michael Menor. 2020. "Journeys to St. Malo: A History of Filipino Louisiana." *Rethinking History: The Journal of Theory and Practice* 25, no. 1: 77–114. DOI: 10.1080/13642529.2020.1831279.

Samui, Pijush, Barnali Dixon, and Dieu Tien Bui, eds. 2020. *Basics of Computational Geophysics.* Elsevier.

Smith, Michael E. 2012. *The Aztecs.* 3rd ed. Wiley Blackwell.

Spinoza, Baruch. 2002. *Spinoza: Complete Works.* Translated by Samuel Shirley. Hackett.

Whitehead, Alfred North. 1985. *Process and Reality (1927–1928).* Free Press.

Zhuang, Yijie, Xiaohu Zhang, and Junjie Xu. 2023. "Aquatic Landscape and the Emergence of Walled Sites in Late Neolithic Central Plains of China: Integrating Archaeological and Geoarchaeological Evidence from the Guchengzhai Site." *Archaeological Research in Asia* 33: 100428. DOI: 10.1016/j.ara.2022.100428.

PART 4

Introduction to Part 4:
Rivers and Floods

You cannot build a city without excavating. Materials must be extracted from the earth, foundations dug. Yet the labors of excavation, and the massive craters they leave, are routinely ignored in histories of architecture that dwell only on the triumphs of erection. What would it take to reverse this bias, to put pits before edifices, quarrymen before construction workers, foundation builders before architects? And how would it change our picture of the city and the people who live there? Moreover, since no buildings last forever, a city — if it is to perdure over centuries or even millennia — must be a place of constant building and rebuilding. What happens then to the rubble of old buildings as new ones go up? In Chapter 13, Matt Edgeworth invites us to think of the city not as a ready-made fabric, but rather as a megamachine that continuously gnaws at the substrate, leaving huge toothmarks, even as it regurgitates the masticated remains of its fabrications into the very earth from which they had once been extracted. Rising thus on its own ruins, the city is a machine for the production of what Edgeworth calls the *archaeosphere*.

Far from being laid down as a passive deposit, the urban archaeosphere is permeated by forces of its own, which interact
with the forces of the atmosphere, hydrosphere, biosphere, and
geosphere, within the earth system as a whole. Neither fixed nor
mappable, it better resembles a viscous, shape-shifting mass that
is inclined to splash out, or "splurge," as the machine relentlessly
grinds on. Its growth, or swelling, is almost organic, as in the
formation of *tells* — city mounds that have risen on their own
rubble, over many thousands of years — on the alluvial floodplains of the Near East and Middle East. But what becomes,
then, of rivers? Since rivers cannot climb hills, they are either
submerged or forced to run through increasingly narrow channels, as built-up banks close in from either side. Here it is a case
of land overflowing water, rather than vice versa. Could this en-
croachment of land on water have shaped our idea of what it
takes to be a *real* river? It is in the nature of rivers, we think, to
flow with a pronounced current, between well-defined banks.
To be blessed by such a river, running right through the center,
can be a mark of a city's identity and prominence. But a river
whose current is lost or weakened, or whose banks are indeter-
minate, appears more like a curse.

This is the curse of the flood, of river waters that — indifferent to the banks between which they should normally be confined — have spread out over built-up land, bringing their mud,
along with all the wastes they should have carried out to sea,
into houses and homes. Typically, flooding events are caused by
intense, heavy rainfall. Ester Gisbert Alemany opens Chapter 14
with an account of such an event, in 2019, when a major rainstorm, of a kind known in the region as *Gota Fría*, led to flooding
around the Mar Menor saltwater lagoon on the Mediterranean
coast of southeastern Spain, while also inundating several towns
in the region when the canal system of the nearby Segura River
burst its banks. Gisbert Alemany shows that a machine is also
at work here; in this case, however, it is not archaeospheric but
atmospheric. This machine achieves naturally what is achieved
artificially — at great cost in terms of equipment and energy ex-
penditure — by desalination plants, which pump water taken

from the sea inland for purposes of irrigation. In the Gota Fría, which typically occurs when the summer heat reaches its peak, seawater is simply desalinated through surface evaporation. Humid air, driven inland by onshore winds and forced upward by the mountainous terrain of the interior, cools and condenses, falling as heavy rain, only to be filtered back toward the ocean through the ground.

The Gota Fría of 2019 not only flooded residential areas around the lagoon. It also filled the lagoon itself with nutrient-enriched mud that stimulated algal growth, starving everything else of oxygen. Fish perished in huge numbers. Gisbert Alemany found an identical process of eutrophication at work in miniature, in a swimming pool she had been working to restore. Tragically, the fish brought in to control the mosquitoes did not survive. How should citizens respond to this kind of ecosystem collapse? Finding themselves viscerally inside the weather machine, caught up in a dialogue between sea, mountains, and atmosphere that is only intensifying with the changing climate, what should they do? Should they attempt to work *with* the machine, rather than seeking to defend themselves *against* it? Instead of treating the cityscape, like the conventional swimming pool, as ready-to-use, might they do better to put themselves back inside the machine and to derive enjoyment from caring for all the living things that keep land and water alive? What if even swimming, like gardening, were to become a practice of care in this sense? Although it goes against the grain of an approach that vests rights of enjoyment in the ownership of property, this could foster real, productive enjoyment in the collective exercise of "response-ability."

There could perhaps be no better example of an urban mega-machine, of the kind described by Edgeworth, than the city of Rio de Janeiro, which we have already encountered in Chapter 5 with Lang's account of inhabiting its mangroves. The city was founded by Portuguese settlers, in the sixteenth century, on the shores of the oceanic bay (at first thought to be a river) of Guanabara, in a landscape of swamps, lagoons, and hills, with its own Indigenous population. But in the following centuries, the machine has violently gouged away many of the hills and used the rubble both to fill the lagoons and to reclaim land along the shore, creating a front to the sea. In the process, old rivers and streams were submerged. Much of the justification for these massive campaigns of earth-moving lay in the idea that lagoons and swamps were a source of "bad air" and disease. However, like the landscape that Gisbert Alemany describes for southeastern Spain, and indeed like the city of Latina in Italy described by Gruppuso in Chapter 2, its waters have not gone away, and every so often they reassert themselves, periodically reminding citizens, who find themselves having to wade through flooded streets, of where they used to lie and of the ways they used to go.

In Chapter 15, Zoy Anastassakis, Caio Calafate, and Paula de Oliveira Camargo set out with their students at Rio's College of Industrial Design (ESDI) to recover the original topography of hills, lagoons, and streams that preceded the emergence of the city as it exists today. From this, they construct alternative stories of the city as it might have been, had not the violence of an urban design culture, for which progress lies in the conquest of nature, been inflicted upon it. The topographic consequences of this violence cannot realistically be reversed, but the fabulation of other pasts, and of the other futures that might have followed from them, offers renewed prospects for a way of thinking that, as Gisbert Alemany also proposes, would work with rather than against the encompassing forces of a liquid world. What was once regarded as good design has turned out, in our times, to have been a harbinger of environmental disaster. But as the chapters in Part 4 show, in the murmurings of liquid water lie other ways of doing things. It is high time we listened to them.

13

Material Flows and the Strata-Producing City

Matt Edgeworth

Introduction

In the early 1970s, twelve ideal cities of the future were imagined by the radical architecture group Superstudio. In addition to presenting an ironic comment on the aspirations of modern consumerist societies, these remarkable thought experiments provide unusual perspectives on the workings of actual cities. Here, the seventh city — the "Continuous Production Conveyor Belt City" — is considered for what it can tell us about flows of materials through cities, the relationship between standing architecture and material deposits in the ground, and the incorporation of rivers into urban conglomerations (fig. 13.1). The interplay of solidifying and liquefying forces is an underlying theme that, though not an explicit focus, is present throughout the discussion.

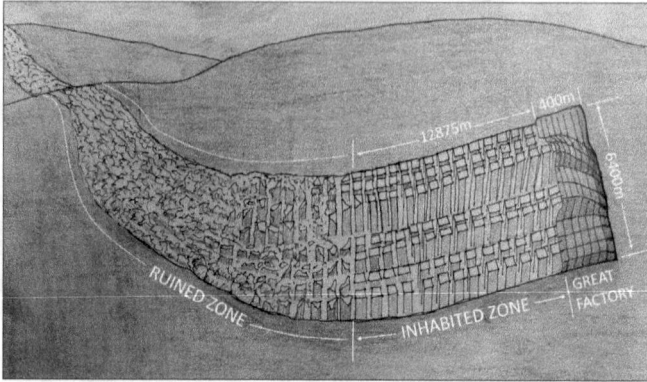

Fig. 13.1. "The Continuous Production Conveyor Belt City," one of twelve ideal cities of the future imagined by Superstudio architects. Adapted and redrawn by Matt Edgeworth from original drawing by Superstudio, "Twelve Cautionary Tales for Christmas (Twelve Ideal Cities)," *Architectural Design Magazine,* December 1971, 740.

The seventh city is mobile. It has a linear form, about 4 miles or 6.4 kilometers wide, and moves across the landscape like a river that has broken out of its old course, carving its own channel, able to run uphill and downhill. It might also be compared to a giant worm-like creature — an organic machine — devouring minerals at one end while excreting material residue at the other. It unrolls "like a majestic serpent, over new lands, taking its 8 million inhabitants on a ride through valleys and hills, from the mountains to the seashore, generation after generation" (Superstudio 1971, 740). To the front is the whirring machinery and cutting heads of the so-called Great Factory, extracting and processing geological material from the ground as the city moves forward, providing necessary building material for constructing buildings. The main body or "inhabited zone" of the city, about 8 miles or 12.8 kilometers long, is composed of skyscrapers, houses, and other urban architecture continuously being built. These crumble into a "ruined zone" at the back as the city moves forward. It takes only four years for houses to go from newly made to abandoned and falling apart. Left behind is a trail of ruins, rubble, and occupational debris, extending back as far as the city has traveled over its lifetime.

This seems at first like an impossible object or dystopian dream, more science fiction than reality, bearing little relation to cities in the real world. After all, common sense tells us that cities stay in one place. Barring the "tent-cities" of some nomadic pastoralists and city-size refugee camps, cities are usually fixed in position and commonly made of solid materials, such as concrete and brick. They do not generally flow as rivers do, or slither like snakes across the landscape. Even so, there are significant similarities. This imagined city produces material residue in the form of archaeological remains just as real cities do, in this case leaving a linear trail of ruins behind it as it moves on. It is perhaps no coincidence that the architects of Superstudio were mainly based in the city of Florence, which has a very rich archaeological and building heritage. In referring to the anthropogenic ground that underlies such cities (or, in the case of the mobile Continuous Production Conveyor Belt City, gets left behind in its wake), I use the term *archaeosphere* (Edgeworth 2017, 2018).

Horizontal and Vertical Formation Processes

Superstudio's seventh city exemplifies the processes through which the solid minerals extracted and used to build the urban fabric actually flow through the city and back into the ground again to form the archaeosphere, the more or less permanent stratigraphic trace of urban existence. If one were to follow the trail of ruins backward in the direction from which the city has come, the remains would get older and older the farther one went — the archaeology of the city laid out in a linear horizontal sequence, earliest at one end, latest at the other.

We might well ask how this can be described as stratigraphic. Surely strata are laid down in vertical succession one on top of another rather than laid down from side to side. When we think of a layer of sediment forming at the bottom of the sea, we tend to envisage material falling from above and settling on the ocean floor, rising up through gradual accumulation. But not all layers are formed in an upward direction. Consider a tsunami flow deposit, for example. As a tsunami wave advances over land, sedimentary particles are deposited in a sideways direction rather than from above. Or rather, there is a combination of vertical and lateral growth. As more particles fall down the advancing face of the sediment left behind by the wave, the layer grows forward, with newer material added in front of the older material left in the wake of the tsunami. The same applies to layers left behind by other material flows, such as pyroclastic delta fans or undersea turbidity currents, and indeed to the trail of ruins in the wake of the imaginary Continuous Production Conveyor Belt City.

Having established that the mobile city is producing a stratum or layer behind it, rather as a tsunami flow deposit might form, now imagine what would happen if it ceased its forward motion, with the whirring blades and production lines in the Great Factory reoriented away from the horizontal plane to the vertical dimension. Brought to a juddering halt, yet with the machinery still working, would not the city devour the very ground on which it was situated, while at the same time rising on its own ruins? Unable to leave its detritus in a trail of rubble behind it, it would incorporate waste material into its own foundations, effectively creating a platform on which further construction could take place. The "inhabited zone" would be stacked vertically on top of the "ruined zone" in stratigraphic formations.

This is exactly what happens in Florence and other actual cities; see, for example, descriptions of the urban archaeosphere in Pisa (Bini et al. 2017) and Rome (Luberti 2018). Present-day city dwellers live their lives on the material residue and occupational debris of previous generations, laid down in sequences of layers, cuts, fills, and dumps that have accumulated over centuries into larger archaeospheric formations, sometimes up to tens of meters thick. Instead of a trail of rubble, however, it gets deposited in vertical successions directly beneath the feet of city inhabitants, forming the foundation for further buildings. In the historic core of London there is an average of 6 to 10 meters of archaeological stratigraphy beneath the present street level. Roman-age deposits at the base are compressed beneath medieval layers, which in turn are overlain by postmedieval and modern deposits and surfaces, all of these being cut through and vastly extended downward by shafts of underground metros and sewage systems.

By unraveling the stratigraphic sequences uncovered in urban excavations, archaeologists can read the history of the development of a city through time. Depth in space corresponds to some extent with depth in time. But processes of accumulation, cutting, extraction, and dumping of material, to form vertical stratigraphic sequences, are not limited to ancient cities such as London and Florence. Consider Boston in the United States, for example (Seasholes 2003; Masoud 2021). From the early 1800s, the small settlement of less than 750 acres grew rapidly in size. The five substantial hills of the Shawmut peninsula were leveled as material was extracted to fill in parts of the bay, thereby providing a platform on which streets could be laid out and buildings constructed. Later, more devouring and cutting occurred underground when metro tunnels and sewers were dug, again with spoil going to land reclamation. Some construction material was brought in from sources outside the city, and some waste material exported, but there is still an important sense in which Boston — like the Continuous Production Conveyor Belt City when brought to a halt — at once devoured and created the very land on which it stands and is supported. The fact that it has done so while standing still is perhaps all the more remarkable than if it were moving along.

The expansion of Boston through time reminds us that actual cities are far from still or immobile. They may not be surging through the landscape on a single linear track, but the energy of movement presents itself instead in the form of growth. Urban expansion is a nonlinear kind of movement — more of a radiation outward in all lateral directions than an extension along a unidirectional path. But it can sometimes take a linear form. Imagine for example a city next to a coastline that is being inundated as a result of climate change and sea level rise. The city expands in the landward direction away from the coast, while those parts of the city nearest to the sea are progressively abandoned. In this thought experiment, the city effectively moves through the landscape somewhat in the manner of the mobile Continuous Production Conveyor Belt City, albeit over much longer periods of time.

The urban strata of most cities, however, spread outward in multiple directions from a historic core. They form through a combination of vertical accumulation and lateral expansion. It is as though a stone has been dropped into water, providing the energy that ripples outward in waves, but actually the energy is initially provided by the combined effects of countless human actions in digging material out of the ground and dumping it on the ground, and in constructing and demolishing buildings over the course of many generations, recirculating much of the building material as rubble and hardcore. Liquid words such as "splurge" come to mind in describing urban expansion, with effects retained as accumulated material residue and not entirely dissipated, providing a solid base layer or ground for subsequent development.

The time scale is slow. The splurge-like movement of a city may not be apparent from one day to the next, and it might only begin to be noticeable over decades, yet over centuries the sheer force through which urban growth is propelled can be astonishing. One may, however, have to stand outside the city inhabitant's situated spatiotemporal perspective in order to be able to perceive it. When geologist Eduard Suess (1862) first noticed the urban archaeosphere underlying Vienna — calling it the *Schuttdecke,* "rubble blanket" — he mapped it as if it were a static deposit of fixed and permanent shape. The very process of mapping reinforced this impression. But when he returned to the task more than thirty years later, it became clear that it had undergone expansion and change of overall shape, and needed to be remapped. If it were mapped today, it would be found to have increased its extent and volume many times over (Edgeworth 2016), to have grown through urban expansion to cover large parts of the Danube floodplain, to have risen up through the addition of occupational debris, and to have been extended down through the cutting of subterranean features, such as metro shafts and underground car parks. And it will continue to grow into the future. Like the surface city itself, the urban archaeosphere is a shape-shifting mass for which maps provide only a snapshot in time.

Organic Growth

It must be acknowledged that a key aspect of most cities, in stark contrast to Superstudio's mobile version, is that they are anchored to particular locations. One might even say that they take root. As a growth form, they are analogous to trees, sending out younger roots and branches, as it were, from an older central trunk or core — in constant movement yet still being attached to place, moving at speeds too slow for ordinary human perception to detect. The metaphor of tree roots is appropriate when thinking of rapidly expanding systems of buried utilities, underground transport networks, and other subterranean infrastructures that underlie many larger cities today. Superstudio's Continuous Production Conveyor Belt City, for all its apparent machinic character, somehow invites us to think of the city in organic terms.

Tree roots continually bring minerals and nutrients from deep in the ground into living trunks and branches, and thence into leaves, which fall and decompose on the ground to form soil on the forest floor. In a broadly comparable way, deep tunneling under cities for metros and other infrastructure brings material from deep strata, against the force of gravity, adding to the vertical accumulation of archaeosphere deposits on the surface, both in the city and beyond its boundaries. In Chicago, material extracted from deep tunneling was dumped into Lake Michigan to create new land onto which the city could expand. In London, material from the recent construction of Crossrail tunnels was shipped down the Thames to create the extensive mudflats of Wallasea Island on the Essex coast.

Quarries within the space of the city itself may provide some building material. Even stonework from building foundations in earlier archaeosphere layers can be quarried for reuse. But when local sources are exhausted, materials are typically brought in from outside the urban area. Building stone, clay for bricks, gravel for hardcore, sand and gravel for concrete, and other minerals are extracted from quarries in rural areas in the urban hinterland or imported from further afield. In the case of *tells* in southeast Europe, Syria, and the Middle East, mud for mud bricks was obtained from the surrounding floodplain.

Tells are mounds composed of the accumulated remains of settlements continuously built and rebuilt for thousands of years (Matthews 2015). They can be up to a kilometer wide and 40 meters high. Many started as villages in the early Neolithic (8000–6000 BCE), often being occupied until the Early Bronze Age (3000–1000 BCE). Such settlements are associated with the early development of agriculture and the first known manifestations of urbanism.

The growth of tells upward from flat river floodplains is largely explained by the fact that houses made of mud brick start falling apart after a few decades and decay back into the mud and dust from which they came, the material going on to form the ground on which replacement houses can be built, often on roughly the same footing or ground plan. These eventually decompose to form the ground on which later houses are constructed, and so on. When such processes are replicated across much of the surface area of a tell, and repeated over many generations, the mound inevitably grows, house upon house, occupation layer upon occupation layer. And as it grows, it slowly rises.

Tell formation can be characterized as a version of the Continuous Production Conveyor Belt City, growing upward instead of forward, leaving its trail of rubble and debris below instead of behind. Building materials for new construction are fed into the Great Factory, so to speak, at the top of the tell. That makes it sound as though these are artificial mounds, implying they were deliberately made. But the growth of these mounds is not necessarily intended. On the contrary, it is the largely unintended by-product of countless smaller human intentional acts, and thus perhaps better thought of as organic rather than artificial (Ingold 2013, 75–89).

Submergence of Rivers

Thinking in terms of the Continuous Production Conveyor Belt City model helps us to see the flow of materials through which the urban ground of cities accumulates and grows. This perspective challenges the entrenched notion of archaeological stratigraphy as somehow inert and passive, as merely a material record of the effects of past human actions, with no effects of its own. It is more than just a record. It has energy and momentum, which causes it to impinge on other things and beings in the wider environment. Considered on a global scale, the archaeosphere is an active force, or a set of forces and flows, with the power to interact with other material flows. Though largely overlooked and unacknowledged, it is an influential part of the earth system, intermeshing with the atmosphere, hydrosphere, biosphere, and underlying geosphere (Edgeworth 2018).

For an example of the effect of the expanding urban archaeosphere on the wider environment, consider the burial of rivers and streams. London once had numerous rivers flowing as tributaries into the Thames: the Fleet, Tyburn, Walbrook, and Westbourne on the north side, and the Effra and Falcon Brook on the south side, to mention just a few. These have all been covered over and buried by the rising urban ground. Once sparkling surface streams, they now flow in darkness through pipes and culverts as part of the sewer system, sometimes referred to as the "lost rivers of London" (Barton 1962). Their burial was unavoidable, given that anthropogenic ground was rising so dramatically. Since water cannot flow uphill against the force of gravity, it had either to be redirected around the changed topography of the city or to flow underneath it. This is a case of "solid" ground effectively "drowning" and "submerging" rivers and streams.

Larger rivers such as the Thames have been radically affected too. In former times, much urban waste was disposed of in the metropolis itself, whereas now it is mostly exported to landfills outside the city. In addition to adding to the vertical expansion of the city ground, substantial amounts were pushed out as landfill into the river itself. This had the effect of extending the surface area of the city, creating new riverside land, pushing the banks further into the river, transforming it into a narrower, deeper, and faster-moving current. From Roman times, household and industrial waste mixed with earth, and mud dredged from the river was deposited in specially constructed timber frames built on the edge of the river and then rammed down to form the surface of new quaysides or river frontages. This was repeated numerous times over subsequent centuries, extending the bank farther and narrowing the watercourse even more — a pattern of development that continued right through medieval times into the postmedieval and modern periods (Schofield, Blackmore, and Pearce 2018). We are accustomed to thinking in terms of water inundating land, but this is land overflowing into and inundating water, a process steadily taking place on urban coastlines and riversides throughout the world (Hudson 1996).

By exploring the stratigraphy of this riverside land through excavation, archaeologists can trace a series of timber revetments or embankments, one in front of the other in a long horizontal succession, extending back almost 200 meters from the present river front, representing about 2,000 years of land reclamation and river narrowing. Such evidence points to growth of the archaeosphere through a combination of lateral spread and vertical accumulation of material. The sequence of embankments, the earliest at one end farthest away from the river and the latest at the other end where the present embankment is today, is not dissimilar to the horizontal stratigraphic sequence envisaged to be left in the ground by the Continuous Production Conveyor Belt City.

References

Barton, Nicholas. 1962. *The Lost Rivers of London.* Phoenix House.

Bini, Monica, Marta Pappalardo, Veronica Rossi, Valerio Noti, Alessando Amorosi, and Giovanni Sarti. 2017. "Deciphering the Effects of Human Activity on Urban Areas Through Morphostratigraphic Analysis: The Case of Pisa, Northwest Italy." *Geoarchaeology* 33, no. 1: 43–51. DOI: 10.1002/gea.21619.

Edgeworth, Matt. 2016. "The Ground Beneath Our Feet: Beyond Surface Appearances." In *Mensch macht Natur: Landschaft im Anthropozän,* edited by Gabriele Mackert and Paul Petritsch. Walter de Gruyter.

———. 2017. "Humanly Modified Ground." In *The Encyclopedia of the Anthropocene,* edited by Dominick A. DellaSala and Michael I. Goldstein. Elsevier.

———. 2018. "More Than Just a Record: Active Ecological Effects of Archaeological Strata." In *Historical Archaeology and Environment,* edited by Marcos André Torres de Souza and Diogo Menezes Costa. Springer.

Hudson, Brian. 1996. *Cities on the Shore: The Urban Littoral Frontier.* Pinter.

Ingold, Tim. 2013. *Making: Anthropology, Archaeology, Art, and Architecture.* Routledge.

Luberti, Gian Marco. 2018. "Computation of Modern Anthropogenic-Deposit Thicknesses in Urban Areas: A Case Study in Rome, Italy." *Anthropocene Review* 5, no. 1: 2–27. DOI: 10.1177/2053019618757252.

Masoud, Fadi. 2021. *Terra-Sorta-Firma: Reclaiming the Littoral Gradient.* Actar.

Matthews, Wendy. 2015. "Investigating Tells in Syria." In *Field Archaeology from Around the World: Ideas and Approaches,* edited by Martin Carver, Bisserka Gaydarska, and Sandra Montón-Subías. Springer.

Seasholes, Nancy. 2003. *Gaining Ground: A History of Landmaking in Boston.* MIT Press.

Schofield, John, Lyn Blackmore, and Jacqui Pearce. 2018. *London's Waterfront 1100–1666: Excavations in Thames Street, London, 1974–84*. Archaeopress.

Suess, Eduard. 1862. *Der Boden der Stadt Wien nach seiner Bildungsweise, Beschaffenheit und seinen Beziehungen zum Bürgerlichen Leben: Eine geologische Studie von Eduard Suess*. Wilhelm Braumüller.

Superstudio. 1971. "Twelve Cautionary Tales for Christmas (Twelve Ideal Cities)." *Architectural Design Magazine*. December, 737–42.

14

From Ownership of Land to Care for Water: Some Lessons from a Flooded Costa Blanca

Ester Gisbert Alemany

From Mutual Help to Real Estate

In September 2019, in the alluvial plain that surrounds the Mar Menor, the biggest saltwater lagoon in the Iberian Peninsula, there was a major *Gota Fría* event and several towns were completely flooded. Some days of heavy rains were worsened by the destruction of the Segura River canal system. People responded as they do in a humanitarian crisis, with the focus on repairing the damage and on trying, with the help of thousands of volunteers, to recover property buried in the mud. When the rains began to subside, I joined a group of volunteers who came to Los Alcázares to help people recover their homes. The area had been declared a disaster zone and the army had come to keep things in order and help to restore basic infrastructure. A control center was set up in the town library, and volunteers were sent from there to specific streets from which residents had called for help. But something went wrong, as easily happens in the middle of such chaos, since together with a group of six people I was sent to a house that had already been cleaned. A neighbor saw that we were idle in the middle of the street and told us there was a house whose owner was in the hospital and needed to be taken care of. He had the key and opened the house for us.

No one had been in this semidetached summer house for a while, and it was quite impressive to see the mud covering all its fixtures. While we were pushing the mud out with whatever tools we had, a sense of comradeship grew among us volunteers as we commented on the damage. My companions had arrived the day before and were happy to be able to do something for people who had lost their homes, especially for this woman who was ill in hospital. From the neighbor who would appear now and then to answer questions about what to do with this bed or those chairs, we learned that the woman, who lived in the house only seasonally, might not see it restored — she was about to die. At some point he was able to talk to one of her sons, and through this we learned bit by bit that many months had passed since this woman had last visited what had been her vacation home. We also learned that her sons, who lived in Madrid, were no longer interested in the house, and would probably sell it. I could see my companions losing their spirits, as indeed I did, on hearing this. With no people to support, I felt no incentive to take care of the house. I could feel a growing impatience every time we opened yet another door, to find a bathroom or storage cupboard covered in mud. Everyone was in a hurry to finish up. I was asked to take photos to prove how we found and left things. We had passed from taking care of the house of a sick old woman to cleaning a real estate asset. When we finally opened the back door that led to the inner street and saw the row of holiday homes, someone commented on the many houses like this that must be empty, in the many rows of holiday homes we had passed to come here. The Gota Fría had reduced the suburbs of Los Alcázares to a nonsense.

A Shared Abstract Diagram of Weather Machines

It can happen at other times of year too, but we normally expect the Gota Fría at the end of summer, when Mediterranean temperatures are at their peak. Humid air evaporating from the warm sea rises and condenses, triggering rainfall. Technically, the event is caused by a deviation in the westerly jet stream. Meteorologists call it DANA ("isolated depression at high altitudes"), and it can occur anywhere in the Iberian Peninsula. The more extreme the difference between sea and air temperatures, the more water is stored in the clouds. The Costa Blanca could be described as the land that results from the encounter of the last spurs of the Iberian mountains with the Mediterranean. This combination intensifies these weather events: Levant winds bring the reheated masses of air to the interior, and the mountains force this wind to rise to higher levels, causing it to condense more quickly. The Gota Fría can discharge up to 500 liters per square meter in extremely intense rain episodes. It usually lasts for only a short time, from a few hours to four days. Since the storm is isolated, the water reserves in the clouds are exhausted without being replenished. In a tourism destination that guarantees 300 days a year of sun, this is the most standout weather pattern. It has drawn a landscape of incised gullies that transform into *ramblas* (wide and dry river beds) as they approach the coast, the floodplains in the south of the Costa Blanca, the saltwater lagoons, the dunes, and the cliffs in the north. They also mark our experience of the landscape.

Comparing the water cycles engineered by humans over the last two centuries with the cycle of the Gota Fría, I have been able to think of this event as a "weather machine" that pumps seawater upstream, first desalinating it in the process of evaporation and then filtering it through the ground. In this, I follow Manuel De Landa's (1997, 58–59) explanation of the engineering diagrams of Gilles Deleuze and Félix Guattari. When we think of machines, what first come to mind are infrastructures such as desalination and water treatment plants, but a diagram of the weather pattern of the Gota Fría would look just the same

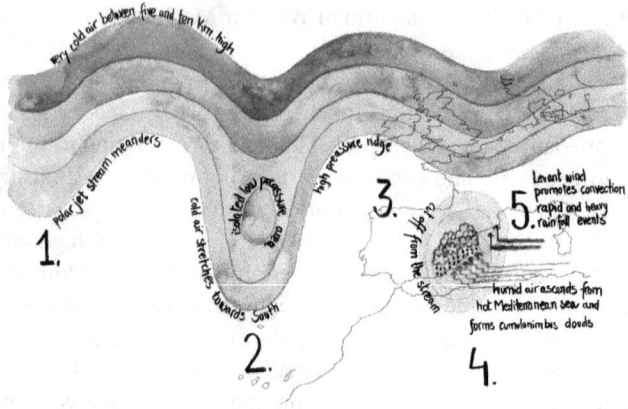

Fig. 14.1. Diagram of the Gota Fría, or DANA, by Alfonso M. Cuadrado and Ester Gisbert Alemany, http://drassana.org.

(fig. 14.1). Where does this parallel take us? For a start, unlike with the electric pumping systems, the diagram of the Gota Fría is felt in the body. This weather machine is all around us. We are immersed in it as big, cold drops, falling on the naked body stretched out on the beach, announce a coming change in atmospheric pressure and humidity. Moreover, the machine is not plugged in; it happens. And it happens more often these days. Meteorologists affirm that there is an increase in DANA formation because of climate change. As the polar jet stream weakens, its thermic contrast is reduced and wind currents meander more, making it easier for these cutoffs to happen. This was also the experience of the neighbor who opened the house for us in Los Alcázares; he had cleaned the next-door house of mud already twice in the last five months. He lived there all year round, and he knew very well that if the house was left full of mud and water it would soon rot, spoiling the walls of his own house.

Cultural theorist Donna Haraway has described the Anthropocene as an era of "destruction of places and times of refuge for people and other critters" (2016, 100), converting the paradigm of a threatening but resourceful nature into one of a vulnerable

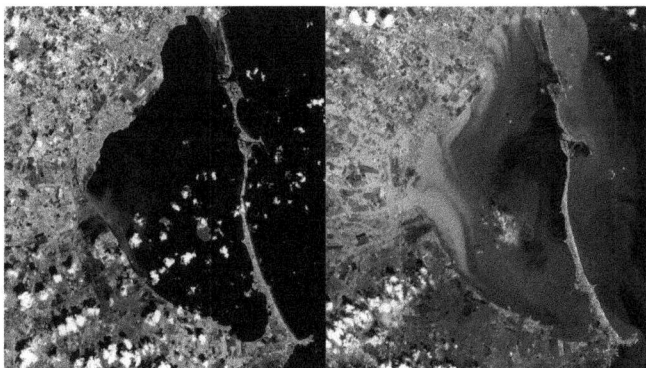

Fig. 14.2. Satellite image of the Mar Menor, September 3, 2019, and September 13, 2019, from Sentinel 2 L2A.

nature in need of care. In the Costa Blanca, a region we would not at first glance consider "natural," having been dedicated to agriculture and tourism for so many centuries, this conversion was highlighted by what happened some weeks after the floods (Romero Díaz and Pérez Morales 2020). Tons of dead fish appeared on the shore, showing us that it was not the human inhabitants of the Mar Menor who had borne the brunt of the extreme weather, and that restoring a living system from the damage inflicted would require more than cleaning the mud after every Gota Fría event, or upgrading the infrastructures that sustain agricultural and tourism development at its current level. The satellite image on the left in figure 14.2 is from ten days before the rains. In an image taken at their height, shown on the right, you can see all the mud brought to the sea from inland. It makes you think of the sea and the land not as divided on either side of a line that can be mapped, but as weaving a line in their oscillations back and forth. In this case, in the Mar Menor, not only does the land spill over the sea, as we see in the image, but the sea also goes under the land through the aquifers that feed tomatoes and other crops adapted to the slightly salted water, on agro-industrial plantations.

Caring for Water

However, my deliberations on the task of taking care of water in response to an environmental catastrophe of such proportions were reflected at a smaller scale. At the time when the floods hit, we (in my architectural practice) were building a swimming pool for a client who wanted to avoid using chemicals in its water treatment. Since it was our first attempt to build what is called a "natural pool," we hired an expert. The idea was to build a wet landscape that keeps water clean enough for people to bathe safely. In practice, however, we found it was not so simple. An excess of nutrients feeds algae, which absorb all the oxygen, choking off everything else. When this happened in the little pool of our client it was a tragedy, not only because of the dirtiness of the water and the smell, but also because we had brought in fish from a nearby lagoon to control the mosquitoes. We used to visit this pool every month, sometimes every week, helping hands-on with all the maintenance tasks, when the pool lost its balance. This was prone to occur in periods of heavy rain or during heatwaves. We helped with removing the gravel from the natural filters, bringing in new plants, emptying the pool completely, and other maintenance tasks. At some point, our client fell pregnant with her second child and realized that she would be unable to take care of the dog, two children, and this other living being that, in its first year, had been as demanding as a newborn. Luckily, we had prepared a design to lower the level of the water and to add chlorine to keep the water clear. This other technology brought time to a close — chlorine and other chemicals are meant to cancel the seasonal variations of the ecosystem. Maybe, at some point, our client will be ready to restart the living system once again.

What interests me here, however, is that the process of eutrophication that led to ecosystem collapse in the pool precisely mirrors what had happened, on a much larger scale, in the eutrophication process that caused the ecosystem to collapse in the inner sea of the Mar Menor. Rendered diagrammatically, it would look just the same. Meanwhile, in the Mar Menor a

Fig. 14.3. Photo collages of the "Scenarios for Climate Change" for Barcelona's metropolitan coast in 2100 by landscape architect Miriam García, 2019 LANDLAB, laboratorio de paisajes SLP.

public campaign was launched to protect and revive the lagoon. In April 2022, the Spanish Congress drafted a law that would confer a legal persona on the salt lagoon, allowing any citizen to go to court to defend it from injury, even if their own legal persona or property is not directly affected. Potential injuries could include toxic spills from surrounding agriculture, or new urban developments. I am fascinated by these efforts. Many people, it seems, are worried and would willingly participate in taking care of the sea. My experience with the pool and how it also reacted to weather events makes me wonder whether these collective efforts could eventually replace the idea of defense against aggression with more affirmative actions.

More Than Nature-based Solutions: Enjoyment

In the Costa Blanca, we can see many images of the sea going over the land when the force of the waves, in winter storms, destroys the line drawn by beach promenades and real estate. Landscape architects are being called in to offer new ideas to work with these amphibious urban landscapes. What I hear more and more, in landscape architecture networks, is that we should work with "nature-based solutions" (NBS). The work on coastal landscapes by architect Miriam García exemplifies very well the technical diagrams I introduced above. She has built up a lexicon for the adaptation of coastal landscapes using NBS. Following this work, she was commissioned by the Barcelona Regional Agency to devise and publish a series of scenarios for the coast a hundred years from now (García García 2019), illustrated with images such as those shown in fig. 14.3.

Our work with the pool, however, has caused me to doubt the way people are depicted in images of this kind. They are shown as passive users of a landscape that — in a way perhaps not so different from the modernist approach to infrastructure — has been prepared for them to enjoy. According to sociologist Henri Lefebvre (2014), architecture cannot produce enjoyment in its user, since enjoyment is not an effect. Architecture, for Lefebvre, can only be enjoyable in its collective coproduction. This, I propose, is what landscape design and regional planning can learn from landscapes of tourism, specifically from the ways people enjoy these landscapes in practice. Elsewhere (Gisbert Alemany 2022), I have discussed how we take care of things as varied as vacation houses and pools, or even whole irrigation systems. I have interrogated the diverse ways in which people take care of property, and of other living beings. In so doing, I have found myself studying the seasons of the landscape, exploring the amazing potential of researching and projecting the city by way of the weather to goad us into action. Here, I have exemplified our experience of this potential with the little natural pool. It puts us human inhabitants *inside* the engineering diagrams, giving us an active role, as shown in fig. 14.4. You might enjoy taking a swim in the pool, but only after you have taken care of the living entities that, just like yourself, keep the water and the land in good shape.

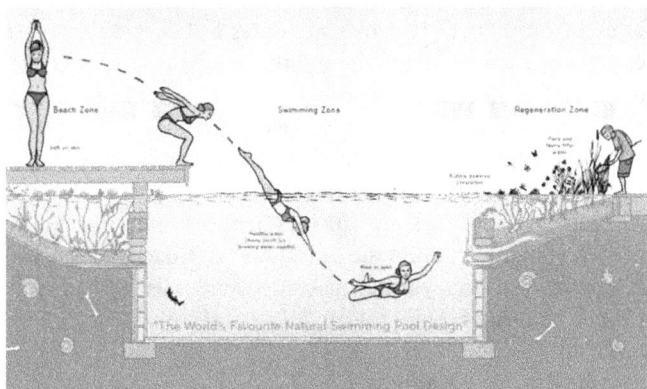

Fig. 14.4. Part of the section of "The World's Favourite Natural Swimming Pool Design" by David Pagan Butler, Organic Pools, UK. http://www.organicpools.co.uk/.

Communities have long known about this potential. In his dissertation on the urbanization of La Manga del Mar Menor, Juan Antonio Sánchez paints an extraordinary picture, with stories from old local newspapers, magazines, and reports, of how a crowd would move every summer toward the Mar Menor, carrying the goods, animals, and materials they would need to build up what would look to us like a temporary city in which to spend the hottest months of the year. In autumn this city would cease to exist, as people returned to the interior (Sánchez Morales 2015, 394–97). We find a similar image of seasonal habitation in many floodplains, as described in Paolo Gruppuso's account of the Pontine Marshes in Italy that, contrary to the Mar Menor, were abandoned in summer (see Chapter 2 of this volume, also Gruppuso 2016, 97–99). In the case of the Mar Menor lagoon, time spent in these normally humid lands in the dry season was a way to get to know and to work these landscapes. This case, together with the little natural pool, the Gota Fría, the sea storms that destroy promenades, and the seasonal cities that used to be built on the shore strain against the fundamental categories of tourism-related coastal developments, such as ownership, maintenance, and resource management. For the owners of every property in the rows of houses in Los Alcázares, real estate was a way to secure the right to enjoy the landscape. For industrial farmers, owning property in the form of agricultural plots surrounding the urbanized belt secured the right to benefit from the produce that came from them. In the Mar Menor, the floods have torn these arrangements apart, just as they did with the traces of the seasonal cities that were built every summer. Beyond the NBS and the ecosystems approach, I argue that our enjoyment of a weather machine could offer another path toward restoring people's role in taking care of these landscapes.

Enjoying Response-ability

I conclude with an image of one of the civil actions of the Mar Menor defense campaign. In August 2021, 70,000 people gathered in a human chain, symbolically to "hug" the lagoon. The event was intended to promote the campaign to protect it. Though it felt a little naïve at the start, I have come to realize that the action holds great potential to show us other ways to relate to the landscape, not just symbolically but literally. To hug the Mar Menor, people had to learn much about its perimeter, places for accessing it, protected areas, and so on. But mostly, they relinquished their laid-back posture, in the sand and under the umbrella, to follow actively the shape of the dying lagoon. This was another way of drawing the coastline, very different from that of the Maritime Terrestrial Public Domain (DPMT), which had separated common and private lands on this coast (Such Climent and Torres Alfosea 1996).

Whereas the DPMT line is drawn on the maps of inherited property that fix the beneficiary rights to land, the lines drawn by the chains of volunteers, formed to sweep mud away or hug the sea, are felt in the bodies of those who have no rights but are willing to take care of the landscape and are capable of so doing. They shift the discussion from rights to "response-abilities." This last notion has been developed by Donna Haraway and other feminist scholars aligned with new materialism, such as Vinciane Despret (e.g., Despret 2008), from whom Haraway

(2016, 7) borrows her definition of "response-ability" as a relational ability that co-constitutes humans and other-than-humans, "rendering each other capable." In this view, the collective that coproduces landscape, as Lefebvre would have it, becomes more-than-human. But drawing on Lefebvre's idea that enjoyment flourishes in tourism-related landscapes, it works the other way too. Not only do unanticipated encounters with more-than-human others nurture our capability to respond, but the exercise of response-ability, in taking up "the unasked-for obligations of having met" (Haraway 2016, 130), also makes for tasks that are mutually enjoyable. And as weather events constantly remind us, it is high time to resume them.

References

De Landa, Manuel. 1997. *A Thousand Years of Nonlinear History*. Zone Books.

Despret, Vinciane. 2008. "The Becoming of Subjectivity in Animal Worlds." *Subjectivity* 23: 123–39. DOI: 10.1057/sub.2008.15.

García García, Miriam. 2019. *The Reinvention of the Coast 2100: Climate Change Scenarios of the Metropolitan Coast of Barcelona*. Barcelona Regional.

Gisbert Alemany, Ester. 2022. "To Do a Landscape: Variations of the Costa Blanca." PhD diss., Universidad de Alicante. http://rua.ua.es/dspace/handle/10045/130306.

Gruppuso, Paolo. 2016. "From Marshes to Reclamation: There and Back Again: Contested Nature, Memories and Practices in Two Wetlands of Agro Pontino, Italy." PhD diss., University of Aberdeen.

Haraway, Donna J. 2016. *Staying with the Trouble: Making Kin in the Chthulucene*. Duke University Press.

Lefebvre, Henri. 2014. *Toward an Architecture of Enjoyment*. Edited by Łukasz Stanek and translated by Robert Bononno. University of Minnesota Press.

Romero Díaz, Asunción, and Alfredo Pérez Morales. 2020. "Before, during, and after the DANA of September 2019 in the Region of Murcia (Spain), as Reported in the Written Press." *Cuadernos de Investigacion Geografica* 47, no. 1: 163–82. DOI: 10.18172/cig.4769.

Sánchez Morales, Juan Antonio. 2015. "Arquitectura ← Interacciones (Críticas y Personales) → Filosofía." PhD diss., University of Alicante. http://rua.ua.es/dspace/handle/10045/50268.

Such Climent, María Paz, and Jose Francisco Torres Alfosea. 1996. "Usos Turísticos y Dominio Público Marítimo-Terrestre en la Provincia de Alicante." In *II Jornadas de Geografía Urbana*. Universidad de Alicante. http://rua.ua.es/dspace/handle/10045/20474.

15

Recomposing Lagoons and Hills in Rio de Janeiro City Center: Speculations, Alternative Pasts, and City-Making

*Zoy Anastassakis, Caio Calafate,
and Paula de Oliveira Camargo*

Remodeling the City

Leveling hills, landfilling beaches, and lagoons — these are radical operations of land modification that have been integral to Rio de Janeiro's history. As such, they have largely come to define an "urban design culture" for the city that has long been characterized by violent, human-led impositions on the "natural" environment. The city center, located in the very area where the European colonizers first settled, is built upon what was once a marshy region between mountains now fallen, hills now destroyed, lagoons now filled with earth, and a shrunken Guanabara Bay. Massive earthworks involving leveling and embankment have strangulated and erased many of the watercourses that had once crossed the territory.

In 2018, along with students in their third year of the under-graduate design course at the College of Industrial Design, State University of Rio de Janeiro (Escola Superior de Desenho In-dustrial, Universidade do Estado do Rio de Janeiro; ESDI/UERJ), architects and PhD candidates Paula de Oliveira Camargo and Caio Calafate joined College Director Zoy Anastassakis in a se-ries of speculative experiments on alternative pasts for the city. The students were given the task of building a physical model of downtown Rio, which would combine the "before" and "after" of the installation of the city, seeking to reveal both the natural environment of the past and the current urban texture. At the same time, we asked the students to develop fictional narratives of alternative pasts. The results of both activities would later be displayed in an exhibition to be installed at the Carioca Design Center (Centro Carioca de Design; CCD), which, like ESDI, is located in the broad stretch of land where the turbulent process of city-making took place. Reconstituting the indeterminacy and fluidity of the boundary between land and sea with our own hands, in the classroom, allowed us to consider other possibili-ties for making cities in environments in which the merging of sea, marsh, and dry land affords no solid foundation.

In Rio, this was precisely the case; the environment did not initially seem promising for the establishment of a new city. The city was founded, in the mid-sixteenth century, in a region lo-cated between the sea, the entrance to a large bay, and a mas-sif of mountains. There were also five lagoons in the area. The land around them was quite unstable, dominated by mangroves, their luxuriant growth fueled by a tropical climate. Abundant rains would frequently flood the drylands across which the In-digenous populations of the region had built paths to link their many villages. This was the environment that first the French and, soon after, the Portuguese sought to colonize. Their strug-gles to contain the waters, and to set up a stable ground on which to establish a European-style city, were intense, recurrent, and frequently in vain.

These efforts, however, were confined neither to the colonial period nor to the region surrounding Guanabara Bay. They were rather part of a campaign of urban intervention that has persisted to this day, and has spread far beyond the limits of the city. Lorelai Kury and colleagues (2020, 50) remind us that "the modern city could only be settled on the piece of land on the margins of Guanabara Bay because lagoons and swamps were filled in, at the cost of the demolition of non-granitic hills, while quarries and even garbage provided the material to fill flooded areas." According to geographer Maurício de Abreu (2014), it is on this physical and symbolic transformation of the material substrate that the "design culture" of the city is founded.

Speculative Fabulations

In our work at ESDI, we were looking for less violent ways for human beings to relate to their environment. Indeed, it seemed to us that the categorical separation of human beings from the environment spells trouble from the start, as the ever-worsening climate crisis reveals. However, raising awareness of the effects of the predatory extraction of planetary materials, as if they were mere resources destined to fuel the human enterprise, does not mean idealizing a pure and untouchable nature. On the contrary, by way of research and design in the classroom, and also in our everyday professional practices, we wanted to better understand and experience the landscape as something that is continually formed and transformed within a matrix of relations in which all its inhabitants are involved. And though the violent actions undertaken in the establishment of Rio de Janeiro irreversibly erased parts of its geographic and social fabric, some traces, even if barely noticeable, insistently resurface in the landscape, and help us perceive its history.

In the exercise we developed with the design students at ESDI, we aimed to investigate this history in practice, such as by walking around the territory, collecting impressions, and interviewing people. These efforts culminated in the collective construction of a model of the region in two overlapping layers. The first layer recomposed the geography of the territory, as documented by the European conquerors who invaded the area

Fig. 15.1. The class works together on reconstituting the shape of Rio de Janeiro's hills and lagoons as they were in the sixteenth century. Photograph by Caio Calafate.

at the beginning of the sixteenth century. The second marked the present conformation of the city (figs. 15.1 and 15.2).

In making the model, the students further investigated the history of some of the places most affected by the urbanization process. Multiple radical geomorphic operations, including leveling hills, landfilling lagoons, and burying water courses, were revealed in this exercise. After identifying these places and their historical backgrounds, the students imagined alternative pasts, or "speculative fabulations" (Haraway 2016), for each of them. These narratives were then graphically assembled to compose an exhibition in which lines linked stories fixed on the wall to the model placed on the floor in the center of the exhibition

Fig. 15.2. Students working with Zoy Anastassakis on the scale model of the Rio downtown area. Photograph by Caio Calafate.

room.[1] There would be much to say about the works developed by the students, but our focus in this chapter is on the historical processes they revealed, especially as they concerned the land on which ESDI is itself located. This is a topic on which all three of us authors have been working in different yet complementary ways. Our researches have involved not only our College of Industrial Design but also other institutions in central Rio de Janeiro.

Importantly, the very location of the College tells much of this story. "It matters what stories tell stories," Donna Haraway (2016, 35) writes. The ground on which ESDI is built plays a part in the processes we are investigating. The land that currently covers this part of the city used to belong to the Tupinambá, one

---

1   The College of Industrial Design (ESDI) in which this work was developed, and the Carioca Design Center (CCD) where the exhibition was to take place, were located in the same area as the one under study. For another speculative approach to the relations between the history of downtown Rio and the installations at ESDI, see Anastassakis and Martins (2022).

of the many Indigenous peoples who inhabited the region long before the Portuguese arrived and called it "Brazil." But unlike the native peoples, the invaders undertook heavy and relentless operations to modify the original geomorphology — along with leveling, landfilling, and watercourse burial, these operations included the violent expulsion of the region's Indigenous inhabitants, both human and nonhuman.

Stories of Radical Urbanization

In the early sixteenth century, before the arrival of the Portuguese and the French, the Tupinambá people inhabited these lands. Walking the region in the wake of colonization, in the 1550s, the French traveler Jean de Lery (1994) counted no less than thirty-two Tupinambá villages in the Guanabara Bay area alone. Two of them, according to writer and journalist Rafael Freitas da Silva (2020), were located in the region surrounding our College. One was Karióka, at the mouth of the now subterranean Carioca River; the other, Gûyragûasu'unaê, was in the region of Morro do Castelo, one of the hills levelled in the late nineteenth century. Several paths linked these and other villages. One of these paths went right past the entrance of the College.

In 1779, after an outbreak of influenza and fever that affected much of the population, one of the five lagoons, Lagoa do Boqueirão, was filled in. In an attempt to justify this radical act, the government claimed that its waters had been responsible for spreading disease in the central region of the city. At that time, Brazil was still one of Portugal's many colonies, and it was the viceroy Dom Luís de Vasconcelos who ordered the lagoon be ground-filled. On top of it, the Crown built the first public garden of the country, right across the entrance to our campus. The garden, called Passeio Público (freely translated as "Public Promenade"), was designed in the French style by the son of a Portuguese diamond trader and a Black woman who had been enslaved and freed, Mestre Valentim.

As the first urbanized area of Rio de Janeiro, and a show-piece for the Enlightenment concept of public health, the Passeio Público was intended to establish a new relationship in the city between humans and nature. Its creators dreamed that the wild nature that had once reigned over formerly fearsome lands would thenceforth be re-created as a monument to knowledge and planning. At this time, before the development of the microbial theory of disease in the second half of the nineteenth century, European medicine still attributed epidemics to the impurity of the air, or to so-called miasmas whose source lay not only in the exhalations of sick people and animals but also in the decaying matter of swampy ground.

However, the waters of the Boqueirão lagoon, which had once flowed into the sea, have not disappeared. With the summer rains, both the park and Passeio Street, onto to which it opens, are often deeply flooded by the lagoon's muddy waters, which stubbornly insist on returning to their place. As they do so, they advance through the entrance of the campus where, in 1962, our College was installed. Many are the occasions on which ESDI's students, professors, and staff found themselves stuck on the premises, faced with the choice of waiting for the flood level to subside or venturing out into the knee-deep waters to find a way through.

The transformations that took place in front of our gates are associated with three particular periods in the history of the urbanization of the city. From the mid-seventeenth and into the eighteenth century, when the city expanded from Morro do Castelo in the direction of its nearest floodplain, five lagoons were ground-filled: Pavuna, Desterro, Santo Antônio, Boqueirão da Ajuda, and Sentinela. All of them suddenly disappeared from the city map. The end of the nineteenth century saw another wave of earth-moving. The leveling of Morro do Senado (literally, "Senate Hill") and Morro do Castelo created extensive flatlands in the central area of the city, and provided the material for landfilling the port region and the new urban front represented by Beira Mar Avenue, expanding the city boundaries to

Fig. 15.3. Map showing ESDI and the historical city center, including its former hills and lagoons. The present urban fabric is shown in red, and the hills and shoreline of the early sixteenth century in black. The dashed black line shows the landfilled shoreline. Drawing by Caio Calafate.

the south. Rocks were drilled, tunnels were created, and Rio's geomorphology was violently redefined.

Once again, in the mid-twentieth century, the city saw one of its main landscape elements levelled, when Morro de Santo Antônio gave way to yet another esplanade, large institutional buildings and the Catholic Metropolitan Cathedral. Along with Morro do Castelo and Morro do Senado, Morro de Santo Antônio ("Saint Anthony's Hill") was one of three small hills, of up to 60 meters high, which had once composed the landscape where the colonizers first resolved to establish themselves, in what is now the most ancient part of town. It was flattened in the decades between 1920 and 1960 in order to provide an open, airy space and a level foundation for new building. The Santo Antônio hill, originally rising from the very point where our College is located, was crossed by the Arcos da Lapa, nowadays one of Rio's main tourist attractions. People lived there, and the Catholic Santo Antônio convent (almost the only part of the hill still preserved) crowned it.

Thinking with Alternative Pasts

Currently, when we walk the ground of Rio's central area, we are stepping on the ruins of land transformed by systematic urban development, which has been proceeding relentlessly since the sixteenth century. In the urbanization of Rio de Janeiro, the wresting of the grounds of the city from nature, whether from its waters, its forests, or its more porous soil, has had consequences. Thiago Florêncio reminds us that these processes have left wounds that remain open, for "the more you fill the land, the more holes you leave: in the flesh, in the soul, in the body-spirit of the city" (Florêncio 2017, 29).

For the most part, passengers, travelers, tourists, and even cariocas who walk the city of Rio de Janeiro do not know the stories of how the land underfoot was formed, or of what was there before. But signs of a forgotten land are still there, if one is sufficiently attentive to look for them. It was from these signs that we — including the students from ESDI with whom we worked in 2018 — tried to imagine alternative pasts, as if the violent geomorphological processes of leveling and landfilling had not occurred. For it seemed to all three of us that, at a time when the very idea of progress is on the verge of the collapse, it is no longer reasonable, to say the least, to continue speaking of the supposed design qualities of sites of urban development as if their value were a given.

It therefore matters that we should question the conditions under which this development was made possible and the violence forced upon the land and upon the beings who lived there. It matters to reveal the histories that have been erased. It matters to refashion with our hands the marshes, lagoons, and hills, forgotten landscapes of earth and water. Even if the work is dull and monotonous, as some students found, it helps to instill a feeling for this carioca land in the minds and bodies of its present inhabitants and visitors. By rebuilding, we bring forth memories of other pasts, of a land that could have been. Instead of assuming that existing land is the inevitable outcome of "good design," we acknowledge that it is also a product of violence and arrogance.

References

Abreu, Maurício de. 2014. *Escritos Sobre Espaço e História.* Garamond.

Anastassakis, Zoy. 2019. "Remaking Everything: The Clash between Bigfoot, the Termites and Other Strange Miasmic Emanations in an Old Industrial Design School." *Vibrant* 16: 1–19. DOI: 10.1590/1809-43412019v16a203.

Anastassakis, Zoy, and Marcos Martins. 2022. *Everyday Acts of Design: Learning in a Time of Emergency.* Bloomsbury.

de Lery, Jean. 1994. *Histoire d'un Voyage Faict en la Terre du Brésil, autrement Dite Amérique.* LDP Classiques.

Florêncio, Thiago. 2017. *De Quem te Protege a Muralha?* Editora Temporária.

Haraway, Donna. 2016. *Staying with the Trouble: Making Kin in the Chthulucene.* Duke University Press.

Kury, Lorelai, Bruno Capilé, Lise Sedrez, and Marcelo Motta. 2020. *Rios do Rio.* Andrea Jakobsson Estúdio.

Silva, Rafael Freitas da. 2020. *O Rio Antes do Rio.* Relicário.

Contributors

Zoy Anastassakis is a designer, and holds master's and PhD degrees in anthropology. From 2016 to 2018 she was director of the College of Industrial Design (ESDI), State University of Rio de Janeiro, Brazil (UERJ), where, since 2012, she has worked as associate professor. At ESDI, she coordinates the Laboratory of Design and Anthropology (LaDA). She is an associate researcher at the Centre for Research in Anthropology (CRIA) in Lisbon, Portugal. Together with Marco Martins, she is coauthor of *Everyday Acts of Design: Learning in Times of Emergency* (2022), published in Bloomsbury's series Design in Dark Times.

Lindsay Bremner is a research architect whose current work focuses on human–nonhuman–monsoonal entanglements in oceanic worlds. Between 2016 and 2021 she led the research project Monsoon Assemblages, funded by the European Research Council (ERC). From 2022 to 2024 she led the project Reimagining the Good City from Ennore Creek, funded by British Academy, and held an ERC/UKRI Proof of Concept grant Climate Cartographics. Bremner began her academic and professional life in Johannesburg, South Africa, where she published, lectured, and exhibited widely on the transformation of Johannesburg after apartheid. She taught architecture at the University of the Witwatersrand in Johannesburg, at Temple University in Philadelphia, and at MIT as a visiting professor, before taking up her current post as professor of architecture at the University of Westminster in London, where she is director of Research and Knowledge Exchange in the School of Architecture + Cities. Bremner holds a bachelor's in architecture from the University of Cape Town, and both a master's and a doctorate in architecture from the University of the Witwatersrand.

Caio Calafate is an architect. He graduated from the Catholic University of Rio de Janeiro (PUC-Rio) in 2010, and holds a master's degree in architectural design from the same institution (2015). In 2022 he gained a PhD from the Postgraduate Program in Design at the College of Industrial Design (PPD/ESDI), State University of Rio de Janeiro (UERJ). His dissertation, "Thinking Ground as an Atlas," was jointly supervised by Zoy Anastassakis and Gabriel Schvarsberg. He is a founding partner of gru.a (group of architects), a studio based in Rio de Janeiro, which, since its formation in 2013, has developed projects and works of different scales and natures, with a special interest in the intersection between architecture and arts. Since 2015, Calafate has been teaching at Santa Ursula University, Rio de Janeiro.

Paula de Oliveira Camargo graduated in architecture and urbanism at the Federal University of Rio de Janeiro (UFRJ) in 2000. She was awarded a master's degree in history, politics, and cultural heritage from the School of Social Sciences at the Getulio Vargas Foundation (FGV) in 2011, and a PhD in design from the Postgraduate Program in Design at the College of Industrial Design (PPD/ESDI), State University of Rio de Janeiro (UERJ), in 2022. Her dissertation, "Times and Crossings: Weaving Lines from Centro Carioca de Design," experiments with the act of writing, mingling historical, political, and discursive aspects of the Carioca Design Centre (CCD) in Rio de Janeiro, where she works, with essays and articles written over the past five years. Paula is the author of *As Cidades, a Cidade: Política e Arquitetura* *no Rio de Janeiro,* (The cities, the city: Politics and architecture in Rio de Janeiro) and coeditor of *Design e/é Patrimônio* (Design and/is heritage), both from 2012. She has been an associate researcher at the Laboratory of Design and Anthropology (LaDA) at ESDI/UERJ since 2017.

Armelle Choplin is professor of geography and urban planning at the University of Geneva. Grounded in long fieldwork in Africa, her research explores how cities are produced and experienced in the Global South, especially in Africa. She currently carries out research on the construction boom, the cement industry, and the political economy of concrete in Africa. She has recently published *Matière Grise de l'urbain, la vie du ciment en Afrique* (MétisPresses, 2020) and *Concrete City, Material Flows and Urbanization in West Africa* (Wiley, 2023).

Riccardo Ciavolella (CNRS, France) is the director of the Laboratoire d'Anthropologie Politique at the School for Advanced Studies in the Social Sciences (EHESS), Paris, where he teaches political anthropology. His ethnographic work mainly focuses on the forms and meanings of politics among marginalized communities in West Africa and the relationship between their being-in-the-world and global crises and ecological, economic, and political transformations. He also writes about the place of anthropology between politics, imagination, and knowledge. He is the author of ethnographic monographs, theoretical essays, handbooks of political anthropology, exhibit catalogs, novels, and children's books.

Matt Edgeworth is honorary visiting research fellow in archaeology at the University of Leicester, UK, and works as a field archaeologist in the commercial domain. He is the author of *Fluid Pasts: Archaeology of Flow* (Bloomsbury, 2011). His research interests include the archaeology of rivers, urban stratigraphy, waste landscapes, and the ecological effects of anthropogenic strata that now cover large parts of Earth's land surfaces.

Ester Gisbert Alemany is an architect and research fellow at the Department of Graphic Expression, Theory and Design of the University of Alicante, Spain. After obtaining a master's of research in social anthropology from the University of Aberdeen, where she was research fellow of the research project Knowing from the Inside: Anthropology, Art, Architecture and Design, she gained her PhD in architecture (2022) with research on the forces and forms of urbanization related to tourism in the Mediterranean. She is founder and partner in the landscape architecture studio Drassana, based in Alicante.

Paolo Gruppuso is an anthropologist interested in nature conservation, urban ecologies, and the environmental and social history of wetlands and land reclamation. He obtained his PhD in social anthropology from the University of Aberdeen in 2016 with a dissertation on environmental contestations in the protected wetlands of Agro Pontino, Italy. Since then he has held positions at different academic institutions across Italy and Germany. He is currently conducting the project Rethinking Wetland, funded by the German Research Foundation at the Rachel Carson Center for Environment and Society (LMU) in Munich.

Martin Hříbek is an assistant professor in Bengali and Indian studies at the Institute of Asian Studies, Faculty of Arts, Charles University in Prague, where he formerly studied Indian philology and ethnology. Besides his alma mater in Prague, he was previously affiliated to the Department of Sociology, Calcutta University, India (2001–2004) and to the Monash Asia Institute, Monash University, Melbourne, Australia (Fall 2014). His research interests include Bengali language and literature, anthropology and sociology of India, Indian nationalism, and the Indo-Pacific.

Tim Ingold is professor emeritus of social anthropology at the University of Aberdeen. He is a fellow of the British Academy and the Royal Society of Edinburgh, and in 2022 was made Commander of the Order of the British Empire (CBE) for services to anthropology. Ingold has carried out fieldwork among Saami and Finnish people in Lapland, and has written on environment, technology, and social organization in the circumpolar North, on animals in human society, and on human ecology and evolutionary theory. His more recent work explores environmental perception and skilled practice. Ingold's current interests lie on the interface between anthropology, archaeology, art, and architecture.

Franz Krause is professor of environmental anthropology at the University of Cologne, interested in the role of water in society and culture. He has conducted research in northern Finland, western England, Estonia, and the Gwich'in and Inuvialuit Settlement Regions in Canada. Krause is coeditor of *Delta Life* (Berghahn, 2021) and *Amphibious Anthropologies* (Washington University Press, 2025), coauthor of *Deltawelten/Delta Worlds* (Reimer, 2022) and *Environmental Anthropology* (Universitätstaschenbuch, 2023), and author of *Thinking Like a River* (transcript, 2023).

Luciana Lang is an anthropologist working in the broad area of socioecological anthropology in urban contexts. Her research interests include age-friendly cities, natural and cultural heritage, and community use of green and public spaces. As a research associate at the University of Manchester with MUARG (Manchester Urban Ageing Research Group), she investigated the role of religious spaces in the age-friendly agenda in Greater Manchester. Lang's doctoral research explored the relationship between an urban fishing community and its surrounding mangroves in Rio de Janeiro, focusing on subsequent transformations as other actors and substances entered that environment, such as plastic, raw sewage, bacteria, oil, new legislations, and institutions. This dialogue between urban communities, the environment, and policymakers informs her research today. In addition to ethnographic methods, she employs map-making techniques, oral histories, and photo-elicitation to tap into people's perceptions of changing landscapes.

Michael Leadbetter is Clarendon Scholar and a doctoral student at the School of Archaeology, University of Oxford. His research focuses on the development of urbanism and settlement patterns across Southeast Asia, and on how archaeology interacts with the social sciences and natural history. Leadbetter teaches archaeology and anthropology at Oxford, and holds the Cyril and Philis Long Fellowship in Social Sciences at Queen's College Oxford. He is co-lead of the Empowering Heritage with Data project, and a member of the SXNCH project (Sites at the Intersection of Natural and Cultural Heritage), funded by the UK Economic and Social Research Council (ESRC) and based in the School of Geography and the Environment, University of Oxford. Previously, he was head tutor of Asian studies at the University of Sydney, and held the Evans Fellowship in Social Anthropology at the University of Cambridge.

Lukas Ley is an environmental and urban anthropologist working at the Max Planck Institute for Social Anthropology in Halle, Germany, where he leads an Emmy Noether research group on the infrastructural lives of sand in the Indian Ocean world, funded by DFG (Deutsche Forschungsgemeinschaft). His research is broadly concerned with marginalization, temporality, and the material environment within urban landscapes. His current research projects the social life of sand and other sediment after extraction and the management of the polluted seabed of Marseille, France. Ley's first book, *Building on Borrowed Time: Rising Seas and Failing Infrastructure in Semarang* (University of Minnesota Press, 2021), was awarded the Social Science Prize by European Association for Southeast Asian Studies and received an honorable mention for the Harry J. Benda Prize of the Association for Asian Studies.

Michel Lussault is full professor of geography and urban studies at the University of Lyon, France. He is the former president of the University of Tours (2003–2008) and University of Lyon (2008–2012). His research focus is on the study of global urbanization as a new milieu and on urban vulnerability in an anthropogenic world. Since 2010, his research has been addressing spatial care in the urban Anthropocene as a new perspective on global change adaptation. In 2017, he was awarded a €10 million EU grant (2017–2022) by the French National Program, called Investments for the Future, to develop a new scientific and graduation program within the University of Lyon, known as the Lyon School of Urban Anthropocene Studies.

Germain Meulemans is an anthropologist at Centre Alexandre-Koyré (CNRS) in Paris, working at the intersection of environmental anthropology and science and technology studies. He obtained his PhD from the Universities of Aberdeen and Liège in 2017, after which he held postdoctoral research fellowships at the Ile-de-France institute for science and technology studies (IFRIS), at Sciences Po Paris, and at the University of Grenoble's School of Urbanism His current research focuses on the significance of urban soils in the soil sciences, urban planning, and gardening activism, and on the development of experimental, collective ethnographies for addressing the politics of urban surfacing. He often works alongside artists, science historians, urbanists, and architects. Meulemans is coeditor of *Back to the Ground: Knowledge, Politics and Practices of Remaking Earth Strata* (2025), and of a special issue of the journal *Revue d'anthropologie des connaissances* titled "Soils, a New Frontier for Environmental Knowledge and Policies" (2020).

Cristián Simonetti is associate professor in the Department of Anthropology and researcher at the Centre for Concrete Innovation of the Pontificia Universidad Católica de Chile. His work has concentrated on how bodily gestures and environmental forces relate to notions of time in science. More recently he has engaged in collaborations across the sciences, arts, and humanities to explore the environmental properties of materials relevant to the Anthropocene. He is the author of *Sentient Conceptualizations: Feeling for Time in the Sciences of the Past* (2018), coeditor of *Surfaces: Transformations of Body, Materials and Earth* (2020), and coeditor of a special issue of the journal

Theory, Culture & Society titled "Solid Fluids: New Approaches to Materials and Meaning" (2022).

Isabelle Simpson obtained her PhD in geography from McGill University in 2022. Her research examines projects to build private cities financed by venture investors and how they take advantage of the financial and political opportunities offered by special economic zones and new technologies, such as blockchain. In addition to academic publications, Isabelle has written for *Rest of World* and *Cabinet Magazine*. She has been quoted in several media, including the *Los Angeles Times,* the *New Republic,* and NBC News. She currently works at a multinational technology company.

www.ingramcontent.com/pod-product-compliance
Lightning Source LLC
Chambersburg PA
CBHW071735270326
41928CB00013B/2691